# TRUTH DECAY

## An Initial Exploration of the Diminishing Role of Facts and Analysis in American Public Life

Jennifer Kavanagh | Michael D. Rich

RAND
CORPORATION

For more information on this publication, visit www.rand.org/t/RR2314

Library of Congress Cataloging-in-Publication Data is available for this publication.
ISBN: 978-0-8330-9994-5

Published by the RAND Corporation, Santa Monica, Calif.
© Copyright 2018 RAND Corporation
RAND® is a registered trademark.

Cover design by Pete Soriano.

## Support RAND
Make a tax-deductible charitable contribution at
www.rand.org/giving/contribute

www.rand.org

# Preface

Much has been written about the growing disregard for facts, data, and analysis in political and civil discourse in the United States. Increasingly, it seems that important policy debates, both within the federal government and across the electorate, are as likely to hinge on opinion or anecdote as they are on objective facts or rigorous analysis. However, policy decisions made primarily on the basis of opinion or anecdote can have deleterious effects on American democracy and might impose significant costs on the public.

The current discourse about the diminishing role of, trust in, and respect for facts, data, and analysis is often hamstrung by the use of conflicting language and unclear or undefined terms. Without a common language with which to discuss the problem—which we are calling *Truth Decay*—the search for solutions becomes more difficult. This report seeks to address this gap by offering a clear definition of Truth Decay and an examination of its drivers and consequences—all with the aim of creating a foundation for more-meaningful discussion of the challenges to U.S. political and civil discourse. The report outlines a research agenda designed to guide further study of Truth Decay and the formulation of responses. The report is the first of several publications that will discuss Truth Decay in different contexts and from different angles.

## RAND Ventures

The RAND Corporation is a research organization that develops solutions to public policy challenges to help make communities throughout the world safer and more secure, healthier and more prosperous. RAND is nonprofit, nonpartisan, and committed to the public interest.

RAND Ventures is a vehicle for investing in policy solutions. Philanthropic contributions support our ability to take the long view, tackle tough and often-controversial topics, and share our findings in innovative and compelling ways.

Funding for this venture was provided by gifts from RAND supporters and income from operations. RAND's research findings and recommendations are based on data and evidence and therefore do not necessarily reflect the policy preferences or interests of its clients, donors, or supporters.

# Contents

Preface . . . . . . . . . . . . . . . . . . . . . . . . . . . . . . . . . . . . . . . . . . . . . . . . . . . . . . . . . . . . . . . iii
Figures and Tables . . . . . . . . . . . . . . . . . . . . . . . . . . . . . . . . . . . . . . . . . . . . . . . . . . . vii
Summary . . . . . . . . . . . . . . . . . . . . . . . . . . . . . . . . . . . . . . . . . . . . . . . . . . . . . . . . . . . . . . ix
Acknowledgments . . . . . . . . . . . . . . . . . . . . . . . . . . . . . . . . . . . . . . . . . . . . . . . . . . . xxi
Abbreviations . . . . . . . . . . . . . . . . . . . . . . . . . . . . . . . . . . . . . . . . . . . . . . . . . . . . . . . xxiii

CHAPTER ONE
Introduction . . . . . . . . . . . . . . . . . . . . . . . . . . . . . . . . . . . . . . . . . . . . . . . . . . . . . . . . . . . 1
What Is Truth Decay? . . . . . . . . . . . . . . . . . . . . . . . . . . . . . . . . . . . . . . . . . . . . . . . . . . 1
A Note on Terminology . . . . . . . . . . . . . . . . . . . . . . . . . . . . . . . . . . . . . . . . . . . . . . . . . 7
Objectives . . . . . . . . . . . . . . . . . . . . . . . . . . . . . . . . . . . . . . . . . . . . . . . . . . . . . . . . . . . . 11
Methodology . . . . . . . . . . . . . . . . . . . . . . . . . . . . . . . . . . . . . . . . . . . . . . . . . . . . . . . . . . 14
Organization of This Report . . . . . . . . . . . . . . . . . . . . . . . . . . . . . . . . . . . . . . . . . . . . 20

CHAPTER TWO
Truth Decay's Four Trends . . . . . . . . . . . . . . . . . . . . . . . . . . . . . . . . . . . . . . . . . . . . . 21
Increasing Disagreement About Facts and Analytical Interpretations
    of Facts and Data . . . . . . . . . . . . . . . . . . . . . . . . . . . . . . . . . . . . . . . . . . . . . . . . . . . 21
A Blurring of the Line Between Opinion and Fact . . . . . . . . . . . . . . . . . . . . . . . 27
The Increasing Relative Volume, and Resulting Influence, of Opinion
    and Personal Experience over Fact . . . . . . . . . . . . . . . . . . . . . . . . . . . . . . . . . . . . 31
Declining Trust in Formerly Respected Sources of Factual Information . . . . 33
Data and Evidence for the Four Trends . . . . . . . . . . . . . . . . . . . . . . . . . . . . . . . . . 38

CHAPTER THREE
Historical Context: Is Truth Decay New? . . . . . . . . . . . . . . . . . . . . . . . . . . . . . . 41
The 1880s–1890s: Yellow Journalism and the Gilded Age . . . . . . . . . . . . . . . 42

The 1920s–1930s: The Roaring Twenties and the Great Depression ....... 51
The 1960s and Early 1970s: Civil Rights, Social Protest, and the
      Vietnam War ................................................................. 61
A Comparison with Today: Similarities and Differences.................... 70
Historical Analogues in Other Countries.................................. 76
Summary.................................................................... 77

CHAPTER FOUR
**Drivers: What Is Causing Truth Decay?** ............................... 79
Cognitive Processing and Cognitive Biases............................... 81
Changes in the Information System ...................................... 95
Competing Demands on the Educational System ......................... 132
Polarization ............................................................ 152
The Question of Agency.................................................. 174
Summary: Truth Decay as a System....................................... 186

CHAPTER FIVE
**The Consequences of Truth Decay** .................................... 191
Erosion of Civil Discourse .............................................. 192
Political Paralysis....................................................... 199
Alienation and Disengagement............................................ 207
Uncertainty ............................................................. 216
Summary.................................................................. 221

CHAPTER SIX
**The Road to Solutions: A Research Agenda**............................ 223
Research Stream 1: Historical and International Analogues.............. 225
Research Stream 2: Data and Trends..................................... 228
Research Stream 3: Mechanisms and Processes ........................... 237
Research Stream 4: Solutions and Responses............................. 244
Summary and Way Ahead .................................................. 253

APPENDIX
**Additional Information About Our Methodology** ...................... 257

**References** .......................................................... 265

# Figures and Tables

## Figures

S.1. Truth Decay as a System . . . . . . . . . . . . . . . . . . . . . . . . . . . . . . . . xvii
2.1. Public Confidence in Institutions, 1973–2017 . . . . . . . . . . . . . . 34
3.1. Public Trust in Government, 1958–2017 . . . . . . . . . . . . . . . . . . 68
4.1. Tweets per Day, 2006–2013 . . . . . . . . . . . . . . . . . . . . . . . . . . . 110
4.2. Share of Visits to U.S. News Websites, by Source . . . . . . . . . . . 115
4.3. Distance Between the Parties Along the
Liberal-Conservative Dimension, 1879–2013 . . . . . . . . . . . . . . . 154
4.4. Percentage of States with Mixed-Party Senate
Delegations, 1913–2017 . . . . . . . . . . . . . . . . . . . . . . . . . . . . . . 155
4.5. Incumbent Reelection and Retirement Rates, 1946–2014 . . . 157
4.6. Number of Landslide Counties in Presidential General
Elections, 1976–2012 . . . . . . . . . . . . . . . . . . . . . . . . . . . . . . . . 158
4.7. Truth Decay as a System . . . . . . . . . . . . . . . . . . . . . . . . . . . . . . 189
5.1. Number of Motions to End Filibusters, 1947–2017 . . . . . . . . . 202
5.2. Percentage of Total Legislation Enacted, 1973–2015 . . . . . . . . 203
5.3. Trends in Political Efficacy, 1952–2012 . . . . . . . . . . . . . . . . . . 209
6.1. Research Agenda Implementation Plan . . . . . . . . . . . . . . . . . . 253

## Tables

S.1. The Four Trends of Truth Decay . . . . . . . . . . . . . . . . . . . . . . . . xi
1.1. Definitions and Examples of Key Terms . . . . . . . . . . . . . . . . . . 8
2.1. Possible New Metrics and Already-Collected Metrics,
by Trend . . . . . . . . . . . . . . . . . . . . . . . . . . . . . . . . . . . . . . . . . . 39
3.1. Assessment of Level of Truth Decay in the 1880s–1890s . . . . . 46
3.2. Assessment of Level of Truth Decay in the 1920s–1930s . . . . . 54

3.3.   Assessment of Level of Truth Decay in the 1960s–1970s...... 64
3.4.   Evidence of Truth Decay in Different Eras...................... 71
3.5.   Characteristics of Three Periods with Similarities to Today....75
6.1.   Research Priorities for Historical and International
       Analogues..................................................... 227
6.2.   Research Priorities for Data and Trends ...................... 229
6.3.   Research Priorities for Mechanisms and Processes ........... 239
6.4.   Research Priorities for Solutions and Responses .............. 247
A.1.   Selected Topic Areas and Search Terms Used in the
       Literature Review ................................................ 262

# Summary

In many areas of American society, facts and data are essential to survival or necessary for success. Complex decisions, even when they require subjective judgments and intuition, can be made with more confidence when anchored by agreed-upon facts and reliable data. Yet in national political and civil discourse,[1] disagreement over facts appears to be greater than ever. Opinions are crowding out and overwhelming facts in the media, and Americans are placing less faith in institutions that were once trusted sources of information. This shift away from facts and data in political debate and policy decisions has far-reaching implications: It erodes civil discourse; weakens key institutions; and imposes economic, diplomatic, and cultural costs.

Despite the consequences of this shift away from reliance on objective facts, little empirical research has investigated the cause of this shift, collected data to ascertain its extent, questioned whether the phenomena behind it are new, or tried to determine what can be done to counter it. Although this report is only a first cut at these issues, it presents a working definition of what we are calling "Truth

---

[1] By *civil discourse*, we mean "robust, honest, frank and constructive dialogue and deliberation that seeks to advance the public interest" (Carli Brosseau, "Executive Session: Civil Discourse in Progress," *Frankly Speaking*, Vol. 1, No. 2, October 27, 2011). Throughout this report, *we*, *our*, and *us* refer to the authors only, not to the RAND Corporation writ large or to all Americans.

Decay,"[2] identifies possible causes and consequences, and proposes a strategy to tackle remaining questions—a research agenda—through which we hope to engage a broader community in understanding and responding to the challenge that Truth Decay poses.

With this exploratory report, we provide a foundation for policy-makers, researchers, educators, journalists, and other interested parties to analyze the concepts and relationships that might be contributing to Truth Decay. We provide a working definition of Truth Decay, explore four related trends in detail, and examine their possible causes (or drivers) and consequences. We also consider whether Truth Decay is a new phenomenon or one that has existed at other points in U.S. history, focusing on three specific eras. Finally, we map out four potential streams of research intended to improve the understanding of Truth Decay and identify potential responses.

Although we separately discuss the trends, drivers, and consequences of Truth Decay, these components work together as a system: Each element influences—and is influenced by—the others. These interactions create a web that increases both the complexity of Truth Decay and the challenge of identifying and implementing workable solutions.

## The Four Trends of Truth Decay

We define *Truth Decay* as a set of four related trends:

1. increasing disagreement about facts and analytical interpretations of facts and data[3]

---

[2] We call the phenomenon "Truth Decay," but we are not actually talking directly about "truth" in the philosophical sense. We use the term "Truth Decay" as a shorthand for the trends identified and focus on the importance of facts and fact-based analysis. The term has been used before in other contexts, but not (to our knowledge) to refer to the specific phenomena considered here. We do not intend to associate our report or research agenda with these previous uses. We thank RAND colleague Sonni Efron for first suggesting the term in this context.

[3] We acknowledge that, although there are certain immutable facts, analytical interpretations of facts and data evolve with new discoveries, the collection of new data, or the development of new technologies that allow for the retesting of even well-established findings. Our focus on

2.  a blurring of the line between opinion and fact
3.  the increasing relative volume, and resulting influence, of opinion and personal experience over fact
4.  declining trust in formerly respected sources of factual information.

Table S.1 summarizes the hallmark characteristics of the four trends and identifies examples of each. Rigorous documentation of and empirical research into these trends are essential to understanding the Truth Decay phenomenon.

**Table S.1**
**The Four Trends of Truth Decay**

| Trend | Example |
|---|---|
| Increasing disagreement about facts and analytical interpretations of facts and data | The shift in opinion about the safety of vaccines and genetically modified foods; public perception of trends in violent crime in the United States |
| A blurring of the line between opinion and fact | Journalistic pieces that do not distinguish clearly between opinion and fact (e.g., "News Page Columns" in the *New York Times*) |
| The increasing relative volume, and resulting influence, of opinion and personal experience over fact | Speculation, opinion, and falsehoods disseminated in traditional media (e.g., newspapers and television) and social media channels that drown out verifiable data (e.g., on such topics as the effect of immigration on jobs and crime) |
| Declining trust in formerly respected sources of factual information | Significant drops in public confidence and trust in government, newspapers, television news, books, the judiciary, and the presidency, as indicated by polls |

Truth Decay does not stem from concern about this evolution, which is a natural and inevitable feature of knowledge accumulation and scientific progress. Nor is it meant as an attack on skepticism or questioning of existing analytical interpretations of facts and data, which is healthy. Instead, we are concerned with the growing imbalance in political and civil discourse between, on the one hand, trust and reliance on facts and analytical interpretations of facts and data and, on the other, opinions and personal attitudes—a balance that seems to be increasingly shifting in favor of the latter. When referring to *increasing disagreement about facts,* we mean increasing disagreement in areas where the existing data or analytical interpretations have not changed, or where they have been strengthened by new data and analysis.

## Historical Context

In our exploratory research, we delved into U.S. history to identify periods that exhibited characteristics of Truth Decay. Our initial inquiry identified three such eras:

- the 1880s–1890s, the Gilded Age, known for newspaper circulation battles and "yellow journalism"
- the 1920s–1930s, the decades of the Roaring Twenties and the Great Depression, known also for "jazz journalism," the birth of the tabloid, and the rise of radio broadcasting
- the 1960s–1970s, the decades of U.S. involvement in and retreat from the Vietnam War, known for "New Journalism"; concern about government and media propaganda; and, later, the resurgence of investigative journalism.[4]

We then explored similarities and differences in the four Truth Decay trends between each of those eras and the most recent two decades (2000s–2010s). In all three periods we studied, we found evidence of two of the four trends identified as part of Truth Decay: the blurring of the line between opinion and fact and the increasing relative volume, and resulting influence, of opinion and personal experience over fact. Both trends were evident in changes in how news was covered and the introduction of new forms of communication: yellow journalism (1880s–1890s); jazz journalism, tabloids, and radio talk shows (1920s–1930s); and television coverage and New Journalism (1960s–1970s). Today, these two trends are evident in all types of news media, from newspapers to online outlets, from cable and network television to social media.

Although we see some evidence that previous eras also experienced a decline in trust in institutions, this trend seems to be more pronounced now than in the past. Distrust of banks and financial insti-

---

[4] "Yellow journalism" refers to sensationalized, exaggerated, and fabricated news stories published in the 1890s and early 1900s. "Jazz journalism" included tabloids that published sensationalized stories of sex, crime, and violence in the 1920s. "New Journalism" was a style of writing that heavily incorporated writers' own opinions and interpretations.

tutions certainly grew in the 1920s–1930s, and the social upheaval of the 1960s–1970s, along with Watergate and the Pentagon Papers, left many questioning the veracity of government. Today, however, we see that lack of trust across the board—in government, media, and financial institutions—and a far lower absolute level of trust in these institutions than in previous eras.

In contrast, we see no evidence in any of these earlier periods of an increase in disagreement about facts and analytical interpretations of facts and data. This trend appears today in the form of disagreement over scientific findings, data and statistics, and objective facts.

Past eras might offer lessons in how to overcome Truth Decay. In each of the eras explored, a revival of fact-based policy analysis or journalism and a renewed interest in holding authorities more accountable helped clarify the line between opinion and fact. In some cases, changes in government policy helped reestablish accountability and transparency, thereby restoring some trust in government institutions. The quieting of social and political upheaval in these eras could also have reduced the societal pressures that had contributed to Truth Decay trends. Further analysis is needed to understand these trends more fully, and other eras that bear the marks of Truth Decay might be revealed in the process.

## What Causes Truth Decay?

We have identified four drivers, or potential causes, of Truth Decay.

1. **Characteristics of cognitive processing, such as cognitive bias.**[5] The ways in which human beings process information and make decisions cause people to look for opinions and analysis that confirm preexisting beliefs, more heavily weight personal

---

[5] To be clear, cognitive bias and other aspects of cognitive processing have not changed in recent years. However, other drivers of Truth Decay, such as changes in the information system and polarization, as well as intentional actions by agents of Truth Decay, have heightened the importance and consequence of these cognitive biases and thrown into stark relief their effects on how people understand and process information.

experience over data and facts, and rely on mental shortcuts and the opinions of others in the same social networks. These tendencies contribute to the blurring of the line between opinion and fact and, in some cases, allow opinion to subsume fact.

2. **Changes in the information system.** These changes include
   a. the rise of social media, which drastically increases the volume and speed of information flow, as well as the relative volume of opinion over fact
   b. the transformation of the media market facing traditional newspapers and broadcasting companies, including the shift to a 24-hour news cycle, the increasing partisanship of some news sources, and the intensification of profit motives
   c. wide dissemination of disinformation and misleading or biased information.

3. **Competing demands on the educational system that limit its ability to keep pace with changes in the information system.**[6] As the information system has become increasingly complex, competing demands and fiscal constraints on the educational system have reduced the emphasis on civic education, media literacy, and critical thinking. Students need exactly this type of knowledge and these skills to effectively evaluate information sources, identify biases, and separate fact from opinion and falsehood. This gap between the challenges of the information system and the training provided to students drives and perpetuates Truth Decay by contributing to the creation of an electorate that is susceptible to consuming and disseminating disinformation, misinformation, and information that blur the line between fact and opinion. In this context, Truth Decay flourishes.

4. **Political, sociodemographic, and economic polarization.** Polarization contributes both to increasing disagreement regarding facts and analytical interpretations of facts and data and to the blurring of the line between opinion and fact by creating opposing sides, each with its own narrative, worldview, and

---

[6]  We focus primarily on the kindergarten–12th grade educational system in this report.

facts. The groups on each side can become insular in their thinking and communication, creating a closed environment in which false information proliferates. Data suggest that political, social, and demographic polarization are not only severe and worsening in the contemporary United States but also overlapping and reinforcing one another.

## Agents of Truth Decay

Although these four drivers of Truth Decay are largely unintentional—a function of human nature or born of circumstance rather than purposeful action—*agents* can play an intentional or unintentional role in exacerbating Truth Decay for their own political or economic gain. For instance, some media organizations rely on punditry and opinion-based news rather than hard-news journalism because the former are relatively inexpensive and allow content to be tailored to specific audiences. However, such programming contributes to a blurring of the line between opinion and fact and thus contributes to Truth Decay. Academic and research organizations can also contribute to Truth Decay, particularly when the pressure to publish—or, in some cases, the agendas of powerful donors—lead to the publication of misleading or incorrect findings that contribute to the blurring of the line between opinion and fact or between fact and falsehood and that erode trust in institutions as information providers. Domestic political actors and government institutions, including especially federal agencies, Congress, and even state and local executive and legislative bodies, also play a role by not keeping promises or spinning facts to the point of fiction, thereby undermining public confidence in institutions. Lastly, foreign actors play a role in blurring the line between opinion and fact and increasing the relative volume, and resulting influence, of opinion and personal experience over fact through the dissemination of false information.

## Consequences of Truth Decay

The consequences of Truth Decay manifest in many ways. We identified the following as potentially the most damaging:

- **The erosion of civil discourse.** Without a common set of facts, it becomes nearly impossible to have a meaningful debate about important policies and topics. As a result, the quality of policymaking declines and the decisionmaking process slows.
- **Political paralysis.** Uncertainty and disagreement about facts create increasing difficulties in agreeing on the terms of the debate, and they prevent compromise. Lack of trust in government strengthens the position of interest groups that can further interfere with government decisionmaking. Political paralysis results in delays in political appointments, lapses in oversight and investigative tasks, and an inability to make fiscal decisions. This dysfunction imposes serious costs on the economy, foreign policy, diplomatic relationships, and government credibility.
- **Alienation and disengagement of individuals from political and civic institutions.** As trust in government declines, so does civic involvement—a process that can increase people's sense of alienation. Public civic engagement often serves as a check on political representatives by fostering transparency, accountability, and community participation.
- **Policy uncertainty at the national level.** Not basing policy on facts and analysis leads to uncertainty when individuals, corporations, adversaries, and allies lack objective data and benchmarks on which to base decisions and are unable to trust key institutions as sources of information. Uncertainty can have significant economic costs in the form of deferred economic investment, and it can also lead to a loss of international credibility—and to challenges in diplomatic relations—if allies and adversaries come to question U.S. commitments.

Figure S.1 depicts the relationships among Truth Decay's four trends, its drivers and agents, and consequences.

**Figure S.1**
**Truth Decay as a System**

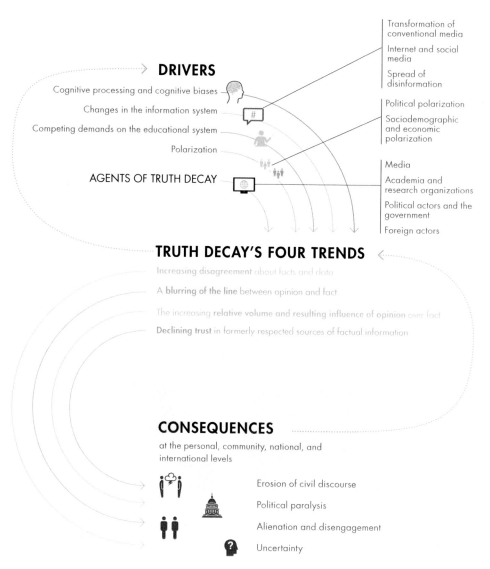

## Research Agenda

Unraveling the complex system of Truth Decay will require multi-faceted and interdisciplinary efforts to develop a clear understanding of the problem and devise possible solutions. We have identified four streams of research, along with corresponding priorities and preliminary questions, that can be pursued independently or together to shed light on the problem of Truth Decay and work to combat it.

### Stream 1: Historical and International Analogues

This stream would look more deeply into how Truth Decay has manifested in the past at home and abroad. Questions include the following:

- What are the similarities and differences between past periods and today, domestically and around the world, in areas relevant to Truth Decay?
- Are the trends observed today unique, or are they continuations of the past?
- What lessons can be learned?

### Stream 2: Data and Trends

This stream covers seven priorities that would examine Truth Decay and its trends, how information spreads, the media industry, the educational system, polarization and political gridlock, civil discourse and engagement, and uncertainty. Questions include the following:

- In which areas has disagreement about facts or analytical interpretations of facts and data become most pronounced? In what ways have opinion and fact become blurred?
- How have content and consumption of information changed over time?
- In the media, how have sources, content, and reporting changed over time?
- How have civics education and media literacy changed across demographic groups?

- What metrics could be developed to assess changes in social and political polarization? What are the costs of that polarization?
- How have the quantity and quality of civil discourse changed, and what are the costs?
- How has uncertainty at the individual and policy levels changed, and what are the costs?

## Stream 3: Mechanisms and Processes

This stream lies at the core of understanding Truth Decay. Its six priorities would analyze information dissemination, processing, and consumption; institutions, authorities, and intermediaries; polarization, engagement, and discourse; the benefits and challenges of technological advancement; agency; and Truth Decay as a system. Questions include the following:

- How can cognitive biases be reduced? How can information be weaponized?
- What causes severe loss or retention of trust in institutions?
- How does political gridlock contribute to declining civil discourse, alienation, and loss of confidence in institutions?
- How does technology affect information dissemination and the spread of disinformation?
- How much of Truth Decay is caused by intentional and unintentional agents, both domestic and foreign?
- What are the ultimate drivers and consequences of Truth Decay?

## Stream 4: Solutions and Responses

This stream would search for ideas on how to address some of the challenges posed by Truth Decay. Its seven priorities would consider educational interventions; improving the information market; institutional development and rebuilding; bridging social divides; harnessing new technologies; behavioral economics, psychology, and cognitive science; and organizational self-assessment. Questions include the following:

- How can civics education and training in critical thinking be provided more effectively to children and adults?

- What policy, legal, or technological interventions might slow the flow of disinformation? What might ensure better delineation between opinion and fact?
- How can the research profession (e.g., academia, think tanks) be altered to better promote transparency and accuracy and to guard against conflicts of interest?
- How can social and demographic polarization be reduced? What types of forums are needed to restore civil discourse?
- How can new technologies be used to improve U.S. democratic processes, including participation and representation, and tamp down Truth Decay trends?
- Can situations in which people process information, make decisions, or exchange views be structured to facilitate effective use of facts and data?
- How can an organization's institutional quality standards be improved to better promote transparency, accuracy, and objectivity?

## Looking Forward

The challenge of Truth Decay is complex, and this research agenda is ambitious. Pursuit of this work will likely require both partnerships among research organizations and the involvement of political actors, media companies, and individuals interested in responding to this phenomenon. We envision this research agenda as a starting point, and we acknowledge that research, data, and analysis alone will not be able to reverse Truth Decay.

We will pursue this research agenda with the objectivity and non-partisanship that lie at RAND's core, and we invite others to take on pieces of the agenda. Because of the vital threat that Truth Decay presents to the health and future of U.S. democracy, we urge interested individuals and organizations to join with us in identifying ways to study Truth Decay and to promote the need for facts, data, and analysis in civic and political discourse—and in American public life more generally. The challenge posed by Truth Decay is great, but the stakes are too high to permit inaction.

# Acknowledgments

Many people contributed to the writing of this report. Susan Gates, RAND's Director of Research Quality Assurance, developed and managed a staged review process designed to ensure that the report meets RAND's *Standards for High-Quality Research and Analysis*.[7] She also provided feedback on an early draft before sending it out for peer review. The first stage of this peer review was conducted by four anonymous RAND researchers with a range of career experiences and expertise in the relationships between media and politics, artificial intelligence, machine learning, social media, the role of information in decisionmaking, and public opinion surveys. Through two rounds of detailed technical reviews, these reviewers provided recommendations designed to ensure that the report meets RAND's quality standards and to offer suggestions for improvement. Upon completion of this formal, technical review, Gates asked two external reviewers to comment on the report's tone and articulation and invited approximately 40 RAND staff members to provide feedback on both tone and specific substantive aspects. In addition, the team reached out to individuals outside of RAND for feedback on the report.

The authors are grateful for the insightful comments provided by all of the anonymous technical reviewers; by Jay Cole and William Getty, who formally reviewed the document in the second round; and by the following additional readers: Marjory Blumenthal, Win Boerckel, Richard Danzig, Lynn Davis,

[7] For more information, see RAND Corporation, "Standards for High-Quality Research and Analysis," webpage, undated-c.

Jim Dobbins, Rick Eden, Susan Everingham, Bryan Frederick, Jayme Fuglesten, Malcolm Gladwell, Chuck Hagel, Laura Hamilton, Karen Elliott House, Joel Hyatt, Michael Leiter, Susan Marquis, Joshua Mendelsohn, Darleen Opfer, Michael Pollard, Donald Rice, Charles Ries, Jack Riley, Henry Willis, and Stephanie Young.

The authors also wish to thank Erin-Elizabeth Johnson for her insightful comments and careful review to ensure the clarity, consistency, and completeness of this report. Her contributions were invaluable.

The authors thank Greg Baumann and Jeffrey Hiday for their strategic recommendations, which helped refine and strengthen the report and the framework it presents. Jen Gould provided insights, support, and valuable feedback throughout the research and writing of this report.

The authors greatly appreciate the RAND colleagues who participated in discussions that helped generate the ideas discussed in this report. We offer special thanks to Sonni Efron, who helped frame the challenge addressed in this report and gather key pieces of evidence; Elizabeth Bodine-Baron, for her assistance in group discussions; Norah Griffin, who provided research assistance; Dori Walker for her help with graphics; Monique Martineau for her assistance with the summary and research brief; Jonathan Blake for his help creating graphs; Rosie Meza and James Henderson, who provided unparalleled administrative support; and Arwen Bicknell, who edited the report.

Finally, special appreciation is due to Lionel Johnson and Michael Tang, who made special efforts to enable us to get feedback about our preliminary ideas from diverse audiences outside of RAND.

The authors are grateful for all those who assisted in the completion of this report. All errors, however, are the authors' own.

# Abbreviations

| | |
|---|---|
| ACA | Patient Protection and Affordable Care Act |
| FCC | Federal Communications Commission |
| FDA | Food and Drug Administration |
| GDP | gross domestic product |
| GMO | genetically modified organism |
| K–12 | kindergarten through 12th grade |

# CHAPTER ONE

# Introduction

## What Is Truth Decay?

In many areas of American society, facts and data are essential to survival or necessary for success. Complex decisions, even when they require subjective judgments and intuition, can be made with more confidence when anchored by agreed-upon facts and reliable data. Architects rely on data to build bridges and buildings that do not collapse. Large manufacturing corporations rely on data to make operations more efficient and to improve products. Military planners use data and analysis to ensure that unmanned spy drones survey the correct target and that aircraft carriers are not lost at sea. Even baseball, football, and basketball teams increasingly rely on data to determine which players to draft, which to play in which situations, and how to tailor strategies to individual opponents.

For businesses and sectors that rely on data, recent advances in technology, computers, communication, and science have already proven advantageous. For example, the ability of super computers and cloud computing to process more data at a faster rate allows for more-advanced analysis of past trends and more-precise forecasts of the future in such areas as business, weather, and traffic patterns. And data-based advances in technology have led to faster and more-robust internet and cable connections that are critical for communication, geolocation, and entertainment.

However, national political debate and civil discourse do not follow this same trend of increased use and reliance on facts and data. Instead, over the past several decades, the opposite trend has emerged: an erosion of trust in and reliance on objective facts in political debate and civil discourse about public policy. This erosion has occurred alongside a sharp rise in political partisanship and polarization and alongside the emergence of 24-hour news cycles and social media platforms. At their best, these latter channels provide nearly constant updates on breaking news and developing stories; at their worst, they create a repetitive blizzard of falsities and opinions. A seeming explosion of misinformation and disinformation also proliferates through conventional and social media channels.[1]

Many observers and analysts have responded to these trends in the political environment by arguing that global society has entered a "post-fact" world or by focusing on the spread of "fake news," broadly defined. We believe that the argument is inaccurate and the focus is misplaced.[2] First, as noted earlier, facts and data have become more important in most other fields, with political and civil discourse being striking exceptions. Thus, it is hard to argue that the world is truly "post-fact." Second, a careful look at the trends affecting the U.S. political sphere suggests that such phenomena as "fake news" are only symptoms of a much more complex system of challenges, one with roots in the ways that human beings process information, the prevailing political and economic conditions, and the nature of the changed media environment. "Fake news" itself is not the driver of these deeper questions and issues, and simply stopping "fake news" is unlikely to address the apparent shift away from and loss of trust in data, analysis, and objective facts in the political sphere. As a result, a narrow focus on "fake news" distracts from a rigorous and holistic assessment of the more-extensive phenomenon—an assessment that might lead to remedies and solutions.

For these reasons, we have adopted the term "Truth Decay" to describe changes currently affecting the U.S. political debate and civil

---

[1]  In this report, we use *conventional media* to refer to cable and network television and to print journalism practiced by local and national newspapers.

[2]  Throughout this report, *we, our,* and *us* refer to the authors only, not to the RAND Corporation writ large or to all Americans.

discourse about public policy.[3] We define *Truth Decay* as a set of four related trends:

1. increasing disagreement about facts and analytical interpretations of facts and data[4]
2. a blurring of the line between opinion and fact
3. the increasing relative volume, and resulting influence, of opinion and personal experience over fact
4. declining trust in formerly respected sources of factual information.

Together, these four trends shape the current state of discourse and status of facts, data, and analysis in American public life—especially its political and civil discourse. We consider these four trends together because our initial research suggests that they are closely intertwined and that, as a set, they accurately describe the changes we have observed in the U.S. political debate and civil discourse about public policy.[5] Although each is certainly important in its own right, we believe that it would be difficult to consider any one in depth without also considering and exploring the others because of the many ways in which the trends themselves (and also their causes and consequences)

---

[3] The term "Truth Decay" has been used before in other limited settings, but not necessarily in the same way or to refer to the specific phenomena considered in this report. We do not intend to associate our report or research agenda with these previous uses. The authors thank RAND colleague Sonni Efron for first suggesting the term in this context.

[4] It is worth noting that disagreements about facts and interpretations of those facts can emerge through the collection of new data or the application of new methodologies that allow for more-sophisticated analysis and possibly new interpretations or conclusions. This is not the type of increase in disagreement that we reference here. We are referring to increasing disagreement in areas where existing data or analytical interpretations of fact and data have not changed, or where the prevailing understanding has even been strengthened by new data and analysis. We will discuss this distinction and its implications for Truth Decay in more detail later in this chapter.

[5] By *civil discourse*, we mean "robust, honest, frank and constructive dialogue and deliberation that seeks to advance the public interest" (Carli Brosseau, "Executive Session: Civil Discourse in Progress," *Frankly Speaking*, Vol. 1, No. 2, October 27, 2011). Within this general topic area, we are particularly interested in discourse surrounding issues related to policy issues and topics related to public well-being, broadly defined.

overlap. By combining all four trends into a single construct, we are able to explore and capture the ways in which the four trends interact with and magnify each other. It is the set of four trends and the way these trends interact, rather than any one trend or even all four considered independently, that most closely represents what we mean by Truth Decay and what we are interested in examining more closely in this report and in future research.

It is worth noting that although we are calling the phenomenon "Truth Decay," we are not talking about "truth" in the philosophical sense and therefore do not offer a specific definition of "truth." There are long-standing debates over the nature of truth, whether there is an absolute truth, and whether the truth is knowable at all.[6] We are aware of these discussions, but we do not engage them directly. Instead, we use the term "Truth Decay" as a shorthand for the trends just identified and focus on the importance of facts and fact-based analysis rather than on "truth."

We also acknowledge that, although there are certain immutable facts, analytical interpretations of facts and data evolve with new discoveries, the collection of new data, or the development of new technologies that allow for the retesting of even well-established findings. This evolution is a natural part of the scientific method, as are skepticism about and questioning of existing analytical interpretations of facts and data. Skepticism and questioning can contribute to the refinement of scientific principles and, in some cases, to the discovery of new facts or better data. Our focus on Truth Decay does not stem from concern about this evolution, which is a natural and inevitable feature of knowledge accumulation and scientific progress. Nor is our effort meant as an attack on skepticism or questioning of existing analytical interpretations of facts and data, which is healthy. Instead, we are concerned with the growing imbalance in political and civil discourse between, on the one hand, trust and reliance on facts and current ana-

---

[6] For additional information on these debates, see, for example, Alexis G. Burgess and John P. Burgess, eds., *Truth*, Princeton, N.J.: Princeton University Press, 2011; Richard L. Kirkham, *Theories of Truth: A Critical Introduction*, Cambridge, Mass.: MIT Press, 1992; Wolfgang Künne, *Conceptions of Truth*, Oxford: Clarendon Press, 2003.

lytical interpretations of facts and data and, on the other, opinions and personal attitudes—a balance that seems to be increasingly shifting in favor of the latter. This is not to say that informal and unsystematic forms of information—such as opinions, experiences, and personal attitudes—are invalid, but rather that they should be verified using the scientific method and after a common set of facts and data has been agreed upon.

This erosion of trust in and reliance on facts, data, and analysis has affected not just political and civil discourse: It has also invaded other spheres, including trust in science and even individual decisionmaking in such areas as health and financial planning. This report is primarily concerned with the effects of Truth Decay in the areas of political and civil discourse and its implications for public policy. In order to clarify our argument, we draw examples from a broad range of topics that are currently debated within these spheres, including the safety of vaccines and genetically modified organisms (GMOs), climate change, immigration policy, trends in national crime rates, and health care.

Some of the trends that constitute Truth Decay, and some of the forces driving it, might not be entirely new or unique to contemporary American society. Indeed, historians have observed some of the trends associated with Truth Decay in the past in the United States, such as during periods of economic recession, rapid sociodemographic change, and significant technological advances that change the way information is consumed and the types of information available. In many cases, there is a lack of systematic empirical evidence to explicitly measure the extent to which the Truth Decay that we observe in contemporary society is different from similar phenomena in previous periods. As we discuss later in this report, this is a gap that should be addressed by future research—however, analysis of historical analogues can already provide some insights into similarities and differences between the past two decades and previous eras. Understanding historical analogues can contribute to an assessment of the extent to which Truth Decay is new, contains new elements, or is something that we have seen before in its entirety. If it has existed in the past, an assessment of historical analogues can also provide insights into the course of the phenomenon (e.g., its duration and natural progression), its precursors, and the specific factors that might reverse or ameliorate it.

Even if some of Truth Decay's characteristics existed in the past, the current iteration's consequences still appear real and damaging to today's society. Truth Decay does not just erode Americans' ability to have meaningful political debates about important topics; it also contributes to political polarization and paralysis, undermines civic engagement, perpetuates the proliferation of misinformation and disinformation, and leads to widespread uncertainty and anxiety throughout the U.S. electorate. Each of these consequences has real-world costs in the areas of politics and governance (in the form of delays in key policy decisions) and effects on the lives of Americans (due to wasted resources, policy setbacks, and forgone opportunities). For example, attacks on vaccines—an issue that has become increasingly politicized—are based almost entirely on false information. Yet some parents' resulting refusal to vaccinate their children has real consequences, including new deadly outbreaks of diseases that had previously been nearly eradicated, such as measles.

Although there is evidence that this phenomenon is also occurring elsewhere, especially in Western Europe, we focused our research and analysis for this report primarily on understanding the trends, drivers, and consequences associated with Truth Decay in the United States. A better understanding within this narrow focus will provide the foundation for a more nuanced assessment of Truth Decay in other countries, including differences and similarities between Truth Decay at home and abroad.

Because the consequences of Truth Decay appear to directly affect the health of American democracy and have the potential to harm U.S. national security and personal health, it is essential that we gain a clearer understanding of the trends occurring as part of Truth Decay, their drivers, key mechanisms, and specific consequences.[7] Despite the

---

[7]  However, we would be remiss if we did not note that one of the reasons for tackling Truth Decay is that its four constituent trends might imperil RAND's mission of helping to improve policy and decisionmaking through research and analysis. Because we believe in and are committed to this mission, we hope that exploring Truth Decay and understanding its drivers and consequences will allow us to reduce any negative effects that these changes could have at the national and individual levels while continuing to pursue our institutional objectives.

significant amount of time, energy, and space that have been devoted to lamenting the declining reliance on facts, the proliferation of disinformation, and the erosion of trust in key institutions, there have been few systematic or rigorous attempts to precisely define relevant trends, to identify or study the drivers, or to assess the extent and scope of the problem and its consequences. It is not surprising, then, that there have also been few effective or innovative solutions or responses proposed or implemented.

## A Note on Terminology

Throughout this report, we refer frequently to different types of information, including facts, data, analysis, and opinion. To be explicit about what we mean by each of these terms, we provide a taxonomy of definitions and examples (drawn from a single field, health care, to make comparisons easier) in Table 1.1.

As we describe in later chapters, a central component of Truth Decay is people's inability or unwillingness to distinguish between and assign different values to different types of information (e.g., facts versus opinion, disinformation versus anecdote). Greater precision and distinction between these different terms will be necessary to address the challenges that Truth Decay poses. To take a step in this direction, we have endeavored to use these terms precisely and consistently throughout the report, adhering to the definitions and distinctions presented here.

In this discussion, we have already referenced the distinction between facts, which are objective pieces of information that can be proven or verified, and opinions, which are views, beliefs, and attitudes. There are also interpretations, which are not themselves facts but are based on analysis of facts and data. Many scientific findings can be considered interpretations because these findings are based on analyses of empirical data—analyses that are repeated multiple times to reduce uncertainty. Although interpretations themselves are not facts, when a given interpretation is reached repeatedly by many different groups of people, uncertainty can fall to a point where that interpretation can be

**Table 1.1**
**Definitions and Examples of Key Terms**

| Term | Definition | Examples (from health care) |
|---|---|---|
| Analysis | A detailed and thorough investigation or study of a specific topic designed to deepen understanding or identify component parts | • Articles in top-ranked academic journals that assess the effects of insurance-premium increases on the number of people with health insurance |
| Anecdote | Narrative of a biographical incident experienced by a person directly or indirectly through family or peers. This is similar to experience and might be a fact but is not generalizable. | • Narrative about a person's ordeal with rising premiums and medical bills<br>• Narrative about a young, healthy man who never bought insurance and was fine |
| Commentary | An article or statement expressing opinions, assessments, or explanations about events or a specific situation. This is similar to an op-ed. | • See, for example, Casey Mulligan, "How Many Jobs Does ObamaCare Kill?" Wall Street Journal, July 5, 2017 |
| Data | Factual information—such as measurements, counts, statistics, or qualitative observations—that is collected to be studied or analyzed | • The number of people with health insurance in any given year<br>• The number of people in the United States with a particular medical condition |
| Disinformation | False or misleading information spread intentionally, usually to achieve some political or economic objective, influence public attitudes, or hide the truth. This is a synonym for propaganda. | • False information about the provisions of a new health care bill, intentionally misrepresented by those for or against it |
| Editorial | An expression of opinion on a given topic by a newspaper, magazine, or other media editor or publisher | • See, for example, "A Scary New Health Care Bill," New York Times, July 17, 2017 |
| Evidence | Facts, data, or other information supporting a belief, argument, or view. This can be empirical (based on observation or experiment) or episodic (based on occasional or unsystematic observation). | • Empirical: data on the average cost of insurance premiums over time<br>• Episodic: observations about the number of major companies that do and do not offer health insurance to their employees |

**Table 1.1—Continued**

| Term | Definition | Examples (from health care) |
|---|---|---|
| Experience | Something a person has directly encountered or lived through. This is similar to anecdote and might be a fact but is not generalizable. | • A person's interactions with insurance companies during a long illness |
| Fact | Objective information that can be proven and verified and is consistent with reality | • The statement, "people who are age 65 or older, have been U.S. citizens or residents for at least five years, and have paid into Social Security for at least 10 years are eligible for Medicare" |
| "Fake news" | Newspaper articles, televisions news shows, or other information disseminated through broadcast or social media that are *intentionally* based on falsehoods or that *intentionally* use misleading framing to offer a distorted narrative | • A newspaper article criticizing an insurance company for raising premiums when the article's author is aware that premiums have not, in fact, been raised<br>• A television broadcast that knowingly misreports the number of uninsured Americans to advance a political narrative |
| Falsehood | Information that is inaccurate, inconsistent with reality, or is based on fabrication or fallacy | • An inaccurate report about total government spending on health care that overestimates or underestimates the true total |
| Information | Knowledge, statements, descriptions, attitudes, or messages communicated or shared about a particular circumstance, set of events, relationship, person, object, or phenomenon. An umbrella term that can encompass most things in this taxonomy. | • List of companies currently operating in the health care market (also a fact)<br>• A report summarizing changes to the health care market under the Patient Protection and Affordable Care Act (ACA) |
| Information system | Collective areas where information is shared, disseminated, and communicated, including social media, conversations, televised debates, television news shows, and newspapers | • Blog posts discussing the implications of different health care plans<br>• Television interviews with the leaders of health insurance companies about premium costs |

**Table 1.1—Continued**

| Term | Definition | Examples (from health care) |
|---|---|---|
| Interpretation | An explanation or understanding of a topic or issue that is based on facts, past experience, and analysis. This is not fact itself but is based on fact. | • A doctor's explanation for why a patient is affected by a given set of symptoms |
| Misinformation | False or misleading information that is spread unintentionally, by error or mistake | • False information about the requirements for signing up for health care, reported in error |
| Op-ed | An article outlining a person's views or attitudes on a subject, printed in a newspaper or other media source. This is similar to commentary. | • See, for example, Marc Short and Briane Blase, "The Fundamental Error in the CBO's Health-Care Projections," Washington Post, July 14, 2017 |
| Opinion | A belief, view, or judgment about a particular issue | • A person's attitude about the role of government in health care |
| Propaganda | False or misleading information spread intentionally, usually to achieve some political or economic objective, to influence public attitudes, or to hide the truth. This is a synonym for disinformation. | • False information about the provisions of a new health care bill, intentionally misrepresented by those for or against it |

SOURCE: Definitions are based on those provided by Merriam-Webster, home page, undated. We have modified some to better fit the way they are used in this report, but our definitions remain consistent with those provided by Merriam-Webster.

widely treated as a fact. It is also worth noting that, when we refer to facts or analytical interpretations of facts and data, we are not talking only about quantitative data. We also include systematically collected qualitative data, well-conducted case studies, and other types of rigorous qualitative empirical assessments.

Another important distinction is that between anecdote and evidence. Anecdotes are narratives told by individuals or groups that were directly or indirectly experienced but that are not generalizable. On the other hand, evidence is based on facts, data, or other information supporting a belief, argument, or view that is broadly replicable. Like facts, evidence can include qualitative information and quantitative data. Evidence can be empirical (based on observation or experiment rather than theory or logic) or episodic (based on a series of unsystematic observations). Unlike anecdotes, evidence comprises a set of observations or experiments that permit a more generalized statement or interpretation. Although certain types of information described thus far and elsewhere in the report might be more reliable and trustworthy than others (for example, systematic evidence of a theory might be more convincing than a single contradictory anecdote), even facts and evidence can be misleading if they are presented without context. The use of facts in intentionally misleading ways is as much a part of Truth Decay as the blurring of the line between opinion and fact or any of the other trends that constitute Truth Decay.

## Objectives

In this report, we contend that Truth Decay is a phenomenon that has historical roots; is exacerbated and accelerated by recent changes in U.S. information and political systems; and threatens democracy, societal discourse in the United States, and even individual well-being. Despite—and to combat—a lack of clear research on this issue, RAND has synthesized a strategy to investigate and potentially correct the negative consequences of Truth Decay. We describe this research agenda in Chapter Six.

Our report intends to provide a foundation for discussing, researching and analyzing, and responding to Truth Decay and the challenges it presents to contemporary American public life. We focus especially on political and civil discourse and on policy formulation, implementation, and evaluation. The report has three main objectives. First, the report aims to provide a foundation that policymakers, researchers, journalists, educators, and all members of the general public can use for more-effective and more-rigorous discussion of the phenomenon of Truth Decay and the challenges it presents—and can use to work toward solutions. Although not referred to as Truth Decay until now, the set of trends described in this report have been noticed and described by others, including researchers, policymakers, and journalists. However, the current discourse at all levels of American society about the erosion of trust in and respect for facts, data, and analysis is often hamstrung by the use of conflicting language, unclear or undefined terms, or words used to mean one thing by one group of people and something else by another. Without a common language with which to discuss a problem, the search for solutions becomes more difficult. This report seeks to address this challenge by offering a set of clearly defined terms, concepts, and relationships that can serve as this foundational lexicon going forward.

Second, the report aspires to present a working definition of Truth Decay and to identify and discuss its possible drivers and consequences. It collects and assesses existing episodic and empirical evidence for each element of the Truth Decay framework and identifies areas where more information is needed. Importantly, this is an exploratory report that proposes a framework for thinking and talking about Truth Decay and an agenda for further researching it, but it is not intended to be the last word on the subject. Instead, we hope that this report serves as a starting point for further discussion and research on this topic. Other organizations are also grappling with many of the challenges highlighted in this report, including such issues as changes brought on by technological developments in the information system and the role played by cognitive bias.[8] By developing a framework that defines the relationships among these different factors, and by exploring key elements of this framework, we hope to move the conversation forward and work toward a more complete understanding of Truth Decay that supports the identification of solutions. We expect that the framework proposed here—including the definition, the discussion of drivers, and the presentation of consequences—will be continually refined and elaborated upon based on the results of these discussions and relevant research. This report will be followed by others that further explore specific aspects of the framework and that refine and explore the broad research areas that we have defined in this report.

The report's third aim is to define a research agenda for the further study of Truth Decay that involves the broader research and policy communities. This agenda includes not only a set of research priorities but also an opportunity for all research organizations, as well as media companies and political actors, to consider how they themselves can better advance and promote the importance of objective facts, data, and analysis. It also intends to identify policy and other responses that might address some of the more severe challenges presented by Truth Decay, with the ultimate goal of strengthening the trust in and respect for facts, data, and analysis throughout American society and public life. Finally, the research agenda could also be relevant to interested individuals who wish to consider the role in their own lives of facts, data, and analysis and who are looking for ways to advance civil discourse surrounding these topics.

This report is intended for all audiences interested and engaged in the formulation, implementation, and evaluation of effective public policies. Because it is intended as a basis for further discussion and research and analysis on the topic of Truth Decay, this report should be of particular interest to the broader research and academic community. It is also intended for all citizens outside of these communities who are interested in understanding the drivers and consequences behind observed changes and who seek ways to address attendant challenges.

---

[8]   Kelly Born, "The Future of Truth: Can Philanthropy Help Mitigate Misinformation?" Hewlett Foundation, June 8, 2017.

We hope that readers will employ the framework and research agenda proposed in this report to build and sustain a constructive discussion and begin a systematic assessment of the ways in which public confidence in facts, data, and analysis can be restored and increased.

We believe that the problem at hand is severe and dangerous, and that it requires an immediate and far-reaching response. Without agreement about objective facts and a common understanding of and respect for data and analytical interpretations of those data, it becomes nearly impossible to have the types of meaningful policy debates that form the foundation of democracy. Without clear standards for the types of information that are disseminated by news media, political actors, and research organizations—and a shared framework to evaluate the veracity and credibility of this information—it is likely that Truth Decay will worsen, further degrading U.S. institutions, increasing alienation, and deepening divisions among the U.S. electorate. Unless action is taken to restore trust in and respect for facts, data, and analysis, much of the basis for the internal stability and prosperity of the United States could be at risk. This report responds to that challenge and proposes a research agenda whose purpose is both to deepen the understanding of Truth Decay and to identify responses that can be taken in the near and medium terms.

## Methodology

### Structured Discussions

To construct, define, and substantiate the Truth Decay framework presented in this report, we conducted several research activities. First, we held structured discussions with approximately 170 staff, including 145 RAND researchers from a wide variety of disciplines. These discussions (some conducted in groups of eight to ten people, and some conducted one on one) each covered a specific set of topics—including appropriate definitions of Truth Decay and its causes, consequences, and implications—and each surfaced ideas for future research in this area. Although details varied from session to session, we used a list of guiding questions and prompts to steer the discussions and elicit participant views. (The appendix lists guiding questions and prompts.)

We selected participants for these discussions to capture a diversity of perspectives and types of expertise. We included individuals from across academic disciplines (e.g., sociology, political science, mathematics, information science, engineering, management science, economics, health, education, law) and with varying levels of experience. We included individuals from RAND's three largest offices: Pittsburgh, Pennsylvania; Santa Monica, California; and Washington, D.C. Many participants are considered top experts in areas directly relevant to topics touched on in this report, such as information science, human cognition, political institutions, and education. Others were able to provide insights based on previous experiences in journalism, government, education, or the military. The group of RAND staff included in these discussions was diverse in some ways, including political views, but less diverse in others, such as educational background.[9]

In addition to RAND staff, we also spoke with a number of RAND-affiliated and external audiences, including educators, journalists, and entrepreneurs, as we developed and refined a framework for defining and discussing Truth Decay. The RAND-affiliated audiences included RAND donors and trustees, as well as people who have been involved in RAND's many outreach events. We also presented earlier versions of this work to a variety of external audiences whose varied economic and geographic backgrounds and political perspectives enabled them to provide unique perspectives on Truth Decay and its causes.[10]

We recognize that even this broader sample is not fully representative of the entire U.S. electorate and might leave certain segments of the population underrepresented. Our initial discussions were intended only as a starting point for an exploration of Truth Decay and we did

---

[9] For more on RAND's diversity, see RAND Corporation, "Overview of RAND Staff," webpage, undated-b; and RAND Corporation, "Diversity at RAND," webpage, undated-a.

[10] For a sampling of Michael Rich's earlier remarks on Truth Decay, see Michael D. Rich, *Erosion of Truth: Remarks from Politics Aside 2016*, Santa Monica, Calif.: RAND Corporation, CP-875, 2016a; Michael D. Rich, "Policymaking in a Time of Truth Decay," UCLA Law School event (via YouTube), September 23, 2016b.

not set out to capture a nationally representative population in this first cut at the issue. As this research continues, we hope to include the views of a broader cross-section of the U.S. population through RAND's American Life Panel and other survey and interview-based research projects, and incorporate additional types of diversity (including economic, educational, and geographic) that are likely very relevant to perspectives on Truth Decay.[11]

Each group or individual discussion generated new ideas, but a small number of common and recurring themes and insights emerged. To identify these insights, we organized key insights from each discussion into several broad categories: definitions, drivers, consequences, historical analogues, and research questions. We used a coding framework that allowed us to group statements referencing similar ideas into narrower subcategories. This coding framework included such categories as "critical thinking," "polarization," "trust in science," "fact versus opinion," "social media," and "disinformation." (The appendix lists the codes used in this process.)

Once the information was coded, we analyzed the information in each subcategory to identify a working definition for the set of trends in which we were most interested and to generate sets of hypotheses about potential drivers and consequences of these trends. To develop a definition of Truth Decay, we examined the different ways in which individual participants in our discussions defined the phenomenon and compared these definitions with our own. We looked primarily for areas of commonality where many people we spoke with agreed and focused on definitional elements that came up repeatedly or seemed to have resonance among other participants. This process suggested four trends that constitute Truth Decay. We used a similar process to identify the key drivers and consequences in our framework. Our initial framework was also shaped by literature reviews of other academic works and articles on such topics as "fake news," "post-truth," and related terms.

---

[11] For more on the American Life Panel, see RAND Corporation, "Welcome to the ALP Data Pages," webpage, undated-d.

As alluded to earlier, this initial phase of our research was not intended to fully elaborate Truth Decay's causes and consequences. Rather, we aimed to define broad areas of interest that could be further explored in subsequent research activities. The initial framework developed through our many discussions served as a set of hypotheses that we examined in more detail through a review of relevant literature and data.

**Literature Reviews**

Areas explored in the literature reviews were chosen based on our working Truth Decay framework (definitions, causes, and consequences), but we also explored other areas that arose in our structured discussions. We reviewed more than 250 articles and books from sources identified using online databases, such as Social Science Abstracts, PubMed, and JSTOR; the appendix contains a curated list of primary search terms.[12] Topics explored during this analysis included cognitive biases, social media and social media networks, partisanship in news media, information consumption and dissemination, training in critical thinking, civics education, political knowledge, political efficacy, demographic sorting, polarization, social capital, civic participation, and policy uncertainty, among many others. The sources we used varied based on the specific topic, but we relied on a mix of academic journal articles and books, newspaper articles, public opinion data and research, and reports from research institutions and government agencies.

When searching for relevant data, we relied on publicly available data sets stored and provided by the Inter-University Consortium for Political and Social Research (e.g., the General Social Survey) and data from such organizations as the Pew Research Center and Gallup. Both Pew and Gallup have well-established polling methodologies that allow for broadly representative cross-sectional samples, and both outfits ask the same questions repeatedly over time to allow for time-series analyses. The General Social Survey is similarly well established and has been used in social science research for decades to track attitudes

---

[12] Our review was iterative in that we conducted many supplementary searches for specific articles or citations that we referred to or encountered. Selected terms are provided in the appendix.

about social, economic, and political issues within the U.S. electorate. Although no survey is perfect, these three organizations use rigorous survey methodologies that have been refined over time. To guard against errors, we have, where possible, compared related and similar trends across several data sources to assess similarities and differences and to identify and exclude outlier results that might be untrustworthy. We also focused less on numerical results and more on trends over time, and we were careful to consider margins of error when interpreting results. Finally, all three of these organizations are widely considered nonpartisan and are not affiliated with advocacy groups.[13]

We used what we learned in these literature reviews to further refine our framework. We rejected no hypotheses and discarded no factors as completely irrelevant. All factors on our initial list proved to be relevant in some way. But we did alter, revise, and recombine these hypotheses to clarify the framework and reflect key findings from relevant research and additional discussions with experts in such areas as cognitive processing, education, and information technology. For example, we initially debated whether political polarization should be considered part of the definition of Truth Decay or a driver of it. Ultimately, we decided that polarization fit better as a driver: Although polarization can survive on its own, it is possible that Truth Decay requires polarization to survive. However, we also believe the relationship between the two is likely complex and involves feedback in both directions. As another example, we expanded an initial focus on confirmation bias as a driver to a broader focus on cognitive biases and processes. We incorporated disinformation as an aspect of a driver of Truth Decay focused on changes in the information system rather than a consequence of Truth Decay (where we had originally put it) based on additional reading about the scope and effects of disinformation and propaganda. We also narrowed our focus on education: Rather than emphasize the system itself, we focus on competing demands that crowd out such areas as civics and (sometimes) social studies. These refinements resulted in our proposed framework.

---

[13] For more on these three surveys, see Pew Research Center, "About Pew Research Center," webpage, undated; Gallup, "About Us," webpage, undated; General Social Survey, "About the GSS," webpage, undated.

However, it is appropriate to consider the framework and relationships presented in this report as tentative and subject to further revision based on additional research and analysis, including material proposed in the research agenda.

## Historical Analysis

Finally, we sought to identify periods in U.S. history that we could consider analogues to the present. We looked for evidence of the trends that constitute Truth Decay as we define it, focusing on the two that are the most observable and for which there is the most extensive and robust data. Specifically, we looked for evidence of widespread blurring of the line between opinion and fact (often triggered by changes in the information system that have affected the consumption and dissemination of information) and periods of declining trust in key institutions as sources of information. Initially, we conducted broad historical surveys and then focused in on specific periods using additional sources and available data. of quantitative data were useful, we had to rely largely on qualitative information (e.g., general histories of the media industry) for the years prior to about 1945. This allowed us to identify three periods that appeared to show promise as historical analogues, which we then explored in more depth to identify both similarities and differences with the present in terms of Truth Decay's four trends. Exploring these similarities and differences is key to understanding Truth Decay more clearly and identifying important lessons from the past that can be used to improve the present and future. It is worth noting that there could be other periods that warrant further investigation; we did not try to exhaustively identify all periods in U.S. history that might apply but instead focused on three that showed the most promise during our initial review. The three eras explored in this report are a starting point, and we recognize that additional research, including archival work, will be essential to fully assess the possible existence of Truth Decay's four trends in previous decades.

## Synthesis

After completing these tasks, we performed literature reviews and synthesized all the information that we could gather on each element of our proposed framework, which helped to identify and prioritize areas that have not been heavily researched (or that have not been researched at all) that require further exploration. Further work on these areas will add to our understanding of Truth Decay and how to address it. These gaps served as the basis for the research agenda. We organized these research topics into broader categories and streams (presented in Chapter Six). Importantly, our initial discussions with RAND staff were relevant; we asked participants to generate possible research ideas. Where applicable, these were also incorporated into the research agenda. As we note in Chapter Six, the research agenda should, like the rest of the material presented, be considered a first step and should be refined as the understanding of Truth Decay progresses and as ongoing or future work suggests additional areas that should be included and addressed.

## Organization of This Report

Chapter Two begins with a discussion of Truth Decay's four trends, including illustrations of how Truth Decay influences the types of information that are spread by media sources, shared in discourse, and relied on for important policy decisions. Chapter Three presents our historical analysis, focusing on three analogous periods and tracing the similarities between each of these periods and the current one. Chapters Four and Five present the drivers and consequences of Truth Decay that constitute the bulk of our framework. In those chapters, we summarize relevant literature and data on each element of the framework and identify shortcomings and gaps in that literature. Chapter Six outlines a research agenda—a list of research priorities and specific questions that must be addressed to improve the understanding of Truth Decay as a process and to identify effective solutions and responses. RAND hopes to pursue this research agenda and to find partners in this research in the coming years.

# CHAPTER TWO

# Truth Decay's Four Trends

In this chapter, we discuss and present examples of each of the four trends of Truth Decay, with two objectives. First, for each of the four trends, we provide a definition and illustrative examples that provide clarity. Second, we describe the evidence indicating that each of these four trends is real and present in the United States in 2017. Importantly, although there is an abundance of episodic indications that this is the case, there is a shortage of empirical evidence derived from rigorous and systematic analysis—where possible, we provide examples of both. Collecting additional data and providing empirical evidence of the trends that constitute Truth Decay are core goals of the research agenda described in Chapter Six.

## Increasing Disagreement About Facts and Analytical Interpretations of Facts and Data

The first trend in our definition of Truth Decay concerns an increasing disagreement about facts and analytical interpretations of facts and data. To be clear, this trend focuses on increasing disagreement about two different but related types of information. First, there are objective facts that can be verified and are observably consistent. Examples include the attendees at a meeting, the contents of a letter, or the amount paid for a service or good. Second, there are analytical interpretations of objective facts, such as inferences drawn from scientific data or conclusions based on statistical analysis. Analytical interpretations of facts are different than objective facts because the former inherently contain some degree of uncertainty attributable to scientific or human error or some other limitation. However, the degree of uncertainty attached to interpretations of facts and data varies. Some interpretations are highly uncertain (for example, emerging findings about the benefits of new cancer treatments), while others are more established (for example, the link between smoking and cancer). In this report, we are primarily concerned with increasing disagreement about objective facts and about the second type of analytical interpretation—specifically, those interpretations that are widely supported by data and evidence but where disagreement nonetheless appears to be increasing.[1]

As noted earlier, agreement about certain types of facts and analytical interpretations of those facts can erode, change, or face skepticism and challenges for legitimate and constructive reasons. For instance, new data might emerge, or new methods of analysis might provide nuance to previous understanding. For example, new technology allows for retesting of DNA evidence in criminal cases that can lead to the reversal of (or cast significant doubt on) convictions that had been widely accepted. This is not the type of increasing disagreement to which we refer here. Instead, we refer to increasing disagreement in areas where the prevailing understanding has not changed, or where it has even been strengthened by new data and analysis. Examples include skepticism about the accuracy of basic statistical information, such as the unemployment rate or the demographic makeup of the United States. It also refers to increasing disagreement or doubt about the interpretation or analysis of data and statistics in areas where supporting evidence has not changed or has strengthened, such as the science supporting the safety of vaccines, discussed in more detail later. In these cases, disagreement might increase as a result of dissemination of disinformation; personal

---

[1]   At points in this report, we use the shortened phrases *increasing disagreement about facts or declining agreement about facts* to capture increasing disagreement about both objective facts and the analytical interpretations of facts and data.

opinion, emotion, or experience; or the development of misinformed biases that reject prevailing facts, data, or analysis.[2]

One example of increasing disagreement about analytical interpretations of facts and data, despite an increasing amount of confirmatory evidence, is the recent rise in skepticism about the safety of vaccines.[3] Although there have always been vaccine skeptics, there was considerable agreement until about ten years ago that the benefits of vaccines outweigh the risks. This has changed, however—due in part to a since-retracted study and in part to celebrities who lobbied vocally against vaccines and called more attention to the issue. Public opinion data show that, in just the last few years, the extent of this agreement has significantly eroded, particularly within certain segments of the population. Now, decreasing numbers of Americans report that getting their children vaccinated is "extremely important." In a 2015 Gallup survey, 54 percent of respondents reported that it is extremely important for parents to get their children vaccinated, down from 64 percent in 2001.[4] This might not seem like a large decrease, but the shift has been significantly greater among specific demographic groups, including younger parents. This is also a sharp change from previous surveys on this topic, where attitudes toward vaccines were more similar across

---

[2]   Although skepticism and disagreement are necessary and important in social and scientific research and innovation and in the development of knowledge, basic agreement about objective and verifiable facts and well-tested and amply supported analytical interpretations of those facts—at least until new research and analysis introduce new facts or interpretations—is necessary for social, political, and economic progress and for democracy itself.

[3]   As noted in the previous chapter, this report is primarily concerned with Truth Decay's effects on political debate and civil discourse about public policy. However, Truth Decay is part of a broader phenomenon that affects other areas as well, including trust in science and individual decisionmaking. We use examples from these areas to define and illustrate Truth Decay's four trends. However, the majority of the report focuses on political drivers and consequences. It is also worth noting that many issues that were not political originally (e.g., vaccines) have become politicized as individual constituents lobby legislatures and school districts to loosen requirements and as courts rule on cases involving parents who decline to vaccinate their children.

[4]   Frank Newport, "In U.S., Percentage Saying Vaccines Are Vital Dips Slightly," Gallup, March 6, 2015.

age and other demographic groups.[5] This declining agreement about facts and data surrounding vaccines among individuals affects both sides of the political spectrum. In the aggregate, parents with conservative leanings are somewhat more likely to distrust vaccines, but a study focused specifically on the antivaccination movement in California found that vaccine refusal rates were highest in some of the wealthiest and most-liberal counties, including Marin and Alameda counties near San Francisco.[6] Studies at the national level confirm that states with the highest vaccine refusal rates are equally split between those won by former President Barack Obama and former Governor Mitt Romney in the 2012 U.S. presidential election.[7] There are certainly reasons, as we will discuss in more detail, why people might distrust the science surrounding vaccines. However, it is less clear why this distrust would begin rising even as the data in favor of vaccines grow stronger.[8] It is this phenomenon, we argue, that is a core component of Truth Decay.

Another example of a case where agreement about analytical interpretations appears to have decreased involves attitudes toward foods containing GMOs. Despite an increasing consensus among scientists that GMOs are safe for human consumption, public attitudes on the topic are growing increasingly divided. A 2015 survey found that 11 percent of scientists in the American Association for the Advancement of Science believe that GMOs are unsafe for human con-

---

[5]   Monica Anderson, "5 Facts About Vaccines," Pew Research Center, July 17, 2015b.

[6]   Anderson, 2015b; Tracy Lieu, G. Thomas Ray, Nicola Klein, Cindy Chung, and Martin Kulldorff, "Geographic Clusters in Underimmunization and Vaccine Refusal," *Pediatrics*, Vol. 135, No. 2, February 2015. It is worth noting that, although agreement among California voters has declined, state policy and the views of policymakers have moved in the opposite direction, with the state adopting a strict vaccination law in 2015. See Lucy Perkins, "California Governor Signs School Vaccination Law," NPR, June 30, 2015.

[7]   Alex Berezow, "Are Liberals or Conservatives More Anti-Vaccine?" *RealClear Science*, October 20, 2014.

[8]   See, for example, Centers for Disease Control and Prevention, "Vaccine Safety," webpage, August 14, 2017, which notes that "[d]ata show that the current U.S. vaccine supply is the safest in history."

sumption.[9] Trends among the public, however, are starkly different. In 2001, 25 percent of Americans believed GMOs were unsafe for human consumption. This number increased to 27 percent in 2004, then rose to 57 percent in 2015.[10] This is another area where partisan affiliation has little effect on individual attitudes.

A final example of increasing disagreement about facts, data, and analysis relates to beliefs about trends in violent crime in the United States.[11] Data from the Bureau of Justice Statistics show a steady decrease in violent crime rates since 1993. Attitudes about whether there is "more crime in the United States than one year ago," however, have not followed this same trend. Attitudes tracked closely with reality, as measured by the trend in violent crimes committed per 1,000 persons (over 12 years of age), until about 2000. After this point, agreement that crime rates in the United States were declining began to erode, and an increasing number of respondents reported that they perceived *more* crime in the United States than in the previous year, despite clear evidence to the contrary.[12] In other words, an increasing

---

[9] Cary Funk and Lee Raine, "Public and Scientists' Views on Science and Society," Pew Research Center, January 29, 2015a.

[10] Pew Initiative on Food and Biotechnology, "Americans' Opinions About Genetically Modified Foods Remain Divided, but Majority Want a Strong Regulatory System," press release, December 8, 2004; Cary Funk and Lee Raine, "Public Opinion About Food," Pew Research Center, July 1, 2015b. Note that these data refer specifically to consumption of GMOs and not to other safety-related issues (e.g., environmental impact) or in other areas. While issues such as the environmental impact of GMOs are essential to a comprehensive understanding of attitudes toward GMOs, existing data concentrate primarily on the issue of consumption. Changes in question wording may explain part of this change over time, but even acknowledging this, there still appears to be a clear upward trend in the number of people who believe GMOs are not safe for consumption.

[11] There are also examples of disagreements about more-basic facts, such as the attendees at a meeting or a sequence of events, that can be easily verified. However, we choose to focus on examples that, although they might be slightly more complicated, have more-direct implications for civil and political discourse, public policy, and individual decisionmaking.

[12] Bureau of Justice Statistics, "Data Collection: National Crime Victimization Survey (NCVS)," webpage, undated; John Gramlich, "Voters' Perceptions of Crime Continue to Conflict with Reality," Pew Research Center, November 16, 2016; David Frum, "The Coming Democratic Crack-Up," *The Atlantic*, September 21, 2015b.

number of respondents question existing data on trends in crime even as data collection and documentation methods become more advanced.

Together, these three examples illustrate areas where skepticism and disagreement about facts and analytical interpretations (1) have increased and (2) extend beyond partisan lines. This skepticism and disagreement focus not only on facts that are objective and verifiable but also on issues where uncertainty surrounding a given analytical interpretation is relatively low. Furthermore (at least, in these examples), increasing disagreement about the interpretations of facts, data, and analysis appears to be creating a divergence between public attitudes on the one hand and facts and data emerging from scientific research on the other. This divergence might partly reflect the rejection of facts and data in favor of experience, anecdote, or the opinions of others; however, other forces might also be relevant. First, broader skepticism about experts and scientific research, driven in part by past errors and outcomes or concerns over conflicts of interest, could contribute to doubt about even well-proven scientific findings.[13] Second, a lack of information could cause people to distrust scientific findings. A large number of Americans report knowing little about GMOs— many of whom also report believing that GMOs are not safe. These people hold views about GMOs that diverge from existing data even though these people might not have intentionally rejected those data or related facts.[14] It is worth noting, however, that the percentage of Americans feeling uninformed about GMOs over the past 15 years has not changed while the proportion holding the belief that they are not safe has increased.[15] This suggests, at the very least, increasing skep-

---

[13] We address the issue of agency as it relates to Truth Decay in more detail in Chapter Four.

[14] William Hallman, Cara Cuite, and Xenia Morin, "Public Perceptions of Labeling Genetically Modified Foods," New Brunswick, N.J.: Rutgers School of Environmental and Biological Sciences, Working Paper 2013-01, November 1, 2013. As above, this discussion and underlying data refer specifically to consumption of GMOs and not to other safety-related issues (e.g., environmental impact). While issues such as the environmental impact of GMOs are essential to a comprehensive understanding of attitudes toward GMOs, existing data concentrate primarily on the question of consumption.

[15] Cary Funk and Brian Kennedy, "Public Opinion About Genetically Modified Foods and Trust in Scientists Connected with Those Foods," Pew Research Center, December 1, 2016b;

ticism about related facts and data or the source of these facts and data. Another factor could be risk aversion, which causes people to fear things that are unknown and potentially dangerous, even when science attests to their safety.

## A Blurring of the Line Between Opinion and Fact

The second trend in our definition of Truth Decay is a blurring of the line between opinion and fact in a way that makes it difficult to distinguish between the two.[16] This can be dangerous when it contributes to the acceptance of opinion as fact, even when data and analysis suggest otherwise.[17] Some of the strongest examples of the blurring of the line between opinion and fact come from print and cable news sources. One manifestation of this blurring of the line between opinion and fact in today's context is the increasing use—even by established newspapers—of stories that combine opinion and fact without clearly demarcating which is which. One such example is the *New York Times'* use of "News-Page Columns," described as having "a distinctive point of view" and offering insight and perspective on the news. These columns, which might appear similar to straight news stories to average readers, include opinion and commentary about a set of facts or specific issues

---

Pew Initiative on Food and Biotechnology, 2004.

[16] It is worth noting at the outset that defining the line between opinion and fact can be difficult, especially because there is a gray zone between the two: that of interpretation and analysis of facts and data. This area of interpretation and analysis is neither strictly fact nor strictly opinion. There can be many interpretations of a given set of facts and instances when multiple interpretations might be correct. However, there is a clear difference between, on the one hand, statements of objective fact and, on the other, opinions or assessments based on experience, beliefs, and attitudes. When we refer to a blurring of the line between opinion and fact, we refer to cases where these two types of information—objective facts and opinions—are intermingled and confused, rather than to this gray zone of interpretation.

[17] We do not mean to suggest that people are not entitled to their opinions or to using subjective information in making decisions about complex matters. Instead, we highlight the current trend toward presenting opinions *as* facts or using them *instead* of facts, and we argue for the importance of having a set of objective, agreed-upon facts as the basis upon which people form opinions and beliefs about important political and social issues.

without a clear delineation between the two. The presentation makes it difficult to parse the objective facts from the writer's perspectives and evaluations.[18] In fact, this specific type of column was criticized by the *Times*' public editor as early as 2008 because such writing often made it difficult for readers to distinguish between opinion and fact.[19] This is not to suggest these pieces are not valuable or insightful or that they are not based on fact. However, because they contain commentary and interpretation, they are fundamentally different from stories that present only the facts and even from stories that present a writer's interpretation of a set of facts. This difference is often glossed over or blurred, creating ambiguity about the different types of information contained.

Another example is the increasing use of "sponsored content" in major news publications. Sponsored content, a form of advertising, often looks nearly indistinguishable from actual news stories; as a result, it can easily mislead readers who consume the content as they would an article based on reporting. Such content appears in many print and online newspapers across the political spectrum.[20] Cable news programming also presents examples of the eroded distinction between fact and commentary. Such programs as those hosted by Sean Hannity, Rachel Maddow, and Jake Tapper include a mix of facts and opinions, both from hosts and invited guests, without clear delineation of what information is based on objective fact and what reflects interpretation or opinion.

Changes in the types of stories produced by conventional media (both television and print) also provide an example of how opinion and fact have become blurred. Content analysis of evening news broadcasts and news magazines between 1978 and 1998, for example, found a shift toward entertainment, celebrity, and lifestyle pieces and away

---

[18] See "Help: Readers' Guide," *New York Times*, webpage, undated.

[19] Carl Hoyt, "The Blur Between Analysis and Opinion," *New York Times*, April 13, 2008.

[20] See, for example, T Brand Studio, "Cities Energized: The Urban Transition," *New York Times*, undated; Institute for Responsible Technology, "The Great GMO Cover-Up #2: Companies Hide Dangers; Attack Scientists," *The Hill*, April 12, 2016; "CMO Today," *Wall Street Journal*, webpage, undated-a.

from government policy and foreign affairs.[21] Another study estimated that soft, non–policy-related news increased from 35 percent to about 50 percent across approximately one decade.[22] These stories often contain fewer facts and tend to be filled with opinions and anecdotes presented as generalizable facts—yet another instance of the ways in which opinion and fact are intermingled in contemporary news media. Although data limitations prevent an assessment of how the 1998 distribution of content compares with today, an unsystematic review suggests that, if anything, the situation has gotten worse.

Some blurring of the line between opinion and fact also reflects the significant increase in the volume of information available and the relative concentration of opinion (versus fact) disseminated through conventional media sources and social media. This volume creates a challenge for people seeking to distinguish fact from opinion, effectively overwhelming their cognitive capacity, and creating uncertainty and misperceptions about what is true and what is not. Even under the best circumstances, people tend to struggle to distinguish fact from opinion. A November 2016 study found that a group of students was generally unable to distinguish true stories from false ones, to identify advertisements and sponsored content as such, or to consider the bias of an information source when determining whether a statement was fact or opinion.[23] These results provide additional evidence for the blurring of the line between opinion and fact and for the challenges this creates for consumers of information. Notably, there are limited data on whether individual abilities to distinguish facts from opinion might have declined alongside the increasingly blurred presentation of information. An investigation into this topic would contribute to an understanding of Truth Decay generally and this specific trend in particular.

---

[21] Project for Excellence in Journalism, *Changing Definitions of News*, Washington, D.C., March 6, 1998.

[22] W. Lance Bennett, "Gatekeeping and Press-Government Relations: A Multigated Model," in L. L. Kaid, ed., *Handbook of Political Communication Research*, Mahwah, N.J.: Lawrence Erlbaum, 2004.

[23] Sam Wineburg, Sarah McGrew, Joel Breakstone, and Teresa Ortega, "Evaluating Information: The Cornerstone of Civic Online Reasoning," Stanford Digital Repository, 2016.

A number of substantive examples reveal instances in which a blurring of the line between opinion and fact has created uncertainty and influenced public attitudes. One clear example is the question of whether immigration is a net positive or negative for the U.S. economy. There are many avenues by which to approach this question, but there are also certain objective facts, such as the number of immigrants entering the country, where and in what industries immigrants are and are not employed, whether their presence creates higher unemployment among various segments of the American-born workforce, and what percentage of immigrants rely on some kind of state or federal assistance.[24] (For the purposes of this example, what the data say is less important than the fact that there are data, generally of reasonably high quality, that can definitely provide answers.)

There are also a range of opinions on this question. Some are based on facts, others on personal experience, observation, or perception. There are also examples across the spectrum where opinions on the issue of immigration are championed as fact or used instead of facts to make arguments about the benefits or costs of a more or less restrictive immigration policy. Many of these arguments do not rely exclusively on opinion but instead employ a specific set of facts to make the case or use specific data and statistics in a misleading way. For instance, those in favor of increasing immigration might, using aggregate statistics, argue that immigration benefits all workers, choosing not to present data that show sectoral effects on employment.[25] Those in favor of tighter immigration policies might do the opposite, arguing that immigrants are a burden on the welfare system, without clarifying the specific populations considered in the analysis or the fact that only specific immigrant populations are even eligible for welfare benefits.[26]

---

[24] See, for example, Daniel Costa, David Cooper, and Heidi Shierholz, "Facts About Immigration and the U.S. Economy," Economic Policy Institute, August 12, 2014; Michael Greenstone and Adam Looney, *Ten Economic Facts about Immigration*, The Hamilton Project, Washington, D.C.: Brookings Institution, September 2010.

[25] David Frum, "Does Immigration Harm Working Americans?" *The Atlantic*, January 5, 2015a.

[26] Steven Camarota, "Welfare Use by Immigrant and Native Households," Center for Immigration Studies, September 10, 2015; Laura Reston, "Immigrants Don't Drain Wel-

These areas of blurring between opinion and fact become dangerous when they (rather than the objective facts) form the primary basis for policy decisions.

## The Increasing Relative Volume, and Resulting Influence, of Opinion and Personal Experience over Fact

The third trend is closely related to the second: the increasing relative volume, and resulting influence, of opinion and personal experience over fact, disseminated by traditional and social media. A simple comparison of the amount and types of information the average person had access to in 2000 versus today provides both an example of and evidence for this trend. As we discuss in more detail in Chapter Four, some of this increase in the relative volume of opinion and anecdote disseminated through media channels can be attributed to the shift to a 24-hour news cycle. When the length of news broadcasts increased from two to 24 hours per day, there was not a 12-fold increase in the amount of reported facts. Instead, most of this additional time is filled with opinions and commentary. The rise of social media platforms has also played a role in the increased relative volume of opinion disseminated throughout the information system. As a 2004 report from the Project for Excellence in Journalism noted, "Quality news and information are more available than ever before, but in greater amounts so are the trivial, the one-sided and the false."[27] This statement appears to aptly describe the increasing relative volume, and resulting influence, of opinion and personal experience over fact that we define as a part of Truth Decay.

The issue of immigration, introduced in the previous section, provides a good example of what this increase in the relative volume and resulting influence of opinion looks like and how this specific trend has affected policy debates. There is such extensive speculation and opinion

---

fare. They Fund It," *New Republic*, September 30, 2015.

[27] Project for Excellence in Journalism, "The State of the News Media Report: 2004," Pew Research Center, undated.

in traditional and social media channels surrounding such questions as the number of immigrants in the country, the extent to which immigrants take jobs from U.S. citizens, and the amount of crime perpetrated by these immigrants that it can be difficult to identify which pieces of information are fact-based and which are speculation or generalized experience. The fact that immigrants are actually less likely to commit crimes than people born in the United States and the fact that the number of illegal immigrants in the country appears to be decreasing are simply overwhelmed by news accounts and social media conversations filled with personal anecdotes claiming the opposite.[28] In effect, the relative volume of opinion and anecdote has drowned out facts, data, and analysis on this issue. This has consequences: There is a policy debate to be had about the proper approach to immigration, but it is hard to see how that debate can occur—or how clear-sighted policy decisions on the issue can be made—without establishing a set of basic facts and having a debate based on those facts. Furthermore, not addressing the immigration issue leaves the lives of millions of people in limbo, creating uncertainty and suffering that could be alleviated were the issue definitively addressed. Similar phenomena affect other issues as well, including questions about the relationship between globalization and trade and even the science surrounding climate change.

People have always been partial to their own experience and beliefs over disconfirming facts, and political parties have always used carefully crafted narratives to support specific policy positions. However, changes in the information system—especially the advance of social media—have exacerbated these trends by massively inflating the amount of opinion that can be easily and quickly proliferated. This is due both to the size of social media audiences and to the type of information often spread through social media channels. First, social media has the power to reach a majority of Americans almost instantaneously. A 2016 study found that 62 percent of adults in the United States get their news through social media platforms, such as Facebook, Twitter,

---

[28] See, for example, The Sentencing Project, *Immigration and Public Safety*, Washington, D.C., 2017.

and Reddit.[29] Second, studies have suggested that, far from promoting deep knowledge or understanding, the massive increase in the volume of information becomes overwhelming, inhibiting true learning.[30] Furthermore, there is some evidence that much of this information is false. A study of 64 assertions promoted in 24 hours by "UberFacts," a site that disseminates random facts through Twitter as a form of entertainment, found that almost 60 percent of those "facts" are incorrect or misleading.[31] The increasing number of sources and the 24-hour news cycle—both of which are explored further in Chapter Four—also play a role in the seeming explosion of opinion and personal experience available in each person's media channels.

## Declining Trust in Formerly Respected Sources of Factual Information

The final trend in our definition of Truth Decay is declining trust in formerly respected sources of factual information, data, and analysis. Public opinion data depicted in Figure 2.1 show quite clearly that confidence in major institutions, such as government, newspapers, and television news—organizations that used to be primary sources of factual information—has dropped sharply over the past 20 years.[32] According to Gallup, the percentage of people who express either "a great deal" or "quite a lot" of confidence in Congress fell from 22 percent in 1997 to 9 percent in 2016, although it did rise slightly to 12 percent in the

---

[29] Jeffrey Gottfried and Elisa Shearer, "News Use Across Social Media Platforms," Pew Research Center, May 16, 2016.

[30] Nicholas Carr, *The Shallows: What the Internet Is Doing to Our Brains*, New York: W.W. Norton and Company, 2011.

[31] Matt Novak, "24 Hours of UberFacts: So Many Lies, So Little Time," Gizmodo, March 12, 2014.

[32] Many would argue that, because of past problems and mistakes, these institutions are no longer looked to as sources of factual information. Certainly there have always been skeptics who have questioned these institutions and their credibility. Here, we mean to emphasize the extent to which this skepticism has grown to encompass the vast majority of the American public, particularly as it pertains to these institutions' role as providers of information.

**Figure 2.1**
**Public Confidence in Institutions, 1973–2017**

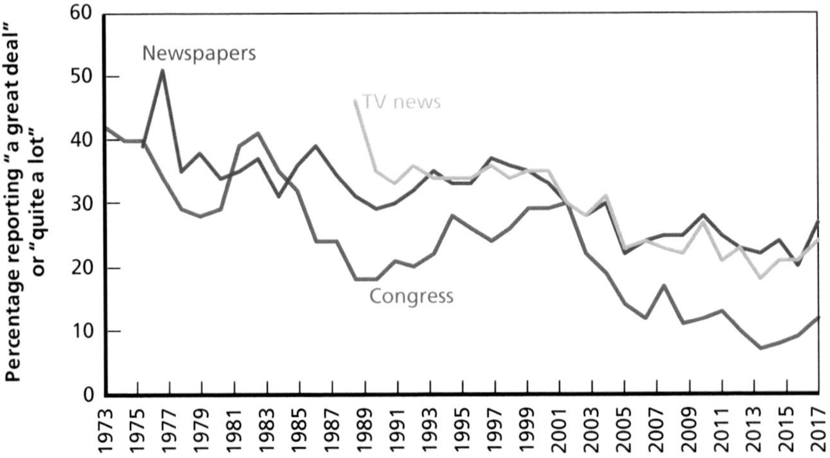

SOURCE: Gallup, "Confidence in Institutions," webpage, June 2016.
RAND RR2314-2.1

early months of 2017.[33] Data from the Pew Research Center similarly reveal that 20 percent of respondents report that they trust government to do what is right most of the time or just about always. This is down from about 43 percent in 2002, and from a high of 77 percent in 1964. Confidence in newspapers has fallen as well: 35 percent of respondents expressed "a great deal" or "quite a lot" of trust in newspapers in 1997, whereas 27 percent did in 2017.[34] This erosion of confidence and trust extends to other organizations charged with providing information, including the presidency, the judiciary, television news, and even books. Furthermore, although new institutions are emerging, there do not seem to be new trusted providers of fact-based information. For instance, trust in social media and news provided on the internet, added to the Gallup survey only recently, is already extremely low.[35]

---

[33] Gallup, "Americans' Confidence in Institutions Edges Up," webpage, June 26, 2017.

[34] Gallup, 2017.

[35] Gallup, 2017.

Not all organizations that provide information have experienced a wholesale decline in trust, however. Trust in the medical community and public schools has remained more or less the same or fallen only slightly. Somewhat surprisingly, given the previously described examples of spreading skepticism about scientific findings concerning vaccines, GMOs, and crime rates, trust in science as an institution has not declined significantly.[36] This suggests that, for some institutions, the decline in trust is targeted less at the institution than at the information it provides. It is possible that people reject or doubt specific scientific findings for other reasons, tied to emotions, fear, experience, social networks, or some other individual-level factor related to the specific topic. Alternatively, it could be that people simply do not know what the science says, either because they lack interest or literacy or because the way science is reported in academic journals, and even in the popular press, is confusing. Still another explanation is that people discount media coverage of new scientific findings due to a basic distrust in the media or the sense that the media exaggerates or misrepresents scientific findings.

Trust in institutions as providers of information has also declined more sharply among some groups than others. Returning to the example of trust in science, survey data suggest that although individuals who self-identify as liberal or independent show no real change (or a slight increase) in trust in science, those who self-identify as falling on the conservative side of the political spectrum show a rather steep decline in recent years.[37] There are three possible interpretations of this trend, all of which are probably relevant. First, it is possible that although trust in science has remained the same on average across the U.S. electorate, this trust might have eroded in certain segments of society, in this case among a particular partisan group. This might occur due to the worldviews and beliefs of the members of that group, the composition of their social network, their past experiences, or some other factor. However, it is also possible that this trend merely reflects sorting over time, with those people who have a generally skeptical view of science aligning themselves

---

[36] Gordon Gauchat, "Politicization of Science in the Public Sphere: A Study of Public Trust in the United States, 1974 to 2010," *American Sociological Review*, Vol. 77, No. 2, 2012.

[37] Gauchat, 2012.

with one particular party, due to the party's position on either this issue or others. Another explanation could be that people trust science as an institution but do not understand the processes by which a body of scientific research is constantly being evaluated, replicated, expanded, and improved and so are skeptical of or overly influenced by isolated findings.[38] Without a clear understanding of how scientific research evolves over time with the addition of new studies, new data, or new methods, people might tire of constant updates and revisions to scientific findings or medical advice. This fatigue might feed a broader degree of distrust in scientific findings more generally. Understanding which of these three explanations is most relevant could be important for understanding the extent to which trust in science as an institution has remained constant and the extent to which it has evolved over time. It might also shed light on the reasons for the decline in trust of other institutions that also provide fact-based information and the implications of eroding trust, where it exists, for individual beliefs more broadly.

This decline in trust in key institutions that provide information might be partially driven by increasing skepticism about and distrust of data and analysis, but it might also be caused by unintentional errors, deception, and malfeasance by many of these institutions themselves. Specifically, at least a portion of the recent decline in trust for institutions, such as government, media, big business, and academic research, might be driven by recent instances of intentional manipulation of information and data by researchers purporting to be unbiased, errors made by government and scientific research organizations, political leaders who do not deliver on promises, and deception practiced by large corporations and banks. A lack of transparency might also be to blame. Although government agencies, banks, research organizations, and other traditional providers of information have always guarded some information as proprietary or sensitive, any sort of secrecy in an environment in which most types of information are becoming increas-

---

[38] A review of how scientific research is conducted, evaluated, reevaluated, replicated, and improved is outside the scope of this report, but interested audiences can find relevant information at National Research Council, *Scientific Research in Education*, Washington, D.C., National Academies Press, 2002 (especially Chapter Three).

ingly available might lead to increased skepticism and distrust.[39] In the next section, we describe in more detail the role played by each of these institutions in contributing to the observed decline in trust and to Truth Decay more broadly. Other developments, such as the role played by partisan media organizations, political partisanship, social and demographic polarization, and a proliferation in disinformation likely also play a significant role.[40] These factors are explored in more detail in Chapter Four. It is also worth noting that the observed decline in trust in institutions as information providers might be driven by the dissemination of not only bad information but also good information: Sound reporting and investigative journalism have helped expose government corruption and malfeasance by other institutions, such as the financial industry in the aftermath of the 2008 financial crisis.

The erosion of trust and confidence in key institutions that previously served as sources of factual information has important implications for Truth Decay. First, the erosion of trust contributes to doubt and skepticism about statistical and other information that these institutions provide, as well as about the analysis and interpretation of this information and the experts who provide them. Although this might be justified and warranted in some cases, in others, this skepticism leads to the rejection of valuable and important data and facts with significant consequences. An example is skepticism and disagreement about the accuracy and credibility of the Congressional Budget Office, a nonpartisan organization, in its estimates of the cost to the government of changes in the health insurance market. Second, it leaves people searching for new sources of credible and objective information and increases uncertainty about basic facts, data, and analysis as people turn to new entities, not all of them trustworthy, to fill this vacuum.[41] In such a situation, with disagreement

---

[39] John Bertot, Paul Jaeger, and Justin Grimes, "Using ICTs to Create a Culture of Transparency: E-Government and Social Media as Openness and Anti-Corruption Tools for Societies," *Government Information Quarterly*, Vol. 27, No. 3, 2010.

[40] Margaret Levi and Laura Stoker, "Political Trust and Trustworthiness," *Annual Review of Political Science*, Vol. 2, 2000.

[41] For a discussion of general trends related to confidence in experts, see Thomas Nichols, *The Death of Expertise: The Campaign Against Established Knowledge and Why It Matters*, New York: Oxford University Press, 2017.

about what is based on fact and who can be trusted to provide facts, it is not that surprising that new areas of disagreement emerge and that the line between opinion and fact becomes blurred.

## Data and Evidence for the Four Trends

As we have noted, although there is a significant amount of episodic evidence for the trends we describe in this chapter and for the effects Truth Decay is having on U.S. political discourse, institutions, and ongoing domestic and foreign policy debates, there is a shortage of empirical evidence based on rigorous analysis. In some cases, this shortage is because of the limited amount of relevant data on a particular topic, often relating to the difficulty of collecting such information. For instance, data on the amount of disinformation present in the information system at any given time are limited. This means that it will be difficult to track the extent to which the volume of disinformation has increased or decreased over time. Being able to more rigorously document these trends and clearly distinguish Truth Decay from the past is an essential part of understanding the phenomenon, and RAND is working toward that understanding as part of the research agenda described in Chapter Six.

However, it might be useful at this point to think more systematically about where good data do or do not exist in relation to each of the four trends that constitute Truth Decay. Table 2.1 summarizes our assessment. The "Possible New Metrics" column lists metrics that might be useful but about which limited data exist; the "Already-Collected Metrics" column highlights areas where good data already exist.

The trend for which there is the most complete information is that of trust in sources of information. There are numerous sources of data on how trust in institutions has declined (e.g., Congress), remained constant (e.g., public schools), or increased (e.g., the military) over time. Although questions remain—e.g., why trust in key providers of information has declined and what the consequences are—the understanding of the basic trends in this area is solid.

**Table 2.1**
**Possible New Metrics and Already-Collected Metrics, by Trend**

| Trend | Possible New Metrics | Already-Collected Metrics |
|---|---|---|
| Increasing disagreement about facts and analytical interpretations of facts and data | • Analysis of existing public opinion data to identify areas where agreement has eroded or strengthened | • Public opinion data on key issues, and analysis of trends |
| A blurring of the line between opinion and fact | • Trends in the proportion of opinion and fact in news media over time<br>• Placement and amount of editorial content<br>• Data on people's ability to distinguish fact from opinion across a range of topic areas and contexts | • Data on people's ability to distinguish fact from opinion<br>• Trends in the mix of topics covered in news media |
| The increasing relative volume, and resulting influence, of opinion and personal experience over fact | • Trends in the proportion of opinion and fact in news media over time | • The relative importance of opinion and fact in individual decisionmaking |
| Declining trust in formerly respected sources of factual information | • Analysis of existing data to explore trends, similarities, and differences across institutions | • Data on public trust in institutions over time |

Existing public opinion data can also identify areas where disagreements about facts and analytical interpretations of those facts appear to be increasing across the electorate. These data exist, but there are few rigorous assessments of these data with an eye toward identifying where some sort of broad agreement exists and where it has weakened over time. Examples of increasing disagreement, discussed in this chapter and elsewhere in this report, include immigration, crime rates, and climate change.[42] This decline in agreement could have policy implications, even if policymakers themselves continue to be able to distinguish between opinion and fact. For instance, in the area of climate change, policymakers seeking political advantage could exploit a

---

[42] Cary Funk and Brian Kennedy, "Public Views on Climate Change and Climate Scientists," Pew Research Center, October 4, 2016a; Bradley Jones, "Americans' Views of Immigrants Marked by Widening Partisan, Generational Divides," Pew Research Center, April 15, 2016a.

lack of trust in facts and data to attract the support of voters sharing a skeptical view, or to attract funding from corporate donors who similarly distrust or ignore existing data and then make policy decisions that similarly disregard data to retain this support. These outcomes could be exacerbated if policymakers are affected by the same trends that affect other people and become unable to distinguish fact from opinion in all cases. Additional data collection might be valuable in identifying additional areas where agreement has declined.

For the other two trends—the blurring of the line between opinion and fact and the increasing relative volume, and resulting influence, of opinion and personal experience over fact—the data are much less rigorous. Systematic analysis of how media content and tone have changed over time, and quantitative metrics documenting growth in the volume of both opinion and fact, would help fill the gaps. Examples include an analysis of changes in the placement and amount of editorial content in major news sources, or an assessment of changes in the topics covered by traditional news sources, including network television stations and newspapers. Better data on people's ability to distinguish opinion from fact could also provide insight into the blurring of the line between opinion and fact. The question of measuring volume is also challenging; it could be difficult to identify metrics of information volume that can be tracked back in time. Study of the information system should include the types of information, disseminators of information, audiences, and forms of media. As study of this system progresses, focus should be placed on a better mapping of the information system and identification of specific issues or issue areas where Truth Decay has had the most and least impact. In addition, the extent of erosion in each of these areas should be documented. We explore these and other areas for additional research in Chapter Six.

# CHAPTER THREE

# Historical Context: Is Truth Decay New?

There is disagreement among political pundits about whether the four trends of Truth Decay—increasing disagreement about facts and analytical interpretations of facts and data; a blurring of the line between opinion and fact; the increasing relative volume, and resulting influence, of opinion and personal experience over fact; and declining trust in formerly respected sources of factual information—are "unprecedented" or have been seen before.[1] Certainly, there are aspects of Truth Decay that appear to be unique and different. However, a closer look at U.S. history reveals several periods—three in particular—that share many similarities with today along a number of dimensions: the 1880s–1890s, the 1920s–1930s, and the 1960s–1970s. Comparing each of those periods with the present day suggests that several of the trends associated with Truth Decay as we have defined it might have been present in some form in previous decades. Although we have not yet collected sufficient evidence to say definitively that Truth Decay existed in those periods, we use this chapter to discuss ways in which these three periods exhibit each of Truth Decay's four trends and ways in which these trends appear different from today. Importantly, although we consider these similarities and differences, we are not able to identify precisely what is unique about trends affecting the country today compared with the trends of previous decades. The research

---

[1] See, for example, William Davies, "The Age of Post-Truth Politics," *New York Times*, August 24, 2016; Francis Fukuyama, "The Emergence of a Post-Fact World," Project Syndicate, January 12, 2017.

agenda proposed in Chapter Six builds on the information presented here to further address remaining and related questions.

An assessment of similarities and differences might ultimately help researchers in the search for responses to Truth Decay, as might lessons or insights drawn from past experience: If periods in the past resemble today, understanding what made it possible to overcome earlier Truth Decay–related trends could suggest possible responses that might work today. Although additional research is needed to tease out the implications of historical analogues for possible responses, we try to highlight areas of promise based on the work we have done thus far. In some cases, limited available data and information make it difficult to draw clear parallels. This is especially true of the early periods, where robust data on public opinion are limited. To address this problem, we use what data we do have to provide as much insight as possible. In each of the three time periods discussed in this chapter, we first provide a general description of the period, including the specific political, economic, and demographic changes, to help set the stage for a discussion of possible manifestations of Truth Decay.

To be clear, the assessment of the extent of Truth Decay in the three periods presented in this report is largely exploratory. This initial review of evidence provides some insight into previous Truth Decay analogues and identifies possible lessons that can be learned from past experience. However, our review of historical manifestations of Truth Decay should not be read as a comprehensive or full history of Truth Decay in the United States. There are likely other examples of Truth Decay's trends in periods and contexts in U.S. history that are not considered here. Instead, we use our exploratory historical analysis to make a preliminary assessment of whether Truth Decay is a new phenomenon or something that has been observed in the United States previously and to identify areas where additional historical research might be valuable.

## The 1880s–1890s: Yellow Journalism and the Gilded Age

### Background
The most striking and formative event of the Gilded Age was the country's rapid industrialization, which included the rise of big business

and factories, mass production of consumer goods, urbanization and changes in the labor market, and the construction of railroads and other infrastructure. This industrialization was driven by such industries as steel, which formed the backbone of new construction and infrastructure. In fact, by 1895, the United States had become the world's leading producer of steel. Industrialization triggered social change as well, including the rise of wealthy business owners and investors—men like John Rockefeller and J. P. Morgan.[2]

However, these changes did not lead to universal gains. Economic inequality grew sharply during this period, and the gap and polarization between the poorer classes and the rich elite grew significantly wider. Although rigorous empirical data on inequality in the 1890s are scarce, what evidence exists paints a picture of widespread income disparity as well as inequality in access to resources and opportunities. Large numbers of agricultural and industrial laborers made on the order of one dollar (in 1890s currency) a day, while large business owners like Andrew Carnegie and Jay Gould acquired large business holdings.[3] Farmers complained that their needs and interests were being ignored for the sake of business owners and laborers. Worse, shifts in currency markets and foreign trade's growing impact on the value of the dollar drove down agricultural prices, causing further economic pain and, later, a severe recession. Business owners prospered while manufacturing grew, but urban laborers fared little better than farmers, earning low wages and experiencing fluctuations and uncertainty in employment that contributed to income inequality and a growing class divide.[4]

Industrialization did not just affect the nation's economy: It also contributed to increased urbanization. By 1900, about 40 percent of

---

[2]  "1878–1899: Business and the Economy: Overview," *American Eras*, Vol. 8: *Development of the Industrial United States, 1878–1899*, Farmington Hills, Mich.: Gale Group, 1997.

[3]  U.S. Department of Labor, *Bulletin of the Department of Labor*, No. 29, U.S. Government Printing Office, July 1900; Matthew Josephson, *The Robber Barons*, New York: Houghton Mifflin, 1962.

[4]  "1878–1899: Business and the Economy: Overview," 1997.

Americans lived in cities, compared with 26 percent in 1870.[5] The number of immigrants increased significantly, with many seeking work in the new factories rising in fast-growing cities. Between 1870 and 1899, about 3.7 million immigrants arrived in the United States, which had a total population of about 50.2 million in 1880.[6] Although the recession in the 1890s slowed the flow of immigrants for a time, new businesses that grew out of industrialization required a ready supply of cheap labor and thus encouraged immigration.

As the number of immigrants grew, U.S. workers protested the influx of immigrants, who were blamed for driving wages down and taking job opportunities from U.S. citizens. Congress responded with laws to limit immigration, including the 1882 Chinese Exclusion Act and the 1882 Immigration Act, which placed limits on the numbers and types of immigrants who could enter the country. In these ways, both the concerns and responses to immigration in the 1880s are very similar to some of the challenges presented by immigration policy in the United States today.[7]

In part as a reaction to new economic pressures and rapid social changes, and as an expression of dissatisfaction with the status quo, the 1880s and 1890s saw one of the early major surges in populism. The surge was led by William Jennings Bryan and the People's Party (also called the Populist Party), which was a major left-wing force in U.S. politics in the early 1890s. Importantly, the populism of the 1890s looked substantially different than the "populism" seen in the 1960s or in the 2016 election, although there are some similarities.[8] The Populist Party

---

[5]  See U.S. Census Bureau, "Table 4: The Urban Population as a Percentage of Total Population, 1790–2010," *Census of Population and Housing 2010*, 2012.

[6]  Linda Alchin, "U.S. Immigration Trends 1880–1900," Emmigration.Info, 2017; Elise Guyette, Fern Tavalin, and Sarah Rooker, "A Brief Timeline of U.S. Policy on Immigration and Naturalization," *Flow of History*, 2013.

[7]  Alchin, 2017; Guyette, Tavalin, and Rooker, 2013.

[8]  Since the 1890s, *populism* has been used to refer to any sort of movement, on the left or the right, that is anti-elite or anti-status and that promotes the interests of the "forgotten common man" over the interests of big banks, big industry, and other technocrats. These principles tend to be the core or essential elements of populism, even as ideas and platforms have varied on the margin over time. In many cases, supporters of populist movements are

of the 1890s represented agrarian interests and campaigned forcefully for agrarian rights and against capitalism, elites, cities, and the gold standard, which put farmers at a disadvantage relative to manufacturers of goods. In the election of 1896, the Democratic Party and leading candidate Bryan adopted many of the principles of the People's Party. Bryan failed to win the 1896 election and, in its aftermath, the Populist Party as an independent entity weakened and receded in importance before disbanding in the early 1900s as an official political party.[9]

### Truth Decay in the 1880s–1890s?

Evidence of Truth Decay, as we define it, in the 1880s and 1890s is mixed. There is fairly strong evidence that *yellow journalism*, which disseminated sensationalized and exaggerated news and information, both blurred the line between opinion and fact and increased the amount of opinion in the mass media of the day. It also seems likely that trust in newspapers as a source of fact-based information declined in this period, especially as stories became increasingly sensationalized. It seems clear that agreement around certain social and political issues declined and that trust in other institutions, such as government, also likely declined, but neither of these trends mirrors what we have defined as Truth Decay. The government lost constituent confidence as a guarantor of welfare, rather than for the accuracy of its information, and disagreement focused less on facts and analysis and more on social and economic policy and norms. Table 3.1

---

well-entrenched in the middle class, rather than being truly destitute, as was the case in the 1890s. Similarities between the populism of the 1890s and "populism" in 2016 do exist, including especially the anti-elite narrative, but there are also clear and important differences, including the agrarian focus in the 1890s and the push for more government regulation that existed in the 1890s and was less prevalent in 2016. Although the populism that emerged on the left side of the political spectrum in 2016 did advocate increased taxes and more social supports (e.g., high minimum wage, free college tuition) in ways similar to the populism of the 1890s, it did not push for federal government regulation in any real sense. The populism that emerged on the right side of the political spectrum in 2016 was even more distinct from that in the 1890s—promoting small government, a reduction in regulations, and tax cuts across the board.

[9]   Paulo E. Colletta, *William Jennings Bryan:* Vol. I, *Political Evangelist, 1860–1908,* Lincoln, Neb.: University of Nebraska Press, 1964.

**Table 3.1**
**Assessment of Level of Truth Decay in the 1880s–1890s**

| Trend | Low | Moderate | High |
|---|---|---|---|
| Increasing disagreement about facts and analytical interpretations of facts and data* | ✓ | | |
| A blurring of the line between opinion and fact | | | ✓ |
| The increasing relative volume, and resulting influence, of opinion and personal experience over fact | | | ✓ |
| Declining trust in formerly respected sources of factual information* | ✓ | | |

NOTES: An asterisk indicates that our assessment relies on limited verified data. These assessments are approximations and should be considered largely in relative terms (i.e., to each other, not across periods).

summarizes our assessment of the extent of the four key trends of Truth Decay in this period. These assessments are based on available information, and an asterisk indicates that our assessment relies on limited verified data. Note that these assessments are approximations and should be considered largely in relative terms (i.e., to each other, not across periods).

### Increasing Disagreement About Facts and Analytical Interpretations of Facts and Data

Limited public opinion data from this period and the decades before it make it challenging to identify the extent to which there was declining agreement about previously accepted facts in the 1880s and 1890s. However, political and social developments during this period provide some indication of areas where disagreement might have emerged. First, although the urbanization observed in this period supported growth in manufacturing, it also led to new social and ideological divides between those who moved to cities and those who remained behind. Social and family relationships in major cities were very different from those in the small towns and villages that had been the hubs of agrarian life. Many who had prospered under the old system—one based on farming, small artisans, and rural communities—resisted the shift to a new means of production and to a life based in cities, decrying the effects on social norms, living conditions, and public safety.[10] The values and priorities of those living in cities and those who remained behind also diverged in ways that might very well have led to declining agreement about social and economic norms. This is different, however, than the eroding agreement about objective facts and analysis that can be observed today.

A second possible indication of declining agreement comes in the area of electoral politics and the rise of populism in the 1890s led by William Jennings Bryan. Populism in the 1890s and early 1900s was largely an outgrowth of the Farmer's Alliance, an organization of farmers formed in the 1880s to promote the interests of farmers at a national level. The Populist Party, as alluded to earlier, campaigned actively for the rights of agrarian workers and lobbied against capitalism, elites, cities, and the gold standard, which put farmers at a disadvantage relative to manufacturers of goods. The party supported graduated income tax, more government regulation and involvement in such areas as railroads and telephones, and labor policy changes (such as limits on the working day). Its supporters were largely poor farmers of the South and the Plains States, although the party was sometimes allied with labor unions as well.[11] The very emergence of a Populist Party to represent the interests of people who felt that their views were no longer represented by mainstream parties might be evidence of declining agreement about previously accepted political facts and increasing disagreement about such issues as the role of government in the economy and the effects of various economic policies on individual well-being. Once again, however, this seems different than the increasing disagreement about facts described in Chapter Two and occurring in contemporary society,

---

[10] John D. Hicks, *The Populist Revolt: A History of the Crusade for Farm Relief*, Minneapolis, Minn.: University of Minnesota Press, 1931, p. 3; Library of Congress, "Rise of Industrial America, 1876–1900," webpage, undated.

[11] Eric Foner, *Give Me Liberty! An American History*, Vol. 2, 2nd ed., New York and London: W. W. Norton & Company, 2005; Matthew Hild, *Greenbackers, Knights of Labor, and Populists: Farmer-Labor Insurgency in the Late-Nineteenth-Century South*, Athens, Ga., and London: The University of Georgia Press, 2007.

where the disagreement is about basic and objective facts in areas where agreement was previously common and even unquestioned.

Thus, there is not clear evidence to support the notion of declining agreement about facts and data in the 1880s and 1890s. There appear to be some indications of possible fissures in society that might have led to divergent views in areas where agreement used to be the norm. What is not clear is the extent to which this increasing disagreement was about facts or analytical interpretations of those facts, as is the case with Truth Decay, and to what extent it was about changing values and norms. This is an area where future research could be valuable.

### A Blurring of the Line Between Opinion and Fact, and the Increasing Relative Volume, and Resulting Influence, of Opinion and Personal Experience over Fact

The 1880s and 1890s saw a clear manifestation of the blurring of the line between opinion and fact and an increasing relative volume, and resulting influence, of opinion and personal experience over fact with the rise of yellow journalism and more-general changes in the ways information was disseminated and consumed. The 1890s saw a rapid increase in the reach and circulation of mass-produced newspapers and monthly journals. Between 1890 and 1905, for example, the circulation of monthly journals increased from 18 million to 64 million, amounting to a significant increase in access to information.[12] The newspaper market was dominated by two men, William Hearst and Joseph Pulitzer, whose competition for market share, subscribers, and profits led each to print and promote sensationalized stories about crime and political intrigue. The result was yellow journalism, essentially an early form of "fake news" in which false or misleading stories were used to attract subscribers and advertisers in order to secure economic profit and advance personal political ends, much as has occurred in today's disinformation campaigns.[13] News outlets adopted clear stances on political and other issues, vilified the other side, and used misleading or false information for support.

---

[12]  Rick Musser, "History of American Journalism," University of Kansas, December 2007.

[13]  W. Joseph Campbell, *Yellow Journalism: Puncturing the Myths, Defining the Legacies*, Westport, Conn.: Praeger, 2001; Musser, 2007; W. A. Swanberg, *Pulitzer*, New York: Charles Scribner's Sons, 1967.

Although some historians believe yellow journalism is partly to blame for the Spanish-American War, most historians dismiss this argument. However, the "fake news" of the time did complicate political arguments and cause both confusion and distrust of media and government in the mid- to late 1890s.[14] Whether or not yellow journalism led to war, it seems fairly clear that it did contribute to a blurring of the line between opinion and fact and an increase in the relative volume of opinion and commentary compared with fact in news media during this period.

What caused the end of yellow journalism is still unclear, but research suggests a number of possible explanations. For instance, the start of the Spanish-American War might have played a role, creating a unifying nationalism that papered over the competition fueling yellow journalism and the social and economic dislocation caused by industrialization and urbanization. The Spanish-American War also seems to have precipitated a shift in journalistic norms and practices and the rise of the "muckrakers"—journalists who conducted deep investigations to uncover evidence of government or corporate corruption, a predecessor of today's (usually respected) "investigative" journalism.[15] Reporters might have been doing investigative journalism while yellow journalism was thriving, but their articles seem to have been overwhelmed by other, less-rigorous reporting. The attention muckrakers paid to collecting and exposing all the facts might have shifted the pendulum away from sensationalized news stories and back toward facts and analysis, reducing uncertainty and increasing confidence in the media and other institutions. It is also possible that a return to economic prosperity and a gradual adjustment by farmers and workers to the new social and economic realities of the time played a role by reducing political polarization and increasing consensus in ways that reduced some of the angst and distrust that fed into the phenomenon and culture of yellow journalism. These hypotheses should be further investigated.

---

[14] Campbell, 2001; Musser, 2007.

[15] Herbert Shapiro, ed., "The Muckrakers and American Society," *Problems in American Civilization*, Vol. 52, Lexington, Mass.: D. C. Heath, 1968.

### Declining Trust in Formerly Respected Sources of Factual Information

Verified public opinion data on public attitudes toward institutions from this period are limited, but evidence suggests several areas where trust in institutions might have declined. First, because of their poor economic position and the fact that they felt left behind by urbanization and related trends, Populist Party supporters had low trust in government and its ability to provide for constituents.[16] Second, despite the promise of the new industrializing economy, the United States experienced a serious recession in the 1890s, triggered by a panic and run on the banks in 1893. The recession led to sharp declines in employment and hurt the nascent manufacturing industries in the United States, as well as farms and small businesses.[17] The recession might also have undermined confidence in economic institutions, including banks and even new manufacturing firms. Finally, the rise of yellow journalism, discussed in the previous section, might have undermined trust in newspapers as people became less certain that what they read was an accurate representation of the facts.[18] Once again, however, limited data on public attitudes at the time preclude a definitive statement about the extent of any decline in trust that occurred.

Importantly, with the exception of newspapers, the situation in the 1880s and 1890s was less a loss of trust in institutions as providers of factual information, which is the focus of Truth Decay, and more a general loss of confidence in the ability of such institutions as government and banks to protect the economic well-being of Americans. This is one possible difference between Truth Decay in the current period and similar phenomena in the past: Today, people are not only losing trust in the ability of government and banks to protect individual interests but are even questioning the accuracy and transpar-

---

[16] Hild, 2007.

[17] Charles Hoffman, *The Depression of the Nineties: An Economic History*, Westport, Conn.: Greenwood Publishing, 1970, p. 9; Richard H. Timberlake, Jr., "Panic of 1893," in David Glasner and Thomas F. Cooley, eds., *Business Cycles and Depressions: An Encyclopedia*, New York: Garland Publishing, 1997.

[18] Campbell, 2001.

ency of information these institutions provide to clients and constituents. Additional research into the relationship between the past and the present on this dimension would provide additional insight into the aspects of Truth Decay that are unique and those that have been present in the past.

## The 1920s–1930s: The Roaring Twenties and the Great Depression

### Background

The 1920s were a period of fantastic economic growth and development that included the rise of mass-produced consumer products, such as automobiles, clothing, and radios. Government policies favored private business, and the stock market boomed, fueled by the practice of "buying on the margin" (essentially, buying stock by paying a percentage of the asset's value and borrowing the rest of the money from a bank or banker).[19] Although economic growth in the 1920s certainly benefited most Americans, benefits were not distributed equally. In fact, economic inequality in the 1920s reached unprecedented levels, which fueled resentment of the elites among lower classes that did not fare as well. Inequality reached its highest point in U.S. history in 1928, remaining unmatched until 2013.[20] Labor strikes by low-wage workers against their wealthy corporate bosses were just one manifestation of this inequality and the growing social unrest that spread throughout the late 1920s.[21] The prosperity of the 1920s proved unsustainable. The crash of the stock market in 1929 ushered in years of economic downturn and severe hard-

---

[19] George H. Soule, *The Prosperity Decade: From War to Depression: 1917–1929*, New York: Holt, Rinehart, and Winston, 1947.

[20] Drew Desilver, "U.S. Income Inequality, on Rise for Decades, Is Now Highest Since 1928," Pew Research Center, December 2013.

[21] Musser, 2007.

ship. By 1933, industrial output had fallen to 50 percent of its level in 1929, and unemployment peaked at 24.1 percent.[22]

This economic devastation contributed directly to the rise of Franklin Delano Roosevelt, who was elected president in 1932. Although Roosevelt did not campaign as a populist (and was even opposed by populists on numerous grounds), he championed and implemented many pieces of the traditional populist platform, including its anti–status quo, anti-elite, anti–big business stance. In fact, Roosevelt's first major actions in office included implementing more-robust regulation of big banks and business and increasing support for protections to labor unions and individuals.[23] He also advocated social welfare programs and the rights of individuals over large corporations. These policies did not, however, eliminate social unrest. Although good public opinion data from this period are limited, they indicate that trust in institutions, such as government and banks, declined.[24] Other political actors in the 1920s also advanced populist ideals. Huey Long, who served as governor of Louisiana from 1928 to 1932 and was then elected to the U.S. Senate, promoted social policy changes and wealth redistribution to increase economic equality.[25] As was the case in the 1890s, social and economic dislocation led to a surge in demands for social support and redistribution—demands that were also heard in 2016, primarily from populists on the left side of the political spectrum.

The 1930s also saw the rise of economic protectionism. The Smoot-Hawley tariff, for example, significantly increased import duties on goods and led to a string of foreign retaliations that caused a

---

[22] Susan Carter, Scott Sigmund Gartner, Michael Haines, Alan Olmsted, Richard Sutch, and Gavin Wright, eds., *Historical Statistics of the United States: Millennial Edition*, Cambridge, Mass.: Cambridge University Press, 2006; David M. Kennedy, *Freedom from Fear: The American People in Depression and War, 1929–1945*, Oxford and New York: Oxford University Press, 1999, p. 167.

[23] Joseph M. Siracusa and David G. Coleman, *Depression to Cold War: A History of America from Herbert Hoover to Ronald Reagan*, Santa Barbara, Calif.: Praeger, 2002.

[24] Musser, 2007.

[25] William Ivy Hair, *The Kingfish and His Realm: The Life and Times of Huey P. Long*, Baton Rouge, La.: Louisiana State University Press, 1996.

sharp reduction in international trade. This protectionism, supported by special interests, had negative effects, such as prolonging the Great Depression and raising the price of imports.[26] The Great Depression, and the protectionism that accompanied it, was brought to an end by a combination of World War II, which increased demand for U.S. manufacturing and helped increase employment, and the New Deal—a model that lessened political and social unrest and helped restart the economy, partly by creating the start of a social safety net that could protect individuals from falling through the cracks.

**Truth Decay in the 1920s–1930s?**

As in the 1880s and 1890s, evidence of Truth Decay in the 1920s and 1930s is mixed. Once again, there is evidence that changes in the media market—the rise of tabloid journalism and radio—contributed to some blurring of the line between opinion and fact and an increase in the amount of opinion relative to fact disseminated through media sources. However, it is not clear that either challenge was as severe as that experienced in the 1880s and 1890s. Evidence that trust in institutions might have declined is also present in this period. In this case, some of this decline in trust seems to have arisen from the role that such institutions as banks and government played in providing fact-based information, particularly about financial and economic issues. Interestingly, however, there is little evidence that trust in the media itself declined, despite the blurring of the line between opinion and fact that came with the rise of jazz journalism in the 1920s, and its shifting emphasis on sensationalized news as entertainment, rather than facts. As in the 1880s and 1890s, any evidence of declining agreement appears to have primarily centered on political and social issues rather than facts and analysis. Once again, then, there appear to be elements of Truth Decay in this period, but there are also clear ways in which the phenomenon observed today seems distinct. Table 3.2 summarizes our assessment of the severity of the four key trends of Truth Decay in this period.

---

[26] Alfred E. Eckes, Jr., *Opening America's Market: U.S. Foreign Trade Policy Since 1776*, Chapel Hill, N.C.: University of North Carolina Press, 1995.

Table 3.2
Assessment of Level of Truth Decay in the 1920s–1930s

| Trend | Low | Moderate | High |
|---|---|---|---|
| Increasing disagreement about facts and analytical interpretations of facts and data* | ✓ | | |
| A blurring of the line between opinion and fact | | ✓ | |
| The increasing relative volume, and resulting influence, of opinion and personal experience over fact | | ✓ | |
| Declining trust in formerly respected sources of factual information* | | | ✓ |

NOTES: An asterisk indicates that our assessment relies on limited verified data. These assessments are approximations and should be considered largely in relative terms (i.e., to each other, not across periods).

### *Increasing Disagreement About Facts and Analytical Interpretations of Facts and Data*

Limited rigorous public opinion data from this period make it difficult to judge the extent to which disagreement about facts and analytical interpretations of facts and data increased in the 1920s and 1930s. A review of political, social, and economic events suggests that any real decline in societal agreement was likely limited to the 1920s and focused mainly on social issues; the severe depression that took hold in the 1930s likely papered over, or at least deprioritized, some of the internal divisions within the United States. Declining agreement during the 1920s appears to have emerged around several key issues. First, as noted earlier, economic inequality in the 1920s reached unprecedented levels, driving resentment of elites among lower classes that did not fare as well, triggering strikes and unrest.[27] Although the existence of high economic inequality does not directly imply a simultaneous decline in agreement about facts, it might contribute to differing views about the optimal economic policy, evaluations of U.S. economic conditions, and expectations about the role of government in society. More generally, some historians note that the 1920s were characterized by duel-

---

[27] Drew Desilver, "U.S. Income Inequality, on Rise for Decades, Is Now Highest Since 1928," Pew Research Center, December 2013.

ing forces of conservativism (embodied in the push for such policies as Prohibition) and progressivism (advanced by newly wealthy youths living in major cities).[28]

Although there does seem to be evidence that social consensus eroded during the 1920s, this is somewhat different than the increasing disagreement that is a focal point of Truth Decay. Most importantly, the declining agreement in the 1920s appears to have concerned social and political norms and economic policy. The increasing disagreement observed today—and that we are focusing on as part of Truth Decay—concerns the accuracy and legitimacy of basic facts and analytical findings. This might be a fundamental difference between the phenomenon of Truth Decay as observed in contemporary society and similar phenomena witnessed in the past.

### A Blurring of the Line Between Opinion and Fact, and the Increasing Relative Volume, and Resulting Influence, of Opinion and Personal Experience over Fact

Changes in the media environment in the 1920s and 1930s clearly led to some blurring of the line between opinion and fact and to the increasing relative volume, and resulting influence, of opinion and personal experience over fact that are part of Truth Decay. First, the 1920s saw the rise of tabloid journalism, known then as "jazz journalism," which sold sensationalized and even fabricated stories of sex and violence to attract attention and subscribers. Jazz journalism was similar to yellow journalism in that it used sensationalized language and intermingled fact and fiction. It was different, however, in that it focused less on news and more on sex, violence, and alcohol. Media became not only a source of information but also a source of entertainment, opinion, and sensationalism, eroding the line between falsehood or exaggeration on the one hand and objective fact on the other.

The rise of tabloids also challenged more-established newspapers, which were forced to differentiate themselves as "real journalism" while also fighting to keep their readers. To compete, the more-established

---

[28] Paul Aaron and David Musto, "Temperance and Prohibition in America: An Historical Overview," in Mark H. Moore and Dean R. Gerstein, eds., *Alcohol and Public Policy: Beyond the Shadow of Prohibition*, Washington, D.C.: National Academies Press, 1981, p. 157.

publications shifted toward offering a higher concentration of non-news content, such as advice columns, short stories, and other serialized or editorial content.[29] This shift in content increased the volume of opinion and anecdote, often at the expense of facts, and it resembles changes observed more recently among conventional media outlets struggling to compete with newer web-based publications that offer less news but are more appealing. Tabloids continued to thrive in the 1930s but lost favor in the 1940s, as journalists took the responsibility of reporting the events of World War II.[30]

The 1920s and 1930s also saw the rise of radio as a primary player in the media market. Although radio had some clear advantages in terms of providing a wider audience with access to information, it also contributed both to the blurring of the line between opinion and fact and to an increase in wide dissemination of opinions. In 1930, about 40 percent of households in the United States had radios; by 1940, the figure had risen to almost 85 percent.[31] Radio programs ranged in nature from comedy and drama to religious and political. Interestingly, debates and discussion about the effects of radio on society echo many current debates and discussions about the impact of the internet. Although radio gave many more people access to information, some argued that it would lead to social atomization, with people turning away from traditional social gatherings and interactions.[32] Others criticized radio for spreading immorality. Still others praised its ability to elicit new democratic vigor and participation.[33]

Regardless of its ultimate social impact, radio began the process of democratizing access to information but also demonstrated how the power of individual opinion and experience could shape public beliefs. Radio personalities gained large followings, and some used serial-

---

[29] Musser, 2007.

[30] Steve Vaughn, ed., *Encyclopedia of American Journalism*, New York: Routledge, 2008.

[31] Musser, 2007.

[32] We use the term *social atomization* to refer to a process in which individuals become isolated, turning inward and doing things on their own, rather than engaging actively with others.

[33] Musser, 2007.

ized shows to spread their worldviews, much as today's cable television hosts use nightly shows to expound their views on world events. Roosevelt broadcast his famous "fireside chats," which allowed him to reach out directly to the electorate. A particularly formative radio figure was Father Charles Coughlin, a priest who used his show to promote his political and social views, including nationalization of major industries, anti-Semitism, protection of workers, and other principles he called "social justice." His arguments were based on ideology and opinion and took liberty with facts, as sometimes observed today on cable news channels. It is worth noting that Coughlin's views changed often: At different times in his career, he supported and opposed communism, Roosevelt, and capitalism.[34] Although Coughlin's radio show was canceled in 1929, he was one of many personalities who shaped the political and social thought of the day.

Radio facilitated the spread of opinion and commentary to a wide audience and made it increasingly difficult to distinguish fact from opinion. It was difficult to assess the trustworthiness of any individual radio host and even more difficult for listeners to "fact-check" information they heard on a radio program. Radio programs undoubtedly provided people with new sources of fact-based information but also provided access to a wealth of opinions and a forum for people seeking to promote or advance their own ideologies. Although not identical, these trends do seem similar in some ways to Truth Decay.

### Declining Trust in Formerly Respected Sources of Factual Information

With limited public opinion data about attitudes toward institutions, it is somewhat difficult to rigorously evaluate any decline in trust in institutions. However, it is possible to make some general assessments based on the evidence that does exist. First, trust in government as both a provider of information, at least in the economic sphere, and a guarantor of individual welfare most likely declined in the wake of the 1929 crash, which directly undermined and contradicted government posi-

---

[34] Kennedy, 1999; Charles J. Tull, *Father Coughlin and the New Deal*, Syracuse, N.Y.: Syracuse University Press, 1965.

tions, policies, and promises. In the lead-up to the 1928 election, for example, it was widely circulated that, if Republican Herbert Hoover were elected, there would be "a chicken in every pot and a car in every garage." Although Hoover never directly promised this outcome (the slogan was derived from a political advertisement), the perception that he had, combined with the sharply contrasting reality in the early 1930s, might have undermined public confidence in government and the supposedly factual information it provided on economic policy and future promises.[35] The election of Roosevelt and the implementation of New Deal policies fostered an image of the government as both a provider of welfare and information, which somewhat restored public trust in the institution more generally. Additional research on attitudes toward government as an information provider would increase understanding of the extent to and ways in which the events of 1929 undermined trust in government as a provider of fact-based information.

Second, trust in large banks—and in the finance industry more generally—fell sharply during the Great Depression because both were ultimately seen as the cause of the 1929 crash. Large numbers of Americans took their money out of banks that were no longer viewed as safe repositories for assets or as trusted sources of financial information. The entire banking industry was stained as corrupt and dishonest, and this reputation extended to the business that banks conducted, the services they provided, and the information they shared with customers and others about personal and national economic futures.[36] After he became president in 1933, Roosevelt made changes in regulatory policy for big banks a top priority. These policy changes appear to have gone a long way toward restoring mainstream trust in the banking industry.[37]

Government and banks seem to have suffered some loss of trust in the 1920s and early 1930s. But it is unclear that trust in media sources

---

[35] Martin Carcasson, "Herbert Hoover and the Presidential Campaign of 1932: The Failure of Apologia," *Presidential Studies Quarterly*, Vol. 28, No. 2, Spring 1998.

[36] David Leonhardt, "Lesson from a Crisis: When Trust Vanishes, Worry," *New York Times*, September 30, 2008.

[37] Julia Maues, "Banking Act of 1933," Federal Reserve Bank of St. Louis, November 22, 2013.

declined in the 1920s and 1930s, despite the rise of tabloid journalism and the advent of talk radio and its sometimes opinionated hosts. The advent of jazz journalism might have somewhat undermined public confidence in the quality and accuracy of news, but the rise and spread of radio increased access and made listening to news and other programs a central part of the average person's life. If anything, the rise of radio seems to have increased public trust in the media organizations of the time. The 1920s and 1930s were known as the Golden Age of Radio, so named for the outsize influence that radio had as a source of news, connection, and entertainment in society at the time.[38]

Thus, the decline of trust in institutions generally and as information providers specifically bears both similarities to and differences from trends observed in contemporary society. Although there is evidence that trust in government and banks as sources of information might have declined during the earlier period, lost credibility primarily affected economic policy and financial issues. This is somewhat unlike today's environment, where trust in all information coming out of government institutions appears to be on the decline. Also unlike today, it is not at all clear that trust in media organizations fell during the 1920s and 1930s, despite the blurring of the line between opinion and fact and the seeming increase in the relative volume of opinion that occurred at that time. Future research into what allowed media of the time to retain popular trust despite the infusion of sensationalism and opinion would be valuable for its insights into today.

Despite the increasing amount of opinion and commentary disseminated over the radio, there were, starting in the 1930s and 1940s, countervailing forces that pushed toward a greater use of data and analysis, particularly in government policymaking. The increased value placed on research and analysis might have been a primary factor in (1) restoring trust in government and other institutions as information providers and (2) rebuilding the importance of facts and data in other areas of society. A number of specific developments provide evidence of this shift toward greater use and reliance on facts, data, and

---

[38] Francis Seabury Chase, *Sound and Fury: An Informal History of Broadcasting*, New York: Harper & Brothers, 1942.

analysis starting in this period. First, the 1930s saw the birth of an industry focused on collecting and analyzing public opinion data as a way of informing policy and understanding public attitudes and how they evolve over time. Organizations such as Gallup not only made it easier for leaders and policymakers to study and track public opinion but also made this information more readily available to all interested parties.[39] Second, the New Deal brought with it a large number of federal agencies, such as the Farm Security Administration, the Drought Relief Service, the Federal Communications Commission, the Federal Surplus Relief Corporation and others, that were empowered to collect and use data and analysis to guide policy formation, implementation, and later, evaluation. These organizations had their own objectives and purposes but shared a greater reliance on data, research, and analysis as an important and necessary policy tool.[40]

Some organizations were more heavily involved with data and analysis than others. For instance, the Great Depression underscored the need for better and more-complete data on the state of the economy so that governing agencies could monitor progress and address problems before they arose. During the 1930s, the Department of Commerce asked Simon Kuznets of the National Bureau of Economic Research to develop a set of metrics that could be used to track various aspects of the economy.[41] This led to the development of the national income and product accounts and paved the way for the creation of additional metrics that could be used to guide government policy and planning.[42] The introduction of these metrics, and their successful use by economic planners across the federal government, allowed for greater economic stability and economic growth. The benefits of these metrics in the economic sphere contributed to increased use of relevant metrics in other

---

[39] Gallup, undated.

[40] Michael Hiltzik, *The New Deal: A Modern History*, New York: Free Press, 2011.

[41] U.S. Department of Commerce, Bureau of Economic Analysis, "GDP: One of the Great Inventions of the 20th Century," from the January 2000 Survey of Current Business, January 2000.

[42] U.S. Department of Commerce, Bureau of Economic Analysis, 2000.

fields, such as health and military planning.[43] As a second example, building off of scientific research that documented the benefits of crop rotation as a way to enrich soil and increase crop yields over time, the Soil Conservation Service (yet another federal agency) began paying farmers to leave certain fields unplanted; in addition, it educated farmers about data-based ways to improve farming techniques and increase profits and economic well-being.[44] The shift toward data-based planning and policy formulation during this period might reflect a reaction to the negative consequences of governing with misleading, haphazard, or incomplete information as occurred in some areas during the 1920s, and a new recognition of the general value of facts and data in the policymaking process. The shift may also be partly credited with increased respect for and value placed on facts, data, and analysis, which might have combated any Truth Decay that did exist during the Great Depression period. We return to the importance of this development later in this chapter.

## The 1960s and Early 1970s: Civil Rights, Social Protest, and the Vietnam War

### Background

The late 1960s were rocked by social and political protests against the Vietnam War, social ills, racial discrimination, and government institutions. The Vietnam War, for which public support declined after 1968, was the backdrop for this social upheaval, and economic recession and the rise of television played major roles as well. The political, social, and economic developments of the late 1960s and early 1970s were closely intertwined. The period was one of extensive social change. Despite passage of the landmark Civil Rights Act and Voting Rights Act, violence and discrimination persisted. The Civil Rights Movement used protests and civil resistance to pressure the government into adopt-

---

[43] U.S. Department of Commerce, Bureau of Economic Analysis, 2000.

[44] Christopher Klein, "10 Things You May Not Know About the Dust Bowl," *The History Channel*, August 24, 2012.

ing new policies to protect minority populations, especially those who faced discrimination due to race. Although the movement won legislative gains, including protections for immigrants (the Immigration and Nationality Act),[45] African-Americans (the Voting Rights Act), and other nonwhite racial groups, discrimination and violence against these groups persisted, primarily from a white majority that did not want change.[46]

Protests at the time combined anti-establishment and anti-government sentiments with political and economic unrest. Populism surged again in the 1960s, this time under George Wallace, a segregationist and socially conservative governor from Alabama. However, unlike the populism of the 1880s and 1890s, populism in the 1960s contained elements of traditional populism and some unique elements. Wallace advocated for the common man and the working class and for expanding social benefits, but he also embraced segregation, campaigned on a "law and order" platform, and promised an end to the Vietnam War. His success—he won 13.6 percent of the popular vote as a third-party candidate—was evidence of significant disillusionment with the traditional political parties.[47] The 1970s saw the Watergate scandal unfold and, with it, a decline in trust in government from citizens across the political spectrum. Watergate (which suggested government corruption) and the Pentagon Papers (which showed that the government had manufactured information and lied to the public about the Vietnam War) led Americans to

---

[45] The Immigration and Nationality Act abolished the quota system based on national origin and created a new preference system based on immigrants' skills and family relationships with U.S. citizens. It also included provisions to ensure that immigrants were paid a fair wage. Association of Centers for the Study of Congress, "Immigration and Nationality Act," webpage, undated.

[46] Robert Loevy, *The Civil Rights Act of 1964: The Passage of the Law That Ended Racial Segregation*, Albany, N.Y.: State University of New York Press, 1997; Doug McAdam, "The U.S. Civil Rights Movement: Power from Below and Above, 1945–70," in Adam Roberts and Timothy Garton Ash, eds., *Civil Resistance and Power Politics: The Experience of Non-Violent Action from Gandhi to the Present*, Oxford and New York: Oxford University Press, 2009.

[47] Bill Kauffman, "When the Left Was Right," *The American Conservative*, May 19, 2008; Stephan Lesher, *George Wallace: American Populist*, Boston: Addison Wesley, 1994, p. 409.

wonder whether they could really trust the government to tell the truth and to do what was right.[48]

A decade of high federal spending to support social welfare programs, tax cuts, the Vietnam War, and the space program caught up with the U.S. economy in the late 1960s and early 1970s. The 1960s were a period of marked economic prosperity that was driven by a mix of tax cuts and credits, policies to stimulate business, and measures to extend the minimum wage and increase unemployment compensation.[49] Growth was also fueled by new technologies that increased productivity. However, a high federal deficit and an overheating economy (according to many experts, a result of irresponsible fiscal and monetary policy as the decade progressed) drove accelerating inflation and a rising unemployment rate as the economy tipped into recession in the early 1970s.[50] Unemployment reached 9 percent by 1975. The early 1970s also saw the end of the gold standard and economic instability after that decision. The term *stagflation* emerged to describe the simultaneous stagnation and inflation that plagued the economy for a decade. Many have noted similarities between the 1920s and 1960s in terms of their overheated and overvalued economies, which ultimately collapsed.[51] Parallels to the 2000s, prior to the collapse of 2008, are relevant.

### Truth Decay in the 1960s–1970s?

As in the previous two periods, the late 1960s and early 1970s exhibit elements of Truth Decay, but there are meaningful differences between trends observed then and those present now. Evidence of ways in which changes in the media environment contributed to a blurring of the line between opinion and fact and an increase in the relative volume of opinion present in media organizations of the day is robust. New Journalism is one example, as is the use of tele-

---

[48] Gallup, 2016; Musser, 2007.

[49] Robert Collins, *More: The Politics of Economic Growth in Postwar America*, New York: Oxford University Press, 2002.

[50] Gregory Bresiger, "The Great Inflation of the 1970s," Investopedia, undated.

[51] Arthur Okun, "A Postmortem of the 1974 Recession," *Brookings Papers on Economic Activity*, No. 1, 1975.

vision news and images to spread propaganda and (in some cases) advance partisan discourse. The blurring of the line between opinion and fact, and even the change in the amount and influence of opinion over fact, does not, however, seem to be as severe as that observed in the 1880s and 1890s or today. There is also fairly strong evidence for this period of declines in trust in both government and news media, in this case as providers of information and facts. This decline in trust was particularly severe for government institutions. Specifically, a pattern of lies by senior government officials exposed by journalists and others undermined public trust in government institutions. In the case of the media, increased partisanship, activist journalism, and a focus on polarizing civil rights issues contributed to declining public confidence. Importantly, even at its low points, trust in both institutions was substantially higher than it is today. It also seems that social consensus about facts declined in the 1960s and early 1970s—but, again, this declining agreement seems to have concerned social, political, and economic norms rather than facts, data, and analysis. In this period, then, as in others, there is clearly some evidence of a Truth Decay–like phenomenon. But it also seems apparent that the phenomenon observed today could be unique in several ways. Table 3.3 summarizes our assessment of the severity of the four key trends of Truth Decay in this period.

**Table 3.3**
**Assessment of Level of Truth Decay in the 1960s–1970s**

| Trend | Low | Moderate | High |
|---|---|---|---|
| Increasing disagreement about facts and analytical interpretations of facts and data* | ✓ | | |
| A blurring of the line between opinion and fact | | ✓ | |
| The increasing relative volume, and resulting influence, of opinion and personal experience over fact | | ✓ | |
| Declining trust in formerly respected sources of factual information | | | ✓ |

NOTES: An asterisk indicates that our assessment relies on limited verified data. These assessments are approximations and should be considered largely in relative terms (i.e., to each other, not across periods).

### Increasing Disagreement About Facts and Analytical Interpretations of Facts and Data

Once again, a lack of rigorous public opinion data tracking individual attitudes over time makes it difficult to accurately identify the extent to which agreement about facts declined in the 1960s and 1970s. Political and social developments during this period offer some insights into areas where society appears to have been increasingly divided and where it seems likely that social consensus did decline. Still, as in previous periods, it is not always clear to what extent this increasing disagreement occurred around facts or analytical interpretations of those facts rather than around social and political norms.

Social and political protests of the period, which concerned civil rights, economic policies, and the Vietnam War, revealed an increasingly fractured and divided society with conflicting priorities and views on a range of different issues. Questioning of the government, its decisions, and (in some cases) the information it provided became more common than had been the case in the 1950s. By the late 1960s, areas of consensus about government and economic policy were beginning to erode.[52]

Washing over college campuses and other social spaces, the counter-culture of the 1960s and 1970s overlapped and bled into protests against the Vietnam War and then against President Richard Nixon.[53] In the 1960s, President Lyndon B. Johnson's Great Society programs were, in part, a response to many of the complaints raised by protestors regarding ways in which current economic policies did not respond to the reality of individuals' lives.[54] Despite these programs, however, clashes between protestors and law enforcement were common and hint at the extent of disagreement over social and economic policy as well as foreign policy decisions.

---

[52] Louis Hartz, *The Liberal Tradition in America*, New York: Harcourt Books, 1991.

[53] Roger Kimball, *The Long March: How the Cultural Revolution of the 1960s Changed America*, New York: Encounter Books, 2013; John Skrentny, *The Minority Rights Revolution*, Cambridge, Mass.: Belknap Press of Harvard University Press, 2002.

[54] Irwin Unger, *The Best of Intentions: The Triumphs and Failures of the Great Society Under Kennedy, Johnson, and Nixon*, New York: Doubleday, 1996.

The evidence suggests, then, that the 1960s and early 1970s were periods of declining consensus about social and political rights and economic policy. However, this still appears different than the increasing disagreement about facts defined in Chapter Two as part of Truth Decay—one based on disagreement about the fundamental accuracy and legitimacy of facts and analytical findings that at one point were more widely accepted.

### A Blurring of the Line Between Opinion and Fact, and the Increasing Relative Volume, and Resulting Influence, of Opinion and Personal Experience over Fact

Changes in the media environment and in journalism played an important role in the social, political, and economic culture of the late 1960s and early 1970s. They also reveal evidence of the same phenomena that we have described in previous eras: (1) blurring of the line between opinion and fact and (2) the increasing relative volume, and resulting influence, of opinion and personal experience over fact. Two developments were particularly important. The first was the rise of "New Journalism," and the second was the consolidation and spread of television news as a staple of the media market. New Journalism, which reached its height in the late 1960s and early 1970s, is a reporting style that relies on a subjective perspective and privileges personal experience and belief over objective facts. At the time, some critics accused New Journalism of blurring the distinction between reporting and storytelling. Others argued that it was simply the merger of activism and journalism.[55] What is perhaps most interesting about New Journalism from a contemporary vantage point is that this type of subjective manipulation of news stories, the emphasis on commentary over objective facts, and a blurring of the line between opinion and objective fact are clear manifestations in this period of one of the key trends of Truth Decay.

The emergence and dominance of television news and its coverage of major political and social events were also significant changes in the information system. By 1966, 90 percent of Americans had a television in the home, making that medium the primary source of news

---

[55] James E. Murphy, "The New Journalism: A Critical Perspective," *Journalism Monographs*, No. 34, May 1974.

for a majority of households. Although television gave a wider group of people access to more information, that material was still filtered and mediated by major television news networks that decided what would be covered on the nightly news, and the rise of television changed the content of news. The Vietnam War provides a good example of what those changes meant for the media landscape: In the 1960s and early 1970s, both proponents and critics of the war increasingly turned to television news to widely broadcast powerful images designed to stir support for the side in question. Television provided a new way for opinion and commentary to be disseminated and sold to the public, in some cases through reporting and in others through carefully manipulated photos and images. As a result, media coverage of the war played a role in shaping public opinion about the conflict.

Over the course of the war, the pictures painted by the government and the news media increasingly diverged. Both sides took liberties with the facts, in some cases misusing data and statistics to mislead or intentionally shape public attitudes.[56] This led to some blurring of the line between opinion and fact, some uncertainty among the public about what was fact and what was not, and even some distrust of media sources and government. As the war progressed, Americans increasingly began to trust journalists' stories, and investigative journalism rose to prominence. Strong investigative journalism that focused on the war, government corruption, and other important topics of the day increased public trust and confidence in the media so significantly that journalism came to be viewed as a check on the government. In fact, shifting media coverage and investigative analysis that exposed the true nature of events in the government helped turn public opinion against the war and, later, against Nixon.[57]

The resurgence of investigative journalism and its role in helping to rein in and expose government wrongdoing did much to reverse the blurring of the line between opinion and fact and the growing volume

---

[56] Daniel C. Hallin, *The Uncensored War: The Media and Vietnam*, Oxford and New York: Oxford University Press, 1986.

[57] Ronald H. Spector, "The Vietnam War and the Media," *Encyclopedia Britannica*, April 27, 2016.

of opinion and commentary spread by New Journalism and television news. Why investigative journalism thrived in the 1960s and early 1970s is not entirely clear, but the drivers of this shift, and its effect on the value and prominence of objective facts, should be explored in more detail, as doing so might uncover insights that could be applied to today.

### Declining Trust in Formerly Respected Sources of Factual Information

Trust in several major institutions declined in the late 1960s and 1970s for a number of reasons. Most notable was the decline in trust and confidence in the government—its ability to "do what is right," its commitment to protect individual interests, and its transparency and the accuracy of information it provided. Pew Research Center data indicate that trust in government to do what is right "just about always" or "most of the time" fell from a high of 77 percent in 1964 to about 36 percent 1974. This decline, shown in Figure 3.1, was driven by many of the events and forces already described—the Vietnam War, the turbulence created by the Civil Rights and feminist movements, and the

**Figure 3.1**
**Public Trust in Government, 1958–2017**

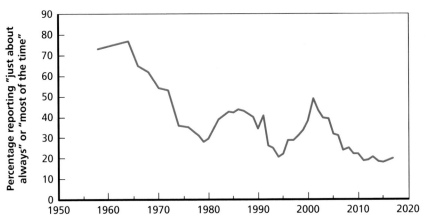

SOURCE: Pew Research Center, "Public Trust in Government: 1958–2017," webpage, May 3, 2017b.
RAND RR2314-3.1

economic recession—and by revelations that the government had lied, such as the release of the Pentagon Papers and the Watergate scandal.[58] In this instance, it was trust not only in government decisions and commitment to individual welfare that declined, but also in government's role as a provider of facts and information, as is also increasingly the case today. It is worth noting that, although the seeds of distrust might have been sown in the late 1960s and early 1970s, and although trust in government clearly declined in this period, it was substantially higher in 1974 than it is today. According to the same Pew data, the 36 percent of respondents in 1974 who reported trusting the government's ability to do what is right "just about always" or "most of the time" dropped to about 20 percent in April 2017.[59]

Rigorous data collection on public trust in news media started in the early 1970s, but there is still some qualitative evidence of the ways that public attitudes toward the news media might have changed over time prior to this period. In the 1950s and early 1960s, trust in news media appears to have been fairly high, especially for specific newscasters and sources. Walter Cronkite, for example, was often called the "most trusted man in America," and his recounting of events was viewed as fact.[60] However, the rise of increasingly partisan news in the 1960s and the growing amount of biased information and propaganda present in mass media sources (including war coverage) at the time appear to have somewhat undermined this trust. Personalized and activist reporting that took on controversial topics contributed to dissatisfaction with newspapers as a source of information, particularly among older generations. Although there are no hard data on attitudes toward newspapers at the time, pollster George Gallup reported in 1968 that they had "never been as poorly regarded by the public."[61] In 1973, about 39 percent of Americans expressed "a great deal" or "quite a lot" of confidence in newspapers.

---

[58] Pew Research Center, "Beyond Distrust: How Americans View Their Government— 1. Trust in Government: 1958–2015," webpage, November 23, 2015a.

[59] Gallup, 2017; Pew Research Center, 2015a.

[60] Jim Poniewozik, "Walter Cronkite: The Man with America's Trust," *Time*, July 17, 2009.

[61] "Newspapers," *Dictionary of American History*, Farmington Hills, Mich.: Gale Group, 2003.

By 1979, perhaps driven by the media's fact-based investigative coverage of Watergate and other events in the mid- and late 1970s, 51 percent of respondents said the same. Once again, however, it is important to note that even depressed levels of trust in the media in the 1970s were likely higher than what we observe today. Aggregate trust in media organizations was about half as strong in 2016 as in 1973, although some media sources experienced an increase in 2017.[62]

Changes in the mid- and later 1970s did much to restore trust in government and newspapers, however. First, policy changes and initiatives in the 1970s were aimed precisely at restoring trust in government. These "good government" bills, intended to reduce corruption and repair some of the distortions in the political process, focused on ethics, fundraising, and financial disclosure. These measures helped rebuild public confidence in government institutions.[63] The Church Committee and Rockefeller Commission, which studied intelligence activities, also might have contributed to the positive image. Second, as noted, the renewal of deep investigative journalism in the early 1970s and its role in helping to rein in and expose government wrongdoing did much to restore trust in the institution of the media. In recent years, we have seen some reemergence of investigative journalism, and the media continue to play a significant role in shaping the opinions and attitudes of society. However, as we discuss later, not everyone views the media as an honest check on the government.

## A Comparison with Today: Similarities and Differences

Table 3.4 lists Truth Decay's four constituent trends and the three periods considered in this chapter, along with today. In each cell, we indicate the level of available evidence that the trend was present in that period. In the case of "reasonable evidence," we wish to note that additional research to gather more-rigorous empirical data will

---

[62] Gallup, 2017.

[63] U.S. Senate Historical Office, "Select Committee on Presidential Campaign Activities," webpage, undated-c.

**Table 3.4**
**Evidence of Truth Decay in Different Eras**

| Era | Increasing Disagreement About Facts and Analytical Interpretations of Facts and Data | A Blurring of the Line Between Opinion and Fact | The Increasing Relative Volume, and Resulting Influence, of Opinion and Personal Experience over Fact | Declining Trust in Formerly Respected Sources of Information |
|---|---|---|---|---|
| 1880s–1890s | No evidence | Reasonable evidence | Reasonable evidence | No evidence |
| 1920s–1930s | No evidence | Reasonable evidence | Reasonable evidence | Some evidence |
| 1960s–1970s | No evidence | Reasonable evidence | Reasonable evidence | Reasonable evidence |
| 2000s–2010s | Reasonable evidence | Reasonable evidence | Reasonable evidence | Reasonable evidence |

NOTE: It would be ideal to compare the severity of each of the four trends across periods, but we do not have sufficient data to make a precise assessment.

be valuable and necessary before drawing definitive conclusions. As this table and our analysis in this chapter suggest, Truth Decay is not entirely unique to the current period, but there are ways in which it appears to be distinct.

Perhaps the clearest similarity across the four periods is that each offers examples of the erosion of the line between opinion and fact and of ways in which the relative volume, and resulting influence, of opinion over fact seems to have increased. This occurred with yellow journalism and again with jazz journalism and New Journalism. As is the case today, the trend toward a blurring of the line between opinion and fact in each period was driven, in part, on the supply side—that is, by newspaper or media publishers and their desire to attract audiences and increase profits. However, the degree to which there was also a demand-side problem (that is, an increase in demand for sensationalized and editorialized news content) appears to vary. It was most clearly present in the 1920s, there to a lesser extent in the 1960s and 1970s, to an even lesser extent in the 1880s and 1890s, but clearly an important factor again today. What is less clear is whether these trends are more severe now than in the past and, if so, why and in what ways. The scope and scale of these phenomena in the present period might be more extreme, but this could be a function of heightened attention or the advent of social media and the internet, which have made examples of both trends easy to find. These are questions where additional and more in-depth research is needed.

We also found some evidence of a decline in trust in institutions as sources of fact-based information, particularly in the late 1960s and early 1970s and in the present day (including not just the current presidential administration but also going back to at least 2000). In both periods, government and media lost or are losing credibility as sources of objective facts because of a lack of transparency and even the dissemination of misinformation, in some cases. In both instances, the decline in trust appears to be fairly severe, but it is important to note, as shown in Figure 3.1, that the absolute level of trust in media and government was substantially higher in the 1970s than it is today. Furthermore, available information suggests that a larger number of institutions have lost public trust as providers of information over the past two decades than during the 1960s and 1970s. There is some evidence that certain institutions also lost the public's confidence as sources of credible information in the 1920s, but, as we noted earlier, this seems to have occurred primarily in the area of economic and financial information. Initial analysis, then, suggests a significantly greater challenge in this area of declining trust in the current period than seen before.

There is the least evidence that previous periods considered in this report experienced the same eroding agreement about facts and analytical interpretations of those facts that appears to be occurring in contemporary society. Although each of the periods explored in this chapter exhibited a significant rise in disagreement over social, economic, and political policies and norms, there is little evidence that agreement about the veracity and legitimacy of basic facts declined in previous eras. However, we do have episodic evidence, presented in Chapter Two, that this trend has been occurring in recent years, although deeper investigation is needed to collect more-rigorous empirical data in this instance as well. This is an important distinction between the current period and previous eras, perhaps even a defining one that sets it apart from the past. Further research is needed to verify and explore this difference, and we return to this point in Chapter Six. Other characteristics of the current period that appear distinct from the past include the severity of the decline in trust in key institutions that used to be sources of factual information, and (potentially) the scope and scale of changes in the information system. Additional research into each of these areas is necessary to confirm and understand these differences and to identify how these differences might lead to solutions. The proposed research agenda in Chapter Six suggests a number of research questions concerning this line of inquiry.

**Why Did Previous Periods Similar to Truth Decay End?**
One question that emerges from these comparisons is why Truth Decay–like phenomena ended in the past. Although further research is necessary, the answer appears to be multifaceted. First, in each previous case, a revival of fact-based and investigative journalism helped reduce the blurring of the line between opinion and fact and championed the primacy of facts over disinformation and opinion. In each period, this shift in the focus and content of news also appears to have increased or at least solidified trust in the media as a provider of facts and analysis. In the 1890s, this shift was triggered by the rise of the muckrakers and an increased emphasis on fact-based reporting during the Spanish-American War. In the 1930s, this change might have been hastened by the increasing use of data in policymaking, governance, and military planning—changes that might have filtered down to journalism as well. The advent of World War II and the desire for fact-based information on events that occurred during the conflict could also have played a role. In the 1970s, large scandals (such as Watergate and the release of the Pentagon Papers) underscored the value of fact-based information and the vital role investigative journalism plays in ensuring transparency. Thus, in each case, an increased focus on and respect for facts and objective analysis appears to have been triggered by a realization of the consequences of not relying on such facts and data (e.g., the Great Depression); a desire to hold authorities more accountable (e.g., muckrakers, the Vietnam War); or a recognition of the value such analysis

can provide, both to journalism and reporting and to policymaking (e.g., war reporting, economic recovery in the 1940s).

Second, in more than one case, changes in government policy to increase accountability and transparency helped restore trust in government as an information provider, again raising the profile of and emphasis on objective facts. This occurred in the 1930s as the government began to rely more heavily on better data and metrics, which, as noted earlier, both improved policymaking and likely made government policy and progress more effective than in previous decades. It also happened to a lesser extent in the 1900s through the Progressive reform movement.[64] In the 1970s, a number of commissions and policy changes improved the accountability and transparency of government processes, although some of the policies put in place at that time have eroded over time. It is worth noting that there were efforts to increase government transparency under the George W. Bush and Barack Obama administrations. The difference appears to be that, in previous eras, fundamental changes to government processes were effective in increasing transparency and creating new mechanisms for accountability. It is not clear that more-recent efforts have been able to alter government processes or measurably increase transparency, at least as it is perceived by the general public. For example, although then-President Obama promised greater transparency at the start of his administration, he was criticized for not delivering on these promises.[65]

Also in each period, an abatement of social and political turmoil reduced the societal pressures that might have contributed to some of the trends that constitute Truth Decay. Each of the periods described here exhibited substantial social and political unrest and upheaval, driven by rapid technological and economic change, immigration, and social developments (e.g., the Civil Rights Movement). It is possible that such phenomena as Truth Decay are a byproduct of these types of unrest and upheaval. However, additional research is needed to verify

---

[64] Lewis Gould, *America in the Progressive Era, 1890–1914*, New York: Routledge, 2001.

[65] Alex Howard, "How Should History Measure the Obama's Administration's Record on Transparency?" The Sunlight Foundation, September 2, 2016.

whether evidence supports this hypothesis and, if so, through what mechanisms it operates.

It is also possible that the end of such phenomena as Truth Decay occurs naturally, in a sort of cyclical or wave-like process. Additional research into each of these areas would prove valuable to those seeking a deeper understanding of Truth Decay and to those looking for solutions to the challenges it presents. Table 3.5 provides a summary of similarities between each of the three periods considered in this report and today, along with possible lessons that can be learned from past periods about how phenomena like Truth Decay have ended in the past.

**Table 3.5**
**Characteristics of Three Periods with Similarities to Today**

| 1880s–1890s | 1920s–1930s | 1960s–1970s |
|---|---|---|
| Yellow journalism and the Gilded Age | Roaring Twenties and the Great Depression | Civil rights, social unrest, and the Vietnam War |
| • Dissemination of sensationalized and exaggerated news | • Tabloids and radio talk shows blur the line between fact and opinion<br>• Distrust of government and financial institutions | • New Journalism places greater emphasis on personal experience<br>• Spread of television as an influential, widely available form of news media<br>• Political scandals (Watergate, Pentagon Papers) erode trust in government institutions |

Responses to emulate?

| 1880s–1890s | 1920s–1930s | 1960s–1970s |
|---|---|---|
| • Muckrakers conduct deep investigative journalism<br>• Progressive reforms increase transparency and accountability of government and corporations | • Birth of data-based policy analysis improves transparency and government accountability | • Resurgence of investigative journalism becomes a public check on the government<br>• Legislation on government ethics, fundraising, and financial disclosure help rebuild confidence in government institutions |

## Historical Analogues in Other Countries

We do not extensively explore historical parallels in foreign countries, but it is worth noting that Truth Decay is not unique to the United States. Other countries are currently experiencing the trends of Truth Decay as well. For example, events in the United Kingdom before the Brexit vote are markedly similar to experiences in the United States over the past several years.[66] In the lead-up to the Brexit vote, parties on both sides used a barrage of misinformation and disinformation to attempt to sway voter attitudes.[67] There was a clear blurring of the line between opinion and fact, and the outcome of the vote was, in part, a response to distrust in both British and European Union institutions.[68] Social media played a role in spreading this disinformation in the lead-up to Brexit. France has also experienced elements of Truth Decay, especially in the run-up to the May 2017 national election, which was affected by misleading statements by political actors and the media, disinformation spread through media channels, and declining trust in status quo political institutions.[69] Perhaps the best-known manifestations were cyber attacks on now-President Emmanuel Macron's political campaign, including leaks of hacked emails.[70] That Truth Decay appears to be a global phenomenon seems to be important because the information system itself appears to be globalizing. This means that

---

[66] The term *Brexit* refers to the June 2016 referendum vote in the United Kingdom to leave the European Union. For more information, see Charles Ries, Marco Hafner, Troy D. Smith, Frances G. Burwell, Daniel Egel, Eugeniu Han, Martin Stepanek, and Howard J. Shatz, *After Brexit: Alternate Forms of Brexit and Their Implications for the United Kingdom, the European Union and the United States*, Santa Monica, Calif.: RAND Corporation, RR-2200-RC, 2017.

[67] Charlie Cooper, "EU Referendum: Immigration and Brexit—What Lies Have Been Spread?" *The Independent*, June 20, 2016.

[68] John Cassidy, "Why the Remain Campaign Lost the Brexit Vote," *The New Yorker*, June 24, 2016.

[69] Chloe Farand, "French Social Media Awash with Fake News Stories from Sources 'Exposed to Russian Influence' Ahead of Presidential Election," *The Independent*, April 22, 2017; Amar Toor, "France Has a Fake News Problem, But It Is Not as Bad as the U.S.," *The Verge*, April 21, 2017.

[70] Eric Auchard and Bate Felix, "French Candidate Macron Claims Massive Hack as Emails Leaked," Reuters, May 6, 2017.

problems in one country or region are likely to spread to others. If this is the case, then a true solution or response to Truth Decay will require not only attention to the phenomenon as it manifests in the United States but also an assessment of its manifestations in other countries. Furthermore, there might be lessons to be learned from the experiences of other countries in the area of Truth Decay. Examples include the types and sources of false information that have affected information systems, the ways in which public trust in national institutions has changed over time, and how institutions responded to Truth Decay–related challenges.

Understanding the ways in which Truth Decay or similar phenomena have affected other countries and observing what has been done to fight it could be a valuable avenue of exploration, especially if it can warn key stakeholders in the United States of ways in which those who benefit from Truth Decay might try to weaponize information as a political tool or perpetuate and extend some of the more negative aspects and consequences of Truth Decay.

## Summary

This chapter has identified aspects of Truth Decay that might have roots in the past, as well as aspects that might be unique to today. The chapter has also identified many areas ripe for further research and has suggested some hypotheses that could help guide this exploration. However, it has also highlighted a number of areas where additional research is needed. First, additional work is needed to determine which aspects of Truth Decay are truly new and which are a continuation of past trends. This chapter has included references to relevant data, but additional investigation to uncover or collect additional data is needed to come to a definitive conclusion about the ways in which Truth Decay is—or is not—new. Second, to the extent that Truth Decay is new, a better understanding of what differences between the current period and the past have allowed Truth Decay to emerge in the form or to the extent that it has will be important in diagnosing the current challenge and responding to it. Finally, research that mines historical analogues (and international analogues, once they have been assessed) for lessons that might support a more effective fight against Truth Decay will be valuable. Exploring these areas will further illuminate what is new and different about Truth Decay and provide insight into both the areas where Truth Decay is most severe and the drivers that might be most relevant to its emergence. The research agenda in Chapter Six proposes additional avenues for research into historical and international comparisons.

Before beginning this historical research, however, we must understand Truth Decay more fully. Research and analysis are needed to thoroughly investigate its extent, progression over time, drivers, and consequences. The next chapter explores four key drivers of Truth Decay, discussing relevant data and summarizing existing literature. This exploration identifies how each driver contributes to Truth Decay and highlights areas where future research is needed to fully understand the dynamics at play.

# CHAPTER FOUR

# Drivers: What Is Causing Truth Decay?

With a definition and a sense of historical context for Truth Decay, we turn to a discussion of the four key drivers—that is, circumstances and changes—that appear to contribute to Truth Decay in contemporary society: cognitive processing and cognitive biases; changes in the information system, including the rise of social media and a transformation of the media industry; competing demands on the U.S. educational system that have prevented school curricula from keeping pace with the challenges of the new information system; and polarization, both political and sociodemographic. These four drivers emerged as particularly relevant to Truth Decay based on our structured discussions; our extensive review of relevant academic and popular literature; and available data on such topics as public attitudes toward government and media organizations, trust in institutions, use of social media and the internet, changes in the dissemination of information, developments in education, electoral trends and trends in policymaking (e.g., laws passed or votes held), and many others.

We synthesized this information, looking for common themes and patterns, to highlight a small set of factors that we hypothesized might be key drivers of Truth Decay as we observe it today. Certainly, there could be other factors that matter, and it is probable that one or two of these factors carry more weight than others. For example, as our discussion will suggest, changes in the information system play an outsize role in the challenges presented by Truth Decay because those changes affect the supply of both fact-based information and disinformation or falsehoods. The role played by political and sociodemographic polarization also seems centrally important because it stirs and sustains the demand for competing narratives and allows misinformation and disinformation to thrive. However, we believe that Truth Decay would not be as pervasive and damaging if it were not propelled by all four drivers identified in this report. In fact, returning briefly to the historical assessment presented in the previous chapter, it might be the confluence of these four drivers at the same time that sets contemporary Truth Decay apart from what we saw in other periods. As research in this area advances, it might become appropriate to identify additional drivers or to replace one or more of the current drivers with others that seem more important, but we believe starting with these four provides a valuable baseline for an exploration of Truth Decay.

In this chapter, we describe each driver, discuss the ways in which it seems to contribute to Truth Decay, summarize some of the recent and relevant research, and identify areas where questions remain. We also discuss the question of agency, describing several types of organizations that have exploited Truth Decay for their own political and economic ends or have otherwise intentionally or unintentionally accelerated the progression of Truth Decay. Drivers and agents are closely related. For example, foreign actors as agents of Truth Decay have been able to exploit changes in the information system (a driver in our framework) to more quickly and efficiently spread targeted propaganda and false information. To differentiate between drivers and agents, we define *drivers* as general conditions or changes that appear to be causing Truth Decay and *agents* as entities that accelerate the trends that constitute Truth Decay, intentionally or unintentionally, in order to advance political, economic, or other objectives.

It is important to note that there is certainly some degree of feedback between each driver and Truth Decay that works in both directions. For instance, we define changes in the information system as one driver of Truth Decay and describe how social media facilitates the spread of disinformation, which blurs the line between opinion and fact and can erode both agreement about facts and trust in institutions. At the same time, in an environment in which there is widespread disagreement about objective facts, disinformation can spread more quickly and gain more traction. We highlight examples of these feedback loops where relevant and discuss them in more detail at the end of the chapter.

## Cognitive Processing and Cognitive Biases

Cognitive biases and the ways in which human beings process information and make decisions cause people to look for information, opinion, and analyses that confirm preexisting beliefs, to weight experience more heavily than data and facts, and to rely on mental shortcuts and the beliefs of those in the same social networks when forming opinions and making decisions.[1] Unlike the other drivers of Truth Decay, cognitive bias and other aspects of cognitive processing have not changed in recent years but are common and consistent characteristics of human cognition. However, other drivers—such as changes in the information system and an increase in political and social polarization—have heightened the importance and consequence of these cognitive biases and thrown into stark relief the effects cognitive bias has on how human beings understand and process information. Cognitive biases can also be exploited by any of the agents of Truth Decay described in more detail at the end of this chapter, including international actors, researchers, partisans, and propagandists. Furthermore, it is not clear that Truth Decay would be as dangerous or persistent absent these characteristics of human cognitive processing. If people were readily willing to update prior beliefs when presented with contradictory facts or relied more heavily on objective facts and analysis in decisionmaking than on social cues, emotions, and heuristics, it would be easier to correct misinformation and disinformation, prevent or break up the

---

[1] *Cognitive biases* can be defined as ways in which a person's beliefs, attitudes, reasoning, or decisions can deviate from reality or strict rationality as a result of patterns and tendencies in human processing. For instance, people may seek to confirm prior beliefs regardless of how well they match reality, or they may make judgments based on heuristics, cues, and shortcuts rather than a full assessment of all facts and data. See Martie G. Haselton, Daniel Nettle, and Damian R. Murray, "The Evolution of Cognitive Bias," in David M. Buss, ed., *The Handbook of Evolutionary Psychology*, Hoboken, N.J.: John Wiley & Sons, Inc., 2005.

formation of echo chambers, and train people to evaluate news media objectively. For these reasons, we begin our discussion of drivers of Truth Decay with an assessment of the ways in which cognitive biases contribute to Truth Decay. This assessment also provides a foundation for understanding the ways in which other drivers, including especially changes in the information system and political and social polarization, have contributed to Truth Decay.

Even if individual cognitive processes themselves have stayed the same, their effects and implications appear to have been magnified by other drivers of Truth Decay. In other words, cognitive bias might be a latent driver—a factor that is always present but does not cause Truth Decay unless activated by other environmental conditions and factors or exploited by actors with specific political and economic motives. Specifically, cognitive biases appear to contribute directly to the decline in agreement about facts and the blurring of the line between opinion and fact by making individuals resistant to facts that conflict with preexisting opinions or experiences. Cognitive bias might also encourage individuals to surround themselves with people who think similarly and to consume information from only those sources with consistently matching beliefs and attitudes. Combined with rising polarization, changes prompted by the ubiquity of social media, the impact of filters, and the characteristics of the 24-hour news cycle, cognitive biases and other characteristics of cognitive processing leave people susceptible to disinformation and increasingly likely to disregard facts in favor of opinion and anecdote. However, we believe that cognitive bias plays such a fundamental role in shaping and feeding Truth Decay that it deserves mention as an independent driver and not a component of other drivers.

## Cognitive Biases and Their Implications for Truth Decay

### Confirmation Bias

An extensive body of empirical research investigates how the heuristics and mental shortcuts that people use to process information affect their beliefs, opinions, and decisions.[2] One of the most important cog-

---

[2]  *Heuristics* are approaches to problem-solving or decisionmaking that rely on cues, shortcuts, prior experience, or rules of thumb in order to produce a satisfactory solution more

nitive biases is the human tendency to hold onto prior beliefs even when presented with information clearly demonstrating that these beliefs are incorrect or misguided. Nyhan and Reifler, for instance, find that individual misperceptions on a range of topics are resilient to corrective information.[3] In fact, people do not just maintain preexisting beliefs: Being confronted with corrective information can make misperceptions more ingrained and cause people to become less willing to consider alternatives.[4] This finding is contested by other research that finds limited evidence that corrective information contributes to such a "backfire effect," but even this research suggests that altering preexisting beliefs can be difficult.[5] This is reflective of the more general human tendency to seek out and give precedence to information that confirms preexisting opinions and beliefs and to reject disconfirming information, regardless of the source.[6] The power and tenacity of this confirmation bias should not be underestimated. Heuristics can have other effects on beliefs and information-processing as well. For example, when making decisions, people tend to give more credence to information that they encounter more often and have read more recently, even where this is unwarranted.[7]

This tendency to hold on to existing beliefs and search for confirming information of these beliefs, also known as motivated reasoning, drives Truth Decay because it means that once a person forms a

---

quickly than would be possible through an in-depth analysis. Examples include using a candidate's partisan affiliation to approximate one's own political views or using a person's attire to guess his or her occupation or income. Heuristics allow for faster and easier decision-making but might not always produce the right or optimal solution.

[3] Brendan Nyhan and Jason Reifler, "When Corrections Fail: The Persistence of Political Misperceptions," *Political Behavior*, Vol. 32, No. 2, 2010.

[4] Nyhan and Reifler, 2010.

[5] Thomas Wood and Ethan Porter, "The Elusive Backfire Effect: Mass Attitudes' Steadfast Factual Adherence," *Political Behavior*, forthcoming.

[6] Amos Tversky and Daniel Kahneman, "Judgment Under Uncertainty: Heuristics and Biases," *Science*, Vol. 185, No. 4157, 1974.

[7] Lisa K. Fazio, Nadia M. Brashier, B. Keith Payne, and Elizabeth J. Marsh, "Knowledge Does Not Protect Against Illusory Truth," *Journal of Experimental Psychology: General*, Vol. 144, No. 5, 2015.

specific belief—whether it is based on fact, disinformation, or misinformation—that belief is likely to endure. For people who hold initial beliefs that are consistent with prevailing data and analysis, confirmation bias is equally likely to strengthen attachment to these initial beliefs even as new data or analyses emerge to challenge those beliefs. Confirmation bias and motivated reasoning have been widely researched and explored in both political and nonpolitical contexts.[8] Kunda suggests that people deciding how and where to seek out information are motivated by a desire to confirm their beliefs. She reports that people will choose search and decision methods that are most likely to lead to desired outcomes or conclusions, not to the best-informed ones. In this way, motivations and desires can have a direct influence on beliefs, behavior, and decisionmaking.[9] We do not mean to imply that emotions and intuition do not have a place alongside facts and data in belief formation or decisionmaking—they do. We are merely suggesting possible ways in which cognitive biases can allow emotions and intuition to fully crowd out facts and data from these processes.

Research shows that people can use many different approaches and strategies to avoid or resist factual threats to worldviews. These include criticizing or disparaging the source of the conflicting information; questioning the validity of the information itself; and framing the rationale for beliefs in terms that are moral, emotional, or religious and thus unfalsifiable, rather than in terms that are fact-based and thus falsifiable.[10] In this way, confirmation biases might contribute not only to declining agreement about facts and an erosion of the line between opinion and fact but also to polarization (discussed later in this chapter) and to a decline in civil discourse (discussed in Chapter Five).

---

[8]   Ziva Kunda, "The Case for Motivated Reasoning," *Psychological Bulletin*, Vol. 108, No. 3, 1990; Arie W. Kruglanski, "Motivated Social Cognition: Principles of the Interface," in E. Tory Higgins and Arie W. Kruglanski, eds., *Social Psychology: Handbook of Basic Principles*, New York: Guilford Press, 1996.

[9]   Kunda, 1990.

[10]   Justin P. Friesen, Troy H. Campbell, and Aaron C. Kay, "The Psychological Advantage of Unfalsifiability: The Appeal of Untestable Religious and Political Ideologies," *Journal of Personality and Social Psychology*, Vol. 108, No. 3, 2015.

Another body of literature examines confirmation bias in the context of political beliefs. Research by Flynn, Nyhan, and Reifler suggests that motivated reasoning can explain at least part of the ferocity with which people hold onto false beliefs. The authors demonstrate that people tend to seek out information that allows them to form beliefs consistent with a preferred political party, rejecting information that does not fit a desired narrative.[11] This might offer one explanation for why "fake news" tends to survive and why some aspects of Truth Decay could prove difficult to overcome. This research also suggests that both partisanship and prior opinions can play a role in providing the "motivation" to maintain preexisting beliefs. The fact that partisanship can feed cognitive bias might explain why misperceptions and cognitive biases seem especially severe in the political arena.[12] Other research confirms the important role of partisanship in belief formation and the perpetuation of bias. Specifically, this work suggests that more-committed partisans hold more strongly onto their beliefs when faced with contradictory information and might spend less time considering conflicting information before making a decision or reaffirming a belief than independents or weaker partisans would.[13] In fact, even the act of voting for a party in an election can have an effect on beliefs and attitudes, as voters seek to bring their beliefs in line with their past voting decisions to reduce cognitive dissonance within their own belief system.[14] Thus, the problem of Truth Decay in the political sphere might be perpetuated not only by cognitive biases but also by the political process itself (almost irrespective of the specific characteristics of that process).

---

[11] D. J. Flynn, Brendan Nyhan, and Jason Reifler, "The Nature and Origins of Misperceptions: Understanding False and Unsupported Beliefs About Politics," European Research Council, 2016.

[12] Flynn, Nyhan, and Reifler, 2016.

[13] David Redlawsk, "Hot Cognition or Cool Consideration? Testing the Effects of Motivated Reasoning on Political Decision Making," *Journal of Politics*, Vol. 64, No. 4, November 2002.

[14] Jorgen Bolstad, Elias Dinas, and Pedro Riera, "Tactical Voting and Party Preference: A Test of Cognitive Dissonance Theory," *Political Behavior*, Vol. 35, No. 3, 2013.

### *The Role of Emotion, Relationships, and Prior Experiences*

A person's beliefs and opinions are also heavily shaped by emotion and personal experience, which, according to some studies, can outweigh the influence of facts in decisionmaking. In fact, a review of psychological studies on the relationship between emotion and decisionmaking suggests that, although rational choice theory is relevant,[15] emotion plays a consistent, shaping, and often determinative role in decisionmaking— one that can overpower fact. This relationship seems especially relevant in areas of high uncertainty.[16] According to research, emotion affects decisionmaking by influencing goals, judgments, relationships, and how people evaluate a given set of options. Mental models—people's conception of how the world works based on their background, experiences, and personal characteristics and values—might also affect how people process information and how receptive they are to new information that conflicts with preconceived notions.[17] For example, someone with a worldview that values tradition and precedent might be less open to new ideas than someone who places more value on change, transformation, and challenging the status quo. Similarly, someone with a worldview that is inherently distrusting of institutions might be more likely to rely on friends and relatives for information than to accept information provided by scientific research organizations. The opposite might be true of a person who has a basic trust for all (or certain) types of institutions, or whose outlook is heavily shaped by

---

[15] Rational choice theory suggests that people always make logical decisions using available data in order to maximize utility or well-being. These theories typically downplay the role of emotion and other factors in decisionmaking.

[16] Jennifer Lerner, Ye Li, Piercarlo Valdesolo, and Karim Kassam, "Emotion and Decision-Making," *Annual Review of Psychology*, Vol. 66, No. 1, 2015.

[17] Dominique Brossard, Bruce Lewenstein, and Rick Bonney, "Scientific Knowledge and Attitude Change: The Impact of a Citizen Science Project," *International Journal of Science Education*, Vol. 27, No. 9, 2005; J. S. Downs, W. Bruine de Bruin, and B. Fischhoff, "Parents' Vaccination Comprehension and Decisions," *Vaccine*, Vol. 26, No. 12, 2008; Shirley S. Ho, Dominique Brossard, and Dietram A. Scheufele, "Effects of Value Predispositions, Mass Media Use, and Knowledge on Public Attitudes Toward Embryonic Stem Cell Research," *International Journal of Public Opinion Research*, Vol. 20, No. 2, 2008; National Academies of Sciences, Committee on Science Communication, *Communicating Science Effectively: A Research Agenda*, Washington, D.C.: National Academies Press, 2017.

the scientific method. The Cultural Cognition Project is exploring the effect of mental models on attitudes and policy beliefs. Specifically, the project asks whether and in what ways cultural values (or *cognition*, in the project's terminology) can shape an individual's policy attitudes on issues ranging from climate change to the death penalty.[18] The project's initial work on this topic has produced evidence that cultural cognition shapes how people form beliefs, what those beliefs are, and the extent to which people believe there is a scientific consensus on issues ranging from disposal of nuclear waste to climate change.[19]

The way information is framed and presented can also strongly influence individual attitudes and beliefs. We use the term *framing* to refer to the process of "contextualizing," or placing a phenomenon, event, or other piece of information in an interpretive schema. A "frame" can be understood as an organizing structure or context that shapes the meaning of an issue or event through the selective emphasis of some details and omission of others.[20] Framing contributes to Truth Decay in two ways. First, people and organizations who intentionally seek to blur the line between opinion and fact can use framing to advance their own interests. Second, because of the power of such frames and interpretative schema to shape public attitudes, these frames can easily lead to the creation of multiple competing narratives about a single issue, thereby contributing to the declining agreement about facts that is part of Truth Decay.

As a practical example, journalists frame issues by using specific descriptors and contextual cues that encourage readers to interpret those issues in particular ways or to accept a particular definition of the problem and implied solution. Consider a journalist writing an article about different ways to respond to violent nationalist actors, such as members

---

[18] For more information, see the Cultural Cognition Project, homepage, undated.

[19] Dan M. Kahan, Hank Jenkins Smith, and Donald Braman, "Cultural Cognition of Scientific Consensus," *Journal of Risk Research*, Vol. 14, No. 2, 2011.

[20] J. Tankard, L. Hendrickson, J. Silberman, K. Bliss, and S. Ghanem, "Media Frames: Approaches to Conceptualization and Measurement," paper presented at the annual convention of the Association for Education in Journalism and Mass Communication, Boston, August 1991.

of the Irish Republican Army. Depending on the author's viewpoint, these people can be alternately described as freedom fighters or terrorists. An account focusing on the freedom-fighter frame might emphasize these individuals' desire for freedom from British rule and the history of discrimination against Catholics in Northern Ireland. An account focusing on the terrorist framework might focus on the use of violence against civilians. By emphasizing different details and contexts, the two accounts would promote different attitudes and different solutions.

Frames can also be manipulated to influence attitudes and sway views regarding a particular issue, individual, or question. Politicians can use frames to influence voters' attitudes.[21] Pollster Frank Luntz, for instance, analyzed and identified words and phrases that he argued would appeal to the interpretive scheme of specific types of voters and therefore allow political candidates to shift these voters' attitudes. He also suggested that political success was based as much on different modes of presentation as on differences in content.[22] Frames become important for Truth Decay when they are used not only to shape attitudes but to intentionally blur the line between opinion and fact or to cast doubt on the veracity of specific facts or institutions.

Finally, social relationships and networks play a large role in the formation of beliefs and attitudes. Research from 2014 on the effect of social settings shows that such surroundings—specifically, the family and friends with whom a person chooses to associate—have an even more significant effect on beliefs than partisan cues.[23] Relying on personal networks of family and friends as a source of information, however, can limit the diversity of information that a person is able to consume or access, leading to the creation of echo chambers in which false beliefs can prosper. These echo chambers can be reinforced by

---

[21] D. A. Scheufele, "Agenda-Setting, Priming, and Framing Revisited: Another Look at Cognitive Effects of Political Communication," *Mass Communication and Society*, Vol. 3, Nos. 2–3, 2009.

[22] Frank Luntz, *Words That Work: It's Not What You Say, It's What People Hear*, New York: Hachette Books, 2008.

[23] Samara Klar, "Partisanship in a Social Setting," *American Journal of Political Science*, Vol. 58, No. 3, July 2014.

social media platforms and internet search filters that impose bias on the types of information to which a person is exposed.[24] The role played by social media, the internet, search filters, and algorithms is considered in more detail in the next section.

### Implications for Truth Decay

These characteristics of human processing are not new, but they are exacerbated by other drivers of Truth Decay, especially changes in the information system and polarization. Rather than seeking out and separating fact from opinion, human cognitive processing encourages people to look for evidence that confirms their preexisting beliefs and opinions and to reject information that might be inconsistent with their personal experience. In an information system with a variety of sources and an almost overwhelming volume of information, it is increasingly easy for people to find the information they need to confirm their own opinions. Social media and its echo chambers (described in more detail in the next section) also make it easier than ever for people to surround themselves with others who share the same beliefs, and this allows people to tune out and avoid exposure to disconfirming information or beliefs. The ability to associate with peers who share similar views and attitudes can be liberating and empowering for many people, particularly those who belong to oppressed minorities and those who feel isolated. However, these networks can become harmful when people refuse to consider or expose themselves to new information or to information that might conflict with preconceived beliefs. Political polarization can deepen the divides between groups and reduce the willingness of individuals in each group to consider the viewpoints of the other side. It also raises the personal and social costs associated with changing one's mind or position. The fact that it is increasingly difficult to identify objective information and to separate this information from anecdote exacerbates this tendency. Thus, cognitive biases are not new, but their importance and impact on beliefs and attitudes might have strengthened because of their interaction with other drivers of Truth Decay.

---

[24] Osonde A. Osoba and William Welser IV, *An Intelligence in Our Image: The Risks of Bias and Errors in Artificial Intelligence*, Santa Monica, Calif.: RAND Corporation, RR-1744-RC, 2017.

## Reducing Cognitive Biases

A response to Truth Decay will require exploring strategies for reducing cognitive biases, particularly those that make human beings unwilling to challenge existing beliefs when confronted with disconfirming evidence and that allow them to privilege opinion over facts and data in assessments and decisions. A growing body of research is investigating methods that can modify an individual's cognitive biases to change behavior and, in some cases, beliefs. Most strategies focus on changing the types of information people pay attention to or the ways in which people interpret and process information. These strategies can include altering attitudes toward a perceived social threat or encouraging people to ignore certain types of stimuli.[25] Methods thus far have typically been lab-based and have involved various techniques to build new cognitive pathways or to teach people new ways to process information. These techniques include manipulating stimuli (such as light, form, color, or sound) or explicitly instructing participants to use a set of cognitive steps to evaluate or process certain types of information.[26] Some research suggests that creating visuals that present all data and evidence in a graphical way can help overcome bias because the availability of information influences the viewer's cognitive process.[27] A number of studies contend that the way information is presented— specifically, its style and framing—can make a difference in counteracting bias. Specifically, information presented in a way that is unexpected or even difficult to process can be powerful in breaking through biases because it forces the individual to slow down and think about the information more carefully.[28] For example, one study found that

---

[25] Colin MacLeod, Ernst H. W. Koster, and Elaine Fox, "Whither Cognitive Bias Modification Research? Commentary on the Special Section Articles," *Journal of Abnormal Psychology*, Vol. 118, No. 1, 2009, p. 89.

[26] MacLeod, Koster, and Fox, 2009.

[27] M. B. Cook and H. S. Smallman, "Human Factors of the Confirmation Bias in Intelligence Analysis: Decision Support from Graphical Evidence Landscapes," *Human Factors*, Vol. 50, No. 5, 2008.

[28] I. Hernandez and J. L. Preston, "Disfluency Disrupts the Confirmation Bias," *Journal of Experimental Social Psychology*, Vol. 49, No. 1, 2013.

people were more likely to adjust both their political attitudes and their attitudes toward court defendants when information was presented in unusual or difficult-to-read fonts because those challenges forced them to consider the information more carefully.[29]

Most fundamentally, however, research suggests that, to reduce cognitive bias, the facts must be presented in a way that is as nonthreatening and neutral as possible.[30] In fact, studies find that information presented in a way that a group might find threatening to its self- or world-perception is more likely to be rejected because the group interprets that information as a threat to identity.[31] However, it is also worth noting that communicating information in a neutral way, especially in a highly politicized environment such as exists today in the United States, can be extremely difficult. This might be partly because experiences, beliefs, and opinions shape the ways in which people communicate and share information. As a result, almost any statement, even one rooted in fact, can take on a political tone based on framing, body language, and intent. Communicating neutrally might also be difficult because of ways in which the polarization and divisions between political parties are crosscutting with social, economic, and demographic polarization (discussed in more detail later in this chapter). Cultural, social, and even factual disagreements can easily become political when political, cultural, and social divisions align with one another. The question of why it seems as if most topics become politicized in today's society is one that deserves further investigation.

Related research focuses on ways to encourage people to be cognizant of their biases, aware of biases contained in information received, and open to alternative viewpoints. Several studies suggest that being aware of bias, either one's own or that of a source, can reduce the effects of cognitive bias. One study found that forcing people to articulate

---

[29] Hernandez and Preston, 2013.

[30] Norbert Schwarz, Lawrence J. Sanna, Ian Skurnik, and Carolyn Yoon, "Metacognitive Experiences and the Intricacies of Setting People Straight: Implications for Debiasing and Public Information Campaigns," *Advances in Experimental and Social Psychology*, Vol. 39, 2007.

[31] Dan M. Kahan, "Ideology, Motivated Reasoning, and Cognitive Reflection: An Experimental Study," Yale Law School, Public Law Research Paper No. 272, 2012.

alternative viewpoints or to cite evidence of a differing explanation can reduce the influence of biases over beliefs by forcing consideration of another perspective and engagement in critical thinking.[32] Another study shows that the effects of misinformation that may create or confirm cognitive biases can be mitigated if there is advance warning that the information may be biased or false, if those warnings are repeated at frequent intervals, and if an accurate account is provided as a replacement.[33] These findings could be particularly relevant to Truth Decay and the search for ways to reduce it by suggesting possible ways to protect people from the effects of "fake news." Corrective information can effectively reduce biases when it has specific characteristics. The corrective information should not directly challenge the target's worldview, might rely on graphs or illustrations, and must provide a rationale for why the disinformation was disseminated and an alternative explanation of the original event or information.[34] These are high standards that are difficult to meet, especially in the current information system, where disinformation is plentiful, polarization is high, and so many issues are easily politicized.

Several reports on the challenges of communicating science to general audiences offer a number of other potential approaches to reducing cognitive bias (in this case, especially those associated with science). This issue is especially relevant because science is an area that has been heavily affected by Truth Decay and dis- and misinformation. Such approaches include building partnerships and relationships that can ease the flow of information (e.g., between researchers and practitioners), using participatory community-based research, attending to

---

[32] Edward R. Hirt and Keith D. Markman, "Multiple Explanation: A Consider-an-Alternative Strategy for Debiasing Judgments," *Journal of Personality and Social Psychology*, Vol. 69, No. 6, December 1995; D. K. Sherman and G. L. Cohen, "Accepting Threatening Information: Self-Affirmation and the Reduction of Defensive Biases," *Current Directions in Psychological Science*, Vol. 11, No. 4, 2002.

[33] Stephan Lewandowsky, Ullrich K. H. Ecker, Colleen M. Seifert, Norbert Schwarz, and John Cook, "Misinformation and Its Correction: Continued Influence and Successful Debiasing," *Psychological Science in the Public Interest*, Vol. 13, No. 3, 2012.

[34] Brendan Nyhan and Jason Reifler, *The Roles of Information Deficits and Identity Threat in the Prevalence of Misperceptions*, manuscript, Dartmouth College, February 24, 2017.

the biases and interests of the audience, and trying to make research findings relevant to individuals' positions and experiences.[35] These reports also suggests that the identity of the messenger plays a role in overcoming or counteracting preexisting beliefs, especially when new information challenges those beliefs and ideas. Specifically, the higher the perceived trust and credibility of the messenger, the more likely a person will be to change his or her mind.[36] The importance the messenger might play in breaking through cognitive biases is one reason why declining trust in institutions that used to be primary sources of information is such an important aspect of Truth Decay. Without information sources that they trust, people might be more likely to maintain their preexisting beliefs.

However, most research on counteracting cognitive biases suggests that, although various interventions might be able to reduce biases in a specific situation or in the short term, it is much more difficult to design interventions that permanently overcome biases or prevent people from developing new biases in the future. Furthermore, research suggests that the optimal modification approach can vary drastically based on the nature of the bias and even the specific individual, and is highly dependent on context. Because most research on reducing cognitive biases occurs in a laboratory context, it is unclear how generalizable these findings will prove.[37] Exploring approaches to reducing cognitive bias that could be implemented

---

[35] Anthony S. Bryk, Louis Gomez, and Alicia Grunow, "Getting Ideas into Action: Building Networked Improvement Communities in Education," in M. Hallinan, ed., *Frontiers in Sociology of Education*, Dordrecht, The Netherlands: Springer Publishing, 2011; National Academies of Sciences, Committee on Science Communication, 2017; V. Tseng, "Studying the Use of Research Evidence in Policy and Practice," *Social Policy Report*, Vol. 26, No. 2, 2012.

[36] S. Bleich, R. Blendon, and A. Adams, "Trust in Scientific Experts on Obesity: Implications for Awareness and Behavior Change," *Obesity*, Vol. 15, No. 8, 2007; D. Brossard and M. C. Nisbet, "Deference to Scientific Authority Among a Low Information Public: Understanding U.S. Opinion on Agricultural Biotechnology," *International Journal of Public Opinion Research*, Vol. 19, No. 1, 2007; Aaron M. McCright, Sandra T. Marquart-Pyatt, Rachael L. Shwom, Steven R. Brechin, and Summer Allen, "Ideology, Capitalism, and Climate: Explaining Public Views About Climate Change in the United States," *Energy Research and Social Science*, Vol. 21, 2016.

[37] MacLeod, Koster, and Fox, 2009.

outside the laboratory setting would be an especially valuable direction for future research. Finally, this research explores many types of cognitive biases, but it does not directly confront the challenge of getting people to privilege objective facts over experiences or opinions or over the beliefs of a wider social network. If anything, research on reducing cognitive bias underscores the important role this bias plays in Truth Decay and how difficult it will be to overcome the challenges that Truth Decay presents. However, more research in this area—including research focused on understanding fully how cognitive biases drive Truth Decay—is necessary to identify targeted responses that are able to reduce the effects of cognitive bias and incentivize people to accept new facts and challenge existing beliefs.

**Cognitive Processing: Areas for Future Research**

Of all the drivers of Truth Decay, cognitive biases and processing are the areas where there is the most existing research and knowledge. However, there are still questions where additional information is needed to deepen the understanding of Truth Decay and help in the development of solutions to reduce these biases. Central among these questions is how cognitive biases can be reduced. While some research has been done on this issue, additional research focused more directly on the types of cognitive bias related to Truth Decay would be valuable. Research in this area could include an assessment of the types of messages or messengers that tend to be most successful in reducing cognitive biases, or an analysis of the issues on which cognitive biases are easiest to successfully challenge. As noted earlier, research into ways to reduce cognitive bias that could be tested and implemented outside of a traditional laboratory setting would also be valuable. Such approaches might include efforts to establish and disseminate standards of objectivity and evidence in structured decisionmaking situations, such as jury deliberations. Other useful exercises would be to (1) formally assess the ways that technology exacerbates cognitive biases and the ways it might challenge or undermine them by altering some of the basic assumptions on which social or other relationships are based and (2) explore whether there are ways to more precisely understand and even measure the costs to a person (e.g., in terms of reputation or social stigma) when he or she changes his or her mind and whether it is possible to design incentives that offset these costs. Relatedly, it might also be relevant to look at costs to individuals of disseminating versus holding information and whether this cost varies based on the cost of information.

Finally, the challenges posed by cognitive biases are compounded at the institutional level, where the biases of many individuals interact. Some organizations—including government agencies, some large universities, and private corporations—have requirements and standards put in place to serve as a check on these biases and to ensure transparency and accountability in decisionmaking. Examples include the public comment period and cost-benefit analyses that are required prior to the enactment of new legislation. However, the extent to which these checks actually serve their purpose is unclear. Research into the types of institutional mechanisms that might reduce the effects of cognitive bias on institutional decisionmaking and a rigorous evaluation of those requirements already in place would be valuable. Answers to these questions will allow researchers and policymakers to develop responses to Truth Decay that target specific beliefs and specific audiences more directly—not to manipulate their opinions but to promote the value and necessity of objective facts. The research agenda in Chapter Six proposes additional avenues for research into cognitive processing.

## Changes in the Information System

Many of the inherent characteristics of human cognitive processing are exacerbated by the nature, speed, and scope of changes in the information system media landscape. These changes, occurring over the past 10–15 years, have been dramatic and multifaceted and are a clear and important driver of Truth Decay. We focus on three key areas: traditional media, social media, and disinformation. Certainly, there have been other changes in the information system, but these three are most directly related to Truth Decay. Toward the end of the section, we discuss areas where additional research is needed to both better understand relevant issues and begin to address some of the Truth Decay–related challenges presented by changes in the information system.

## The Transformation of Conventional Media

Changes in conventional media, both in form and business model, have contributed to Truth Decay in a number ways.[38] Many of these changes have been driven by the need of conventional media outlets, such as television and newspapers, to compete with newer forms of media, including social media platforms. For example, the shift to a 24-hour news cycle and an increase in the number and diversity of news organizations appear to have significantly increased the relative volume of opinions to facts and created incentives for the dissemination of sensationalized and sometimes misleading information. As competition increases and subscribership decreases, shrinking profit margins have also played a role, forcing newspapers and network and cable television stations to focus less on expensive investigative journalism and more on commentary, which is cheaper and appeals to viewers. There are exceptions, but newspapers tend to provide more-detailed information than cable news programs, which often provide more-immediate coverage but without the same level of detail or rigor.[39] Cable news programs might also benefit from a greater reliance on opinion and commentary, which require fewer resources to produce and can be more effective in attracting viewers. The increase in partisan news sources has had a similar effect while contributing to the formation of competing narratives on each side of the political spectrum. These changes have, together, created strong incentives for some media outlets to act as agents of Truth Decay, both to advance economic interests and to promote political agendas. Each of these changes contributes to the blurring of the line between opinion and fact and might contribute to rising distrust of the media as a provider of factual information. These changes, along with others discussed in this chapter (including the rise of social media and the shift to online content), have substantially reduced the com-

---

[38] Changes in the media industry, from consolidation of media companies to the shift to a 24-hour news cycle to the rise of social media, have had profound effects on the demands placed on media corporations. Here we discuss these trends to the extent that they relate to Truth Decay, but do not go into detail on the economics of the media industry. For more on economic changes in the media industry, please see Eli Noam, "Who Owns the World's Media?" Columbia Business School Research Paper, No. 13-22, September 2013.

[39] Michael Schudson, *The Power of News*, Cambridge, Mass.: Harvard University Press, 1996.

mitment to investigative, fact-based journalism both in print and on television. This is significant because investigative journalism, in its ability to reveal corruption and abuses of power and to champion the rights of minority groups whose voices might otherwise not be heard, can serve as an important protector of democracy.

### 24-Hour News Cycles and the Profit Motive

Changes in conventional media have fundamentally transformed the type of news disseminated and the way news is consumed. These changes include the shift to a 24-hour news cycle, a proliferation of sources, the increasing challenge of turning a profit for local and cable television networks and for local and national newspapers (as margins have fallen and competition has risen), and the permeation of partisanship throughout the media landscape. These changes appear to have contributed to Truth Decay in several specific ways. As the 24-hour news cycle forces media organizations to fill more time with content, they are forced to shift away from reporting strictly the facts (of which there are only so many) to providing commentary, increasing the volume of opinion over that of fact and blurring the distinction between the two. Compared with deep investigative journalism, commentary might be a cheaper endeavor, which can help media companies control or reduce costs and increase profits. The increasing number of players in the media market (both conventional sources and newer forms of media, such as social media platforms and blogs) and corresponding competition for audience have driven some media organizations to use sensationalized stories to attract and keep viewers and maximize appeal to advertisers.[40] Furthermore, analysis of the media market suggests that, for the sake of profits, media organizations have an incentive to cater their coverage to audience biases, essentially providing the types of news stories that people want and agree with, rather than focusing on providing high-quality and objective news coverage.[41] This is especially true as the number of media outlets increases and

---

[40] Pew Research Center, *State of the News Media*, Washington, D.C., June 15, 2016a.

[41] Matthew Gentzkow and Jesse M. Shapiro, "Media Bias and Reputation," *Journal of Political Economy*, Vol. 114, No. 2, 2006.

consumption of conventional sources of news, such as newspapers and television networks, is increasingly replaced by social media and online news sources. Journalists confirm this view, with two-thirds reporting as early as 2004 that increased pressure on the bottom line was undermining the quality of news coverage.[42] At the same time, the proliferation of news sources likely makes it easier than ever for people to find news organizations that promote similar views, thus feeding cognitive bias.

### The Spread of Partisan News

There have also been changes in the partisan affiliations of news organizations. To be clear, there has probably never been a time when journalism, whether print or television, has been entirely nonpartisan and objective. The earliest newspapers in the United States were largely local, expressing local opinions and points of view, and were often funded by political parties.[43] Coverage became more nationally focused when advertisers became the primary source of funding for most forms of media. The trend we are observing today, however, seems almost to be a shift away from this national coverage and back toward a more segmented news market in which a large number of sources compete for specific niche markets of consumers by appealing to those viewers with a specific type of content. In many cases, the niches appear to be defined by partisanship, leading to the rise of new and overtly political cable and print media and the shift leftward or rightward on the political spectrum of formerly centrist news organizations. A rise in the number of partisan news sources has implications for Truth Decay because, as we will describe in more detail, it has also led to an increase in biased news coverage that is intentionally skewed or that features more commentary and opinion than facts. Content analyses of the evening news programs of three major broadcast networks revealed a small but consistent Democratic bias in tone and amount of coverage in both 1968 and 1996, but more-recent analyses suggest a picture that

---

[42] Project for Excellence in Journalism, undated.

[43] See, for example, Marcus Daniel, *Scandal and Civility: Journalism and the Birth of American Democracy*, New York: Oxford University Press, 2009.

is more complex.[44] Analysis of the media market reveals a greater diversity of partisan affiliations and increasingly strong political orientations at some outlets. A 2005 study used the research think tanks cited in a newspaper's news stories as a proxy for partisanship and found that the news coverage (excluding editorials) of the *New York Times* and the *Los Angeles Times* were among the most liberal. The more-conservative sources included Fox News and the *Washington Times*.[45] The *Wall Street Journal* is a special case: Although its news coverage was, by the metric of a 2016 study, more liberal, its editorial pages tended to lean conservative.[46] This and other studies show an even more partisan landscape, with the *Washington Post*, the *New York Times*, CNN, and MSNBC on the left, the *Wall Street Journal* slightly to the right of center, and such sources as Fox News and the *Washington Times* further to the right.[47] Local news sources are also often partisan in their tone and coverage, depending on the ideology of the newspaper or station owner or the partisanship of the national affiliate. However, few studies explicitly map the partisanship of these news sources.

Regulatory changes over the past several decades have contributed to changes in the content, partisanship, and objectivity of print and television news shows compared with, for example, the 1970s and 1980s. Perhaps the best example of such legislation was the 1987 decision to stop enforcing the Fairness Doctrine.[48]

The Fairness Doctrine, a policy initially put in place in 1949, required broadcasters to cover important public issues, including those that were controversial, and to do so with coverage that was fact-based,

---

[44] D. D'Alessio and M. Allen, "Media Bias in Presidential Elections: A Meta-Analysis," *Journal of Communication*, Vol. 50, No. 4, 2000.

[45] Tim Groseclose and Jeffrey Milyo, "A Measure of Media Bias," *Quarterly Journal of Economics*, Vol. 120, No. 4, 2005.

[46] Seth Flaxman, Sharad Goel, and Justin Rao, "Filter Bubbles, Echo Chambers, and Online News Consumption," *Public Opinion Quarterly*, Vol. 80, Special Issue, 2016.

[47] Flaxman, Goel, and Rao, 2016; Tim Groeling, "Who's the Fairest of Them All? An Empirical Test for Partisan Bias on ABC, CBS, NBC, and Fox News," *Presidential Studies Quarterly*, Vol. 38, No. 4, 2008.

[48] The Fairness Doctrine was no longer enforced after 1987, but the language implementing it remained intact until 2011.

unbiased, and evenhanded. Television and radio stations therefore had to devote time to covering issues of significance to the public and commit to presenting both sides of the issue fairly through news coverage, discussion-based shows, or other means. However, the rule did not apply to newspapers—or later to cable television. By law, television and radio news coverage had to be objective and cover a story from all angles, not just one. It could not present only one side of the story, skew or distort the opposing side, or apply media spin. The Fairness Doctrine was intended to expose the electorate to a diversity of viewpoints and to ensure that the media did not become biased promoters of one side of a political or other debate. In today's context, this would mean that cable news channels and radio broadcasts would be required to spend a certain amount of time discussing major issues—such as alternative health care policies, immigration, and cyber security—in a manner that a Federal Communications Commission (FCC) observer would consider fair, balanced, transparent, and honest. The decision to stop enforcing the Fairness Doctrine gave broadcasters more freedom, but it also made the public more vulnerable to receiving biased coverage of key issues.[49]

Although proponents of the Fairness Doctrine argued that it promoted fair and balanced news coverage, prevented bias in the media, and made a civic contribution by ensuring Americans were more informed about key issues, those who opposed it raised a number of criticisms. First, most legal scholars argued that it was unconstitutional because it regulated content and had a "chilling effect" on speech.[50] Studies of media content and surveys of media executives found that news outlets, rather than addressing truly controversial issues (which risked either expensive lawsuits from those who felt that coverage was not sufficiently balanced or fines from FCC regulators), did the

---

[49] Brooks Boliek, "FCC Finally Kills Off Fairness Doctrine," Politico, August 22, 2011; Donald J. Jung, *The Federal Communications Commission, the Broadcast Industry, and the Fairness Doctrine: 1981–1987*, New York: University Press of America, Inc., 1996.

[50] Dennis Patrick, "Abolishing the Fairness Doctrine: A Policy Maker's Perspective," speech delivered to the George Mason University Information Economy Project, National Press Club, Washington, D.C., July 18, 2007. The Information Economy Project is now run out of Clemson University.

bare minimum required to meet the law and tried to focus on issues unlikely to raise conflict. Instead of increasing press coverage of important issues, then, the Fairness Doctrine might ultimately have reduced this coverage, compared with an alternative information system without the Fairness Doctrine.[51]

Critics also argued that implementing the Fairness Doctrine was inefficient and logistically difficult. Responsibility for monitoring the compliance of media organizations fell to members of the FCC, who had to decide whether coverage of an issue was truly balanced and whether both sides had been afforded equal coverage (in time or depth), and address other, similarly difficult questions. Furthermore, in some cases, an issue had more than just two sides. FCC members, then, had to evaluate whether media organizations had fairly covered *all possible sides*, a judgment that was often very difficult to make.[52] Finally, those who argued for the removal of the Fairness Doctrine noted that, in some ways, the rule made it easier for incumbent politicians to suppress media criticism, because the doctrine included a provision that allowed incumbents to sue (or, more accurately, to have one of their supporters sue) media organizations that the plaintiff felt covered the candidate in a biased or imbalanced way.[53] It was for these reasons that the FCC made the decision in 1987 to stop enforcing the Fairness Doctrine.

The effects of the end of the Fairness Doctrine on the objectivity and diversity of news sources have evolved over decades. Radio programming was the first to be affected. The 1990s saw the rise of talk radio shows led by charismatic hosts who commanded large followings and often espoused and promoted extreme and partisan views. Regulatory changes also appear to have influenced the content of radio programming in important ways. A study of the number of radio shows and the diversity of topics covered by these shows before and after the end of the Fairness Doctrine showed a dramatic increase in the

---

[51] Thomas W. Hazlett and David W. Sosa, "Was the Fairness Doctrine a 'Chilling Effect'? Evidence from the Postderegulation Radio Market," *Journal of Legal Studies*, Vol. 26, No. 1, 1997; Patrick, 2007.

[52] Patrick, 2007.

[53] Patrick, 2007.

number of news and information-focused shows between 1975 (when the Fairness Doctrine was in place) and 1995 (after it was no longer enforced). This increase can be interpreted as evidence that the regulations included in the doctrine might have had the "chilling effect" that some feared.[54] In addition, it would be incorrect to blame the removal of the Fairness Doctrine for the emergence of some of the more-partisan news sources, located mostly on cable networks, because cable networks were not covered by the Fairness Doctrine.

Regardless of the catalyst or catalysts that triggered the change in media coverage, content, and partisanship, the 1990s and 2000s saw a steep rise on both sides of the political spectrum in the number of sharply partisan news sources that intentionally blurred opinion and fact and manipulated data to advance political agendas. Although there were (and are) both conservative and liberal programs, the volume and reach of conservative talk radio vastly exceeded that of its progressive counterparts. Such hosts as Glenn Beck, Sean Hannity, and Rush Limbaugh developed nationwide followings after national syndication.[55] Research suggests that these shows did, in fact, have significant effects on audience beliefs. For example, one study found that conservative talk radio listeners were more likely than listeners of progressive talk radio to come away with misinformation and incorrect beliefs.[56] In this way, there appears to be some link between this rise in partisan radio broadcasting and some of the early seeds of Truth Decay.

The success of conservative talk radio was a key motivating factor in the creation of Fox News in 1996. Although there had been news channels with political leanings in the past, Fox News was perhaps the most overtly partisan at its inception, pushing a strongly conservative agenda through its conservative primetime talk shows, led by

---

[54] Hazlett and Sosa, 1997.

[55] Abram Brown, "Why All the Talk-Radio Stars Are Conservative," *Forbes*, July 13, 2015.

[56] C. Richard Hofstetter, David Barker, James T. Smith, Gina M. Zari, and Thomas A. Ingrassia, "Information, Misinformation, and Political Talk Radio," *Political Research Quarterly*, Vol. 52, No. 2, 1999.

such hosts as Neil Cavuto, Sean Hannity, and Bill O'Reilly.[57] Research suggests that Fox News has been successful in advancing its partisan agenda. A 2007 study found that the share of Republican votes rose between 1996 and 2000 in districts where the station was broadcast.[58]

There were also efforts to build liberal talk radio and television channels that could promote progressive ideas and agendas. Air America Radio, for example, launched in 2004, led by such liberal personalities as current MSNBC host Rachel Maddow and actress and activist Janeane Garofalo, and hosted shows by Jon Elliott, Marc Maron, Jack Rice, and Nicole Sandler. The network performed well in its first year, gaining a rapidly growing number of followers, but then struggled through a number of scandals, changes in ownership and leadership, and turnover in personalities. It filed for bankruptcy and ceased operations in 2010. There appear to be many reasons for its demise, but the network's inability to capture a wide and stable audience (one of the successes of conservative analogues) is at least partly to blame.[59]

Another example is Current TV, launched in 2005 by Al Gore and Joel Hyatt (who was also its chief executive officer).[60] Current TV was originally promoted as an independent cable news channel and a forum for user-generated content with a commitment to citizen journalism. The hope was that it would become an independent marketplace of ideas that could challenge the near-oligopoly that controls conventional media outlets (e.g., Fox, NBC, ABC). However, that model had limited success, and the channel evolved to become a means of advancing progressive ideals and agendas, covering such issues as climate change and such events as Occupy Wall Street. It worked hard

[57] Scott Collins, *Crazy Like a Fox: The Inside Story of How Fox News Beat CNN*, New York: Portfolio Hardcover, 2004.

[58] Stefano DellaVigna and Ethan Kaplan, "The Fox News Effect: Media Bias and Voting," *Quarterly Journal of Economics*, Vol. 122, No. 3, 2007.

[59] Al Franken, *Giant of the Senate*, New York: Hachette Book Group, 2017.

[60] Joel Hyatt has served as a RAND Trustee since November 1, 2014. For a complete list of trustees, see RAND Corporation, "RAND Corporation Board of Trustees," webpage, September 2017.

to attract younger, liberal viewers and promoted user-generated content in an early form of crowd-sourcing. Like Air America, however, the channel struggled to build a viewership and went through numerous format changes, eventually hiring Keith Olbermann and Jennifer Granholm (a former governor of Michigan) in 2011. More format changes in 2012 led to the firing of Olbermann and the hiring of Eliot Spitzer, Joy Behar, and others. The channel was acquired by Al Jazeera in 2013, becoming Al Jazeera America, at which time the programming lineup and brand as a progressive news outlet were abandoned.[61]

In more-recent years, partisan bias seems to have spread even through media organizations previously considered relatively unbiased. For example, a 2008 study of news coverage of former Presidents Bill Clinton and George W. Bush found that coverage from NBC and CBS was at least as biased as that of Fox News (but in the other direction). ABC was the only network that appeared willing to broadcast equally positive coverage of both presidents.[62] Since that study, the partisan divide of news sources has continued to grow, with outlets on both sides of the spectrum, across forms of media and information platforms, taking increasingly divergent positions on the core issues faced by the American people and policymakers.

### Implications for Truth Decay

Partisan news contributes to Truth Decay because sources on each side present entirely different worldviews to very different audiences. This contributes to the formation of echo chambers, erodes agreement about facts and analytical interpretations of these facts, and plays a role in the formation of beliefs and attitudes that might not be based entirely on fact and that, once formed, might be very difficult to change. Content analysis reveals the wide variation in the stories and frames presented to audiences, and an analysis of the audiences themselves suggests that there is limited overlap in view-

---

[61] "Al-Jazeera Buys Al Gore's Current TV," Associated Press, January 3, 2013; Rob Lowman, "Al Gore's Current TV Network Moves Toward Becoming a 24/7 Channel," *Daily Breeze*, January 29, 2012; Dana Stevens, "Invasion of the Pod People," *Slate*, August 3, 2005. Note: Al Jazeera America shut down in 2016.

[62] Groeling, 2008.

ership, especially among individuals who are "regular" cable news viewers.[63] Demographic and preference analysis suggests that these viewers also have different preferences and social and economic characteristics. Fox News viewers, for instance, tend to favor information that matches their political views; viewers of CNN prefer in-depth interviews.[64] One study found that this polarization of viewers began around 2004. Before that, partisanship was not a significant predictor of choice of cable news channel. After 2004, however, Democrats became more likely to choose CNN and Republicans to choose Fox.[65] This bifurcation and partisanship of news sources and their appeals to very different audiences appears to directly feed Truth Decay by giving rise to competing sets of "facts" and interpretations of those facts, driving the increasing disagreement on key issues, and sowing uncertainty about what is opinion and what is fact. Partisanship might also be contributing to polarization, a concept discussed in more detail later in this chapter. The evidence concerning whether partisan media can actually change people's opinions is mixed, but news channels that present a partisan worldview might be able to *shape* opinions and beliefs that are still being formed and can certainly deepen preexisting divides along political or demographic lines.[66] The strengthening of partisan news sources also challenges the concept of "fact-based journalism" and contributes to the rise of opinion in place of fact throughout the news media, blurring the distinction between the two.

---

[63] Markus Prior, "Media and Political Polarization," *Annual Review of Political Science*, Vol. 16, No. 1, 2013.

[64] Jonathan S. Morris, "The Fox News Factor," *Harvard International Journal of Press/Politics*, Vol. 10, No. 3, 2005.

[65] Morris, 2005.

[66] Kevin Arceneaux, Martin Johnson, and Chad Murphy, "Polarized Political Communication, Oppositional Media Hostility, and Selective Exposure," *Journal of Politics*, Vol. 74, No. 1, 2012; Matthew Levendusky, "Affect Effects: Do Viewers Dislike and Distrust the Opposition After Partisan Media Exposure?" Philadelphia, University of Pennsylvania, working paper, 2012a; Matthew Levendusky, "Do Partisan Media Polarize Voters?" Philadelphia, University of Pennsylvania, working paper, 2012b.

It is worth noting that, in other countries, news sources have long held partisan bias without contributing to the proliferation of misinformation and disinformation observed today both in the United States and elsewhere. Partisan news sources might not, on their own, drive Truth Decay. It is when partisan media coverage combines with many of the other changes and trends described in this report—including the increasing volume of information available, the emergence of social media, and the increase in political polarization—that partisan media becomes an important contributor to the trends that constitute Truth Decay.

### Change in News Content

Alongside the increasing partisanship of news sources and the role played by the profit motive, a shift in news coverage appears to have occurred as well, away from coverage that focuses predominantly on facts and substance and toward coverage that is less comprehensive, less substantive, and often dominated by opinion. Although this shift in content itself might not be evidence of Truth Decay, the accuracy and commitment to facts and data in soft news articles are likely lower than that in intensively researched and high-quality journalism on such topics as politics and finance (this is largely a hypothesis that should be tested)—and this decreased emphasis on facts does seem to drive the increasing relative volume, and resulting influence, of opinion and personal experience over fact and the blurring of the line between opinion and relevant facts. For example, a content analysis of newspapers, evening news, and news magazines from 1978 to 1998 found a shift toward entertainment, celebrity, and lifestyle pieces in place of government policy and foreign affairs.[67] One study estimates that soft news (news with no policy content) rose between 1978 and 1998 from 35 percent of total printed content in analyzed sources to about 50 percent.[68] Although this study is now somewhat dated, it is indicative of trends that appear to have continued. Part of this shift could be due to the drive for increased profit (soft news might be cheaper to produce than hard news), but it could also reflect changing standards or

---

[67] Project for Excellence in Journalism, 1998.

[68] Bennett, 2004.

changing preferences. A more concrete example of this phenomenon is coverage of political campaigns. A content analysis of coverage in 2004 found that airtime was dominated by discussion of the "horse race" rather than the substantive issues. Since at least 2000, coverage of major election campaigns was on the decline—a trend that stopped with the 2016 election.[69] These changes in news content published by even conventional news outlets have also likely influenced the types of information consumed by readers of major national newspapers and viewers of cable and network television. If it has not decreased the amount of fact-based information that viewers consume, it has at least increased the amount of opinion, commentary, and other information they are exposed to. To the extent that these other types of information affect beliefs or lead to misperceptions that are likely to persist, the shift in content might be an important way that changes in the information system contribute to a blurring of the line between opinion and fact and the increasing relative volume, and resulting influence, of opinion and personal experience over fact that are part of Truth Decay.

### Changes in Media Consumption and Trust

Changes in how people consume news might be playing a role in Truth Decay. A 2017 study showed that newspaper subscriptions (both weekday and Sunday) have fallen consistently since about 1990, declining by a total of about 38 percent over the past 20 years. Subscriptions declined 8 percent year over year between 2015 and 2016, a rate that was twice as large as the average year-over-year decreases seen in the previous five years. But cable news viewership actually rose in 2015 and 2016.[70] And this increase was substantial: CNN, MSNBC, and Fox News experienced a 55-percent increase in combined average primetime viewership in 2016 compared with 2015, a large portion of which is likely attributable to interest in the 2016 presidential election.[71] As described previously, in general, cable news coverage is less in-depth and features less-rigorous analysis and more commentary

---

[69] Project for Excellence in Journalism, undated.

[70] Michael Barthel, "Newspapers Fact Sheet," Pew Research Center, June 1, 2017.

[71] Katerina Eva Matsa, "Cable News Fact Sheet," Pew Research Center, June 1, 2017.

blended with fact than newspaper articles, which often include deep investigative reporting.[72] This increase in cable news viewership and the simultaneous decrease in newspaper subscribership might have contributed to an apparent decrease in the weight and importance placed on fact and the increased relative volume of opinion over fact in the information system. In addition, although subscriptions to newspapers have declined, web traffic to the digital and online versions of newspapers appears to have risen slightly between 2015 and 2016.[73] This shift to web-based newspapers could be evidence of the growing predominance of the internet and social media in the information system.[74] In 2017, 93 percent of Americans report that online sources, including websites and social media, are their primary sources of news.[75] The role played by the rise of social media and the internet in changes in the information system and Truth Decay is discussed in more detail in the next section.

This rapid reshaping of the media environment might also have contributed directly to the decline in trust in media organizations, which is at an all-time low across the board—from print journalism to broadcast news. Between 1997 and 2016, the percentage of people expressing "a great deal" or "quite a lot" of confidence in newspapers fell from 35 percent to 20 percent and, for television news, from 34 percent to 21 percent.[76] Confidence in both newspapers and television news increased in 2017, to 27 percent expressing "a great deal" or "quite a lot" of confidence in newspapers and 24 percent saying the same about television news.[77] In comparison, 16 percent expressed "a great deal" or "quite a lot" of confidence about news found on the internet, the first

---

[72] Leonard Downie and Michael Schudson, "The Reconstruction of American Journalism," *Columbia Journalism Review*, November/December 2009.

[73] Barthel, 2017.

[74] Darrell West, *How to Combat Fake News and Disinformation*, Washington, D.C.: Brookings Institution, December 18, 2017.

[75] Galen Stocking, "Digital News Fact Sheet," Pew Research Center, August 7, 2017; Amy Mitchell, Jeffrey Gottfried, Elisa Shearer, and Kristine Lu, "How Americans Encounter, Recall, and Act Upon Digital News," Pew Research Center, February 9, 2017.

[76] Gallup, 2016.

[77] Gallup, 2017.

time Gallup included this metric in its survey.[78] In part, declining trust in media organizations of all types could be attributed to the increasing bias and inaccuracy of news coverage. A 2011 Pew Research Center survey showed a sharp increase since 1985 in the percentage of people reporting that news stories are often inaccurate, biased, or strongly influenced by other powerful organizations.[79] There are, however, some significant partisan divides on this issue. In 2017, Democrats reported trusting the press more than the president to provide accurate information; Republicans reported the opposite.[80] As noted elsewhere, this declining trust in institutions is a core part of Truth Decay, and this is especially true of declining trust in media institutions.[81] Uncertainty about what is opinion and what is fact and the human tendency to privilege opinion over fact both thrive when no institutions are viewed as trusted providers of accurate and honest information. Notably, while trust in conventional media organizations as sources of factual information has decreased, trust in other forms of media, such as social media, have not improved. This does not, therefore, seem to be a case of trust in one institution being replaced by trust in another.[82]

---

[78] Gallup, 2017.

[79] Pew Research Center, "Press Widely Criticized, but Trusted More Than Other Information Sources," webpage, September 22, 2011.

[80] Quinnipiac University Poll, "Trump Slumps as American Voters Disapprove 55%–38% Quinnipiac University National Poll Finds; Voters Trust Media, Courts More Than President," February 22, 2017a.

[81] Despite the one-year increase noted earlier, the overall trend in trust in media institutions is still sharply downward. It is also not clear whether the one-year uptick is a fluctuation or the beginning of a longer increase in trust in these institutions. This is a development worth watching.

[82] It is possible that recent changes in the form of media content and the emergence of new media technologies might undermine trust not only in media organizations but also in traditional institutional hierarchies more generally. Throughout history, new media technologies have challenged the conventional or establishment media that often held a monopoly over information. The best example of this is probably the invention of the printing press, which allowed the publication of a vernacular Bible and works by pre-Christian authors and so sparked both the Reformation and Enlightenment and the emergence of a new set of institutions. See Elizabeth Eisenstein, *The Printing Press as an Agent of Change*, New York: Cambridge University Press, 1980.

## The Internet and Social Media
### The Volume and Flow of Information

The second major change that has affected the information system and contributed to Truth Decay is the rise of the internet and social media platforms, which have drastically increased the volume of information available and the speed with which it can be accessed. These increases reflect perhaps the most significant change in the information system and also one of the characteristics that most sets the present environment apart from those of the past. It is not the increased volume of information, but rather the increased volume of opinion compared with the volume of fact that appears to drive Truth Decay. This increase in the relative volume of opinion is facilitated by social media and the internet. Social media platforms, such as Twitter and Facebook, directly affect the spread of information by making it easier to access and share large quantities of information more quickly. Assessing growth in the volume of tweets per day on Twitter is one way to measure the extent of this information explosion. As Figure 4.1 shows, the number of tweets

**Figure 4.1**
**Tweets per Day, 2006–2013**

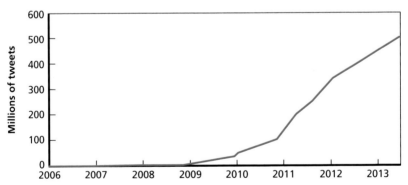

SOURCES: Internet Live Stats, "Twitter Usage Statistics," webpage, undated; Krikorian, 2013; Twitter Engineering, 2011; Weil, 2010.
NOTE: Twitter has not officially updated its tweets per day metric since November 2013. Other unofficial sources suggest that the number of tweets per day has plateaued or even declined since then. See, for example, Jim Edwards, "Leaked Twitter API Data Shows the Number of Tweets Is in Serious Decline," *Business Insider*, February 2, 2016.
RAND RR2314-4.1

per day rose from 5,000 in 2007 to 500,000,000 by 2013, although some sources suggest that growth in tweets per day has plateaued or even declined since then.[83] Although we do not consider detailed data trends for all social media platforms, such platforms as Facebook have shown similar increases in data produced.[84]

Social media platforms can also affect the spread of information, changing the ways in which people engage with information, the patterns through which information diffuses, and even the likelihood that information is proliferated throughout a social network. For example, research suggests that people who receive lots of information shared by friends through social media networks are more likely to also share information than those who exist in networks where information-sharing is less common.[85] To be clear, this increase in the volume and availability of information is generally a positive development because it allows more people to directly consume and evaluate information, rather than waiting for filtered information from centralized sources. As noted above, wider dissemination of greater amounts of information can also be valuable in holding government and corporate leaders accountable and exposing wrongdoing, corruption, or dishonesty within public and private institutions. However, this increased volume and democratized access can also have other outcomes. For example, people tend to be most strongly influenced by their closest friends and family in interpersonal communication but more-distant and weaker relations can be highly influential in social media networks, often serving as the source of new information that can spread through the social group.[86] This might mean

---

[83] Raffi Krikorian, "New Tweets per Second Record, and How!" Twitter Blog, August 16, 2013; Twitter Engineering, "200 Million Tweets per Day," Twitter Blog, June 30, 2011; Kevin Weil, "Measuring Tweets," Twitter Blog, February 22, 2010.

[84] See, for example, Josh Constine, "How Big Is Facebook's Data? 2.5 Billion Pieces and 500+ Terabytes Ingested Every Day," Techcrunch, August 22, 2012; and Kit Smith, "Marketing: 47 Facebook Statistics for 2016," Brandwatch, May 12, 2016.

[85] Eytan Bakshy, Itamar Rosenn, Cameron Marlow, and Lada Adamic, "The Role of Social Networks in Information Diffusion," *Proceedings of the 21st International Conference on World Wide Web*, 2012.

[86] Bakshy et al., 2012.

that there is a higher chance of being exposed to information from an untrusted or mostly unknown acquaintance, which could have implications for Truth Decay. It can be difficult to evaluate the legitimacy of information spread through unknown or new sources encountered on social media platforms and through internet searches, and, as a result, someone's odds of accepting false information could rise. Facebook's announcement in September 2017 that Russian-linked entities created Facebook users and groups to disseminate information and influence attitudes is just one example of how this might occur.[87]

Different types of information can also spread through a network or across social media at different rates and to different extents, with implications for Truth Decay. For instance, one study found that Twitter hashtags associated with politically controversial topics and sports tend to spread further and persist longer on social media platforms than those attached to other topics, such as music and conversational catchphrases (e.g., #FridayFeeling).[88] This finding could be important for understanding the ways in which social media contributes to the blurring of the line between opinion and fact and the increasing relative volume, and resulting influence, of opinion and personal experience over fact. If political controversies and sensationalized political stories do indeed spread the furthest and last the longest, this could help explain why Truth Decay and disinformation currently seem to be strongest in political debate and civil discourse. Finally, information can change as it spreads through a social network, becoming biased or distorted as it passes from person to person.[89] Research on information diffusion confirms that messages evolve as informa-

---

[87] Alex Stamos, "An Update on Information Operations on Facebook," Facebook Newsroom, September 6, 2017.

[88] Daniel M. Romero, Brendan Meeder, and Jon Kleinberg, "Differences in the Mechanics of Information Diffusion Across Topics: Idioms, Political Hashtags, and Complex Contagion on Twitter," *Proceedings of the 20th International Conference on World Wide Web*, 2011.

[89] G. Kossinets, J. Kleinberg, and D. Watts, "The Structure of Information Pathways in a Social Communication Network," *Proceedings of the 14th Association for Computing Machinery Special Interest Group on Knowledge Discovery and Data Mining's International Conference on Knowledge Discovery and Data Mining*, 2008.

tion spreads through a social network and pieces of the network preferentially share certain variants or interpretations of the message and as each person passing the information adds his or her own biases, interpretation, and background.[90] In these ways, social media makes it possible for disinformation and misleading information to spread quickly and widely—and thus feeds Truth Decay by enabling the blurring of the line between opinion and fact and magnifying the relative volume and effect of opinions and beliefs over objective facts. In some cases, people might eventually realize that the information they have been exposed to online is false, but the power of cognitive bias and the strong role of social networks in belief formation might prevent this understanding.

### Access to Information

Another unique aspect of social media platforms and the internet that might contribute to Truth Decay is the removal of information filters and the ease of access that this removal affords to all types of information. In past decades, a handful of national newspapers and network news channels mediated information disseminated more broadly. Local papers and television stations were often affiliated with one of these national papers or networks. Access to many types of information was limited to people who could afford to subscribe to newspapers; others relied almost entirely on the prepackaged information provided by the three major network news channels or major radio stations. Furthermore, publishers and network and radio broadcasters could (and still can) be sued for defamation and were subject to certain standards and regulations. Now, however, almost anyone can instantaneously access large volumes and diverse sources of unmediated information from cable news channels, online publications, and social media on nearly any topic imaginable. Social media and the internet have reduced the authority and removed the primary role of "gatekeeper" institutions that used to be the primary information filters, such as conventional media sources and government. In addition, many newspapers have

---

[90] Lada A. Adamic, Thomas M. Lento, Eytan Adar, and Pauline C. Ng, "Information Evolution in Social Networks," *Proceedings of the Ninth Association for Computing Machinery International Conference on Web Search and Data Mining*, 2016.

shifted to a completely (or partially) online, open-access format that further democratizes access to information. Finally, it is worth noting that cable news and social media, two means of information dissemination that have grown substantially over the past two decades, are subject to fewer content regulations or laws holding outlets responsible for content accuracy than are radio and network television broadcasters.[91]

The loss of information filters or gatekeepers can have both positive and negative implications for quality and access to information. On the one hand, democratized access to information is a positive development that has empowered people across geographic, economic, political, and social groups. It reduces the power of conventional media companies that, although they might have served as a check on misinformation and the quality of content, have also at times served as an oligopoly in their control of media content. Direct access to information and the ability to be a source of information also democratize the information system and might give voice to marginalized voices and minorities. Singer argues that the emergence of blogs and social media has created an interactive relationship between the media and the audience. The audience has now taken on the role of "secondary mediator," meaning that the audience has some discretion over which sources and stories are redisseminated and spread more widely.[92] She characterizes this shift as a good thing, one that empowers individuals to shape their information system.

At the same time, however, the fact that anyone can become a source of information, by posting on Twitter or some other platform, makes it much easier for disinformation to spread, and it also provides a tool for those who might benefit from intentionally fueling Truth Decay. The rise of unmediated news sources, although it might entail benefits, appears therefore to be a key contributor to Truth Decay. Journalists have expressed concerns about the implications of this shift to a more-open

---

[91] See Federal Communications Commission, "Program Content Regulations," webpage, September 29, 2017; Byron Tau, Georgia Wells, and Deepa Seetharam, "Lawmakers Warn Tech Executives More Regulation May Be Coming for Social Media," *Wall Street Journal*, November 1, 2017.

[92] Jane B. Singer, "User-Generated Visibility: Secondary Gatekeeping in a Shared Media Space," *New Media and Society*, Vol. 16, No. 1, 2014.

information environment, focusing on a possible decline in the quality and credibility of information and reporting and of civility in communication; a loss of balance or the use of inappropriate tones; and lack of accountability among secondary disseminators.[93] Whether the change is ultimately positive or a negative, the loss of sources of information authority has significant implications for Truth Decay. Specifically, the loss of key media gatekeepers increases uncertainty about what is generally accepted as fact and what is not. It also allows opinion to overwhelm fact in many areas, especially those that are complex and might require some sort of expert knowledge or experience.

There is even some evidence that social media is one of the primary ways through which people access "fake news" and disinformation. A 2017 study used data on web traffic for the top 609 real-news websites in the United States and 65 fake ones (e.g., sites that produce only or mostly articles based on verifiably false information) and compared how individuals accessed those sources, focusing on such methods as direct browsing and social media. As Figure 4.2 shows, the primary access route for real-news websites is direct browsing (fol-

**Figure 4.2**
**Share of Visits to U.S. News Websites, by Source**

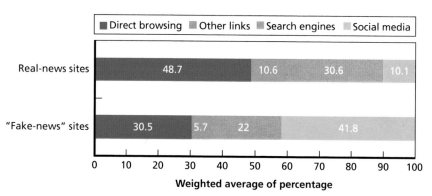

SOURCE: Allcott and Gentzkow, 2017b, p. 222.
NOTE: Sites are weighted by percentage of monthly visits.
RAND RR2314-4.2

---

[93] Singer, 2014.

lowed by search engines), and only 10 percent of traffic gets there via social media. For "fake-news" sites, however, more than 40 percent of traffic comes from social media.[94] This does not mean that social media is inherently a problem—rather it suggests that social media might contribute to the proliferation of disinformation; a blurring of the line between opinion and fact; and the increasing relative volume, and resulting influence, of opinion and personal experience over fact.

The internet and social media have also changed the way the media performs its functions. Like average Americans, journalists are increasingly embracing social media platforms, such as Twitter, both as a source of information for stories and news reports and as a tool for dissemination. Research suggests that, over the past decade, journalists and television news broadcasters have increasingly relied on Twitter as a sole or primary source (although they tended to use only "official" Twitter accounts). A shift to reliance on Twitter or other social media as a source of information for stories and news reports might suffice in many cases, but relying solely on Twitter may undermine the quality of investigative journalism and increase the risk of spreading disinformation, thus worsening rather than improving Truth Decay.[95] The need to distill information into ever-shorter blurbs and sound bites (e.g., for a 280-character tweet) could also be eroding the quality of journalism and the information contained in news reporting and decreasing the importance of facts. Because only so much can be communicated in 280 characters, the factual basis of a story might be lost or distorted in the effort to be concise and pithy and to attract views. The rise of the internet and the shift to a media model in which online publication and social media are now one of the primary ways that people get information have also increased the speed at which news articles are published and reduced the time spent on editing and fact-checking

---

[94] Hunt Allcott and Matthew Gentzkow, "Social Media and Fake News in the 2016 Election," *Journal of Economic Perspectives*, Vol. 31, No. 2, Spring 2017b.

[95] Soo Jung Moon and Patrick Hadley, "Routinizing a New Technology in the Newsroom: Twitter as a News Source in Mainstream Media," *Journal of Broadcasting & Electronic Media*, Vol. 58, No. 2, 2014.

these stories.[96] This has the potential to increase the dissemination of misinformation or misleading information, with implications for the quality of journalism and the level of trust in media institutions (if the number of known errors increases).

Although this discussion has focused on Twitter and Facebook, it is important to note that there are many other social media platforms that exhibit both similarities to and differences with these industry leaders. Examples include Reddit, Snapchat, Instagram, 4chan, LinkedIn, Pinterest, Tumblr, WhatsApp, and YouTube, among many others. Each might have a slightly different business model or appeal to slightly different audiences. For example, Instagram revolves around posted photos, whereas LinkedIn is primarily a professional networking site. Snapchat is popular among younger social media users, whereas Twitter tends to attract a somewhat-older user base. Platforms also differ in the extent to which they contribute to Truth Decay, particularly to the blurring of the line between opinion and fact, the extent to which they proliferate misinformation, and in the degree to which this proliferation is tolerated by those in charge of overseeing or monitoring content.

Some sites, such as Reddit and 4chan, are better known than others for hosting and allowing communities that use the platform to launch intentional disinformation campaigns both on that platform and through other ones. Reddit works through upvotes from other users. Posts that have more upvotes are more prominently displayed on the Reddit homepage, which effectively means that other users are responsible for evaluating the quality and even credibility of a piece of information. Although this seems to be the purest form of democratized access to news, it also has the potential to exacerbate some of the conceivably negative aspects of social media previously described, including a gradual degradation of quality and easier dissemination of misinformation and disinformation.

A closer look at the workings of such sites provides insight into some of these negative implications. Several analyses suggest that Reddit's algorithms and oversight have made the site increasingly inter-

---

[96] Fred Vultee, "Audience Perceptions of Editing Quality: Assessing Traditional News Routines in the Digital Age," *Digital Journalism*, 2014.

nally focused and have allowed it to serve as a breeding ground for echo chambers and harmful subcultures. One ethnographic study of Reddit communities points to ways in which the upvoting system, ease of creating subreddits (which are forums for discussing specific topics), and weak policies regulating offensive content foster what the author calls "toxic technocultures," or subcultures that promote misogynist or otherwise discriminatory perspectives.[97] These same dynamics facilitate the spread of misinformation and disinformation. Reddit and 4chan have done less to regulate these types of intentionally subversive subcommunities than Facebook and Twitter, with the result that such communities continue to thrive in these forums. Although we do not consider social media and the changes it has triggered in the information system to be a negative development overall, this discussion suggests that there are specific social media platforms that seem to be contributing more directly to Truth Decay than others.

It is also worth noting that although a large percentage of Americans now rely heavily on social media sites as a source of news,[98] social media sites themselves are very different in form and intention than the professional journalism that grounded most print and network television news in previous decades. Instead, such corporations as Facebook and Twitter are largely concerned with generating advertising revenue. Thus, they have little incentive to establish standards for content or to guard against the proliferation of misinformation or disinformation. Although both organizations have made some recent efforts to address shortcomings in these areas, changes made thus far have done little to ameliorate the situation.

### Filters and Algorithms

Finally, the filters and algorithms embedded in social media platforms and search engines, such as Google, contribute to Truth Decay—and particularly to increasing disagreement and the blurring of the distinc-

---

[97] Adrienne Massanari, "#Gamergate and the Fappening: How Reddit's Algorithm, Governance, and Culture Support Toxic Technocultures," *New Media & Society*, Vol. 19, No. 3, 2017.

[98] Elisa Shearer and Jeffrey Gottfried, "News Use Across Social Media Platforms 2017," Pew Research Center, September 2017.

tion between opinion and fact—by inserting a bias into the types of information a person is likely to encounter or engage with. Twitter's suggestions to users about other people to follow are one example. These suggestions are based on (and usually very similar to) the types of content and people a user already follows and most regularly retweets or views on the site. However, this system of recommendations encourages people to fill their Twitter feeds with information similar to what people are already consuming and is, in all likelihood, already consistent with their beliefs. The onus is therefore on the individual user to seek out disconfirming voices and information. News aggregators, such as Yahoo, Google, or the iPhone news app, similarly skew the information provided by tailoring the stories they feature to individual users based on the articles these users have viewed in the past. These types of biases imposed by filters and algorithms can contribute to the formation of echo chambers and silos consisting of like-minded people who share a common set of beliefs, consume the same kinds of information, and constantly reinforce each other's beliefs (whether or not they are based on fact).

Even filters and algorithms embedded in social media platforms and internet search engines that appear (or purport) to be unbiased have inherent biases programmed into them that skew the content to which a person is exposed and thus contribute to Truth Decay. As Osoba and Welser note, these filters and algorithms contain the biases of the people who write them, as well as any biases contained in the socially generated data on which that code is tested and refined. This means that even searches on a platform like Google will provide results that are, in some sense, biased—by the algorithm used to run the search and the system used to score and rank the results. The inherent biases of these filters are reinforced by the biases and tendencies of the user. As noted elsewhere, users are likely to search for and focus on information that is consistent with what they already believe and then to pass this information along to others in their social network. This further contributes not only to the emergence of echo chambers but to the creation of a context in which the line between opinion and fact is easily blurred.[99]

Research suggests that people who access news and information using search engines and those who rely on social networks (e.g., social media) for their news tend to consume content that is more segregated and that comes from a smaller number of sources than those who seek information directly (e.g., from a news organization's website). The former group is also likelier to have more-polarized ideological views than the latter.[100] This could be due, in part, to the role played by the filters and algorithms that shape the news stories that social media users are exposed to and to the ways in which these filters and algorithms interact with preexisting cognitive biases. It is also worth noting that, although filters and algorithms may contribute to the formation of echo chambers, users' own choices about which sources and articles to read also play a significant role in shaping the ideological diversity or heterogeneity of the media content consumed.[101]

There is some opposing evidence, however, that suggests that networks and social media platforms, and sometimes even the algorithms programmed into search engines, can also expose people to diverse viewpoints and perspectives.[102] Research on social media networks and communities suggests that the exposure these networks provide to different ideas can be beneficial. Research into how social media usage affects polarization reveals that, among all social media users, polarization increases the least among groups that spend the most time on social media, possibly because these groups are exposed to a wider range of ideas and perspectives, even if not all of these ideas and per-

---

[99] Osoba and Welser, 2017.

[100] Flaxman, Goel, and Rao, 2016; Dimitar Nikolov, Diego F. M. Oliveira, Alessandro Flammini, and Filippo Menczer, "Measuring Online Social Bubbles," *Peer Journal of Computer Science*, Vol. 1, 2015.

[101] Eytan Bakshy, Solomon Messing, and Lada A. Adamic, "Exposure to Ideologically Diverse News and Opinion on Facebook," *Science*, Vol. 348, No. 6239, 2015.

[102] Flaxman, Goel, and Rao, 2016.

spectives are accepted.[103] This could also reflect the fact that younger people are both more likely to spend time on social media and more likely to be open to changing their mind. Importantly, analysis suggests that echo chambers that consist of users with largely homogenous views on key issues exist among both Democrats and Republicans and are thus a bipartisan phenomenon.[104] Regardless of how they form, echo chambers are a driver of increasing disagreement about facts and analytical findings that is a key component of Truth Decay: In many cases, the views that resound in one echo chamber might not match those that dominate another.

Although filters and algorithms play an important role in skewing the information that people consume online and through social media platforms, there is also evidence that each person's own selections play an even bigger role in limiting viewed content to material that conforms with his or her preexisting beliefs. Specifically, Bakshy, Messing, and Adamic looked at 10.1 million U.S. Facebook accounts and observed interactions with socially shared news. They found that individual choices played a bigger role than Facebook's algorithm in determining the diversity of news content consumed.[105] Thus, even with completely unbiased algorithms, it seems likely that many people would continue to view homogenous news content that conforms with their existing ideas and views.

## The Spread of Disinformation

A third change in the media landscape that has contributed to Truth Decay is an apparent increase in the dissemination of disinformation. We define *disinformation* as intentionally misleading or false information proliferated in order to achieve an economic or political goal.

---

[103] Levi Boxell, Matthew Gentzkow, and Jesse Shapiro, "Is the Internet Causing Political Polarization? Evidence from Demographics," Cambridge, Mass.: National Bureau of Economic Research, NBER Working Paper 23258, March 2017.

[104] Elanor Colleoni, Alessandro Rozza, and Adam Arvidsson, "Echo Chamber or Public Sphere? Predicting Political Orientation and Measuring Political Homophily in Twitter Using Big Data," *Journal of Communication*, Vol. 64, No. 2, 2014.

[105] Bakshy, Messing, and Adamic, 2015.

Other forms of dubious information have also spread, including misinformation (information that is unintentionally misleading or false) and various forms of sensationalized or biased information. We define *misinformation* as false or misleading information spread unintentionally, by error or mistake. Both misinformation and disinformation come in many forms. Misinformation includes simple errors, erroneous beliefs, or the sharing of a misleading headline or news story. Disinformation involves outright lies, manipulated facts, story headlines that misrepresent the content of the article, facts or statements presented with a false context, falsified emails and documents disseminated as legitimate, and opinion peddled as fact.[106] As noted earlier, the internet and social media have both motivated and facilitated the spread of disinformation in recent years. Domestic and foreign political actors seeking to achieve their political objectives have spread disinformation, and disinformation has also been exploited by individual actors seeking economic profits.[107] Disinformation contributes to the blurring of the line between opinion and fact by proliferating false information that creates uncertainty about what is accurate and what is not. It also leads directly to the increasing relative volume, and resulting influence, of opinion and personal experience over fact and opinion's ability to subsume fact. However, as the four trends that constitute Truth Decay worsen, it becomes easier and even more profitable for those interested in proliferating disinformation to do so, as it becomes increasingly difficult to distinguish fact from falsehood.

Neither disinformation nor misinformation is new. However, the internet and social media allow misinformation and disinformation to spread further and faster than ever before and so magnify the negative effects and the extent to which this bad information contributes to increasing disagreement about facts and interpretations of those facts and the blurring of the line between opinion and fact. In previous

---

[106] Claire Wardle, "Fake News: It's Complicated," *First Draft*, February 16, 2017.

[107] "Disinformation: A Primer in Russian Active Measures and Influence Campaigns," hearings before the Select Committee on Intelligence, United States Senate, 115th Congress, March 30, 2017; Abby Ohlheiser, "This Is How Facebook's Fake-News Writers Make Money," *Washington Post*, November 18, 2016; Rob Portman, "President Signs Portman-Murphy Counter-Propaganda Bill into Law," press release, December 23, 2016.

eras, the effects of misinformation and disinformation were somewhat limited by their reach (e.g., how many people actually read or heard this information). Today, disinformation and misinformation can spread to millions of people in an instant. Furthermore, the diversity of sources and the depth of polarization (discussed in a later section) create an environment in which it is harder to identify disinformation as such (because there is simply so much information available) and in which people are more likely to accept disinformation as true if it matches their political worldviews. Furthermore, as described in more detail in the discussion of agency later in this chapter, there seems to be an increasing number of actors operating in the information system with the incentives and the means to launch sophisticated disinformation campaigns. This could be because of the prevalence of social media platforms, the increasing number of users, the easily accessed forums provided to interested actors who seek to spread disinformation, or a combination of all three. Over the past several years, for instance, there has been an increase in the proliferation of "fake news" by bots— autonomously run programs that can masquerade as real people on social media and other online platforms and so proliferate information on a massive scale—that are designed to magnify and extend the reach of false information by exploiting technological and human vulner-abilities, as well as an increase in the number of foreign and domestic actors (including both real people and bots) who create and spread false information for economic gain.[108] Recent examples include not only fake stories proliferated about political candidates in the 2016 election but also the significant amount of false information spread about Zika virus.[109] The volume of this disinformation and the speed with which it can spread across social media networks drive Truth Decay by sowing

---

[108] David Lazer, Matthew Baum, Nir Grinberg, Lisa Friedland, Kenneth Joseph, Will Hobbs, and Carolina Mattsson, "Combating Fake News: An Agenda for Research and Action," Cambridge, Mass.: Shorenstein Center on Media, Politics, and Public Policy, 2017; Jacob Ratkiewicz, Michael D. Conover, Mark Meiss, Bruno Goncalves, Alessandro Flam-mini, and Filippo Menczer, "Detecting and Tracking Political Abuse in Social Media," *International AAAI Conference on Web and Social Media*, 2011; West, 2017.

[109] Lydia Ramsey, "5 Biggest Myths and Misconceptions About Zika Debunked," *Business Insider*, August 15, 2016.

uncertainty about what is (and is not) fact and by creating doubt and disagreement in areas where there was previously general agreement.

Good data on the volume of disinformation are limited, as is empirical information on how people relate to and interact with it, especially compared with previous eras. However, as noted previously with evidence from social media platforms, we know that the volume of information and data available overall has increased, and there is some evidence that certain pathways are more likely to promote and advance disinformation than others, including especially social media platforms.[110] Furthermore, the amount of disinformation disseminated through various forms of media appears to have become overwhelming in volume and increasingly sophisticated. "Fake-news" websites, for example, look increasingly similar to those of real-news organizations, and actors bent on proliferating disinformation have developed finely tuned strategies to target vulnerable audiences.[111]

### Efficacy of Disinformation

Disinformation is dangerous because it can sow confusion among media consumers (including in the electorate and among political leaders) and lead to policies that have unintended negative implications or that do not address key issues. However, measuring how effectively disinformation actually changes opinions on political and social issues is difficult in most cases. What research does exist suggests that the effects of disinformation and "fake news" vary based on the context, the information, and the individual—findings that closely follow research on the effectiveness of marketing and advertising campaigns.[112] For example, research on the effectiveness of contemporary Russian disinformation in shaping the attitudes of its own people suggests some

---

[110] Allcott and Gentzkow, 2017b.

[111] Graham Ruddick, "Experts Sound Alarms over News Websites' Fake News Twins," *The Guardian*, August 18, 2017.

[112] See, for example, Christy Ashley and Tracy Tuten, "Creative Strategies in Social Media Marketing: An Exploratory Study of Branded Social Content and Consumer Engagement," *Psychology & Marketing*, Vol. 32, No. 1, 2015; Sandra Ernst Moriarty, Nancy Mitchell, William Wells, Robert Crawford, and Linda Brennan, *Advertising: Principles and Practice*, Melbourne, Australia: Pearson Australia, 2014.

degree of success, especially on such issues as the war with Ukraine and attitudes toward the United States.[113] Russian propaganda in Ukraine and even in Georgia has been effective in shaping the attitudes of specific groups of people toward Russia and Russian activities in those countries.[114] Analysis of Soviet propaganda used during the 1960s and 1970s, however, suggests that there are limits to disinformation's ability to affect beliefs. Specifically, in these cases, disinformation seemed to be powerful in shaping and solidifying beliefs but less effective at changing the minds of people with fully formed beliefs.[115] The form of the disinformation is also a determinant of its effectiveness. Analysis of Russian propaganda suggests that volume, diversity of sources, speed, and repetition are some of the characteristics that make disinformation successful as a tool or weapon.[116] Russian disinformation has also been able to exploit the existing vulnerabilities of a targeted audience and its specific characteristics, as is reported to have happened in the lead-up to the 2016 U.S. election.[117]

As we have noted elsewhere, it remains unclear to what extent disinformation disseminated by Russian-backed and other sources during the 2016 presidential election cycle was able to affect individual voter positions or influence the way they voted.[118] Most empirical research suggests that the effect of this effort was likely not prodigious. One study determined that, "for fake news to have changed the outcome

---

[113] Theodore P. Gerber and Jane Zavisca, "Does Russian Propaganda Work?" *Washington Quarterly*, Vol. 39, No. 2, 2016.

[114] Chris Paul and Miriam Matthews, *The Russian "Firehose of Falsehood" Propaganda Model: Why It Might Work and Options to Counter It*, Santa Monica, Calif.: RAND Corporation, PE-198-OSD, 2016.

[115] Stephen White, "The Effectiveness of Political Propaganda in the USSR," *Soviet Studies*, Vol. 32, No. 3, 1980.

[116] Paul and Matthews, 2016.

[117] Office of the Director of National Intelligence, *Assessing Russian Activities and Intentions in Recent US Elections*, Washington, D.C., ICA 2017-01D, January 6, 2017; Paul and Matthews, 2016.

[118] Hunt Allcott and Matthew Gentzkow, "Social Media and Fake News in the 2016 Election," Cambridge, Mass.: National Bureau of Economic Research, NBER Working Paper No. 23089, January 2017, revised April 2017a.

of the election, a single fake article would need to have had the same persuasive effect as 36 television campaign ads."[119] However, although disinformation might not have changed preexisting beliefs, it could have influenced the initial formation of opinions. An assessment of the 2004 election, for instance, found that media bias and spin in the coverage of candidates prior to the election did indeed affect voter assessments of the candidates.[120] Thus, disinformation in almost any form becomes a driver of Truth Decay because it obscures the distinction between opinion and fact and massively inflates the amount of false information, effectively drowning out facts and objective analysis in some cases.

### The Consequences of Disinformation

Truth Decay driven by disinformation can have significant consequences. Clear examples emerge when disinformation is used to attack and discredit science in such areas as foods that incorporate GMOs, the safety and regulation of drugs, and climate change. In the case of GMOs, as noted earlier, there is a wide scientific consensus that they are safe for consumption (with their benefits affirmed by numerous studies)—especially in areas where food sources are scarce. For example, a 2016 report by the National Academies of Sciences, Engineering, and Medicine concluded that genetically modified foods are as safe and healthy as non–genetically modified foods.[121] Studies show that genetically modified foods can have health, price, and humanitarian benefits in certain contexts. For example, golden rice has been genetically modified so that it produces beta carotene, which could reduce vitamin A deficiency in deeply poor areas where people struggle to get adequate nutrition.[122] Other genetically modified crops can increase

---

[119] Allcott and Gentzkow, 2017a.

[120] Kim L. Fridkin, Patrick J. Kenney, Sarah Allen Gershon, and Gina Serignese Woodall, "Spinning Debates: The Impact of the News Media's Coverage of the Final 2004 Presidential Debate," *International Journal of Press/Politics*, Vol. 13, No. 1, 2008.

[121] National Academies of Sciences, Engineering, and Medicine, *Genetically Engineered Crops: Experiences and Prospects*, Washington, D.C.: National Academies Press, 2016.

[122] Steven Salzberg, "Nobelists to Greenpeace: Drop Your Anti-Science Anti-GMO Campaign," *Forbes*, July 4, 2016.

food yields or withstand inhospitable conditions, making farming and even food self-sufficiency possible in areas currently plagued by hunger and famine.[123]

Despite this and similar evidence, distrust about the safety of GMOs for human consumption exists among people on the political left and the political right. Such organizations as Greenpeace are some of the most vociferous critics of GMOs, arguing that they are simply a way for big agricultural organizations to increase profits.[124] Other critics are opposed to the use of genetic modification technology, arguing that it is unethical and potentially dangerous to "manipulate" nature.[125] Policies that react only to disinformation promoted by people and organizations that seek to discredit both GMOs and the companies that develop them could unnecessarily prevent these beneficial outcomes from being realized.

Climate change affords another example. Despite scientific consensus that climate change is occurring and is caused by human activity, some in the United States, largely concentrated among those on the conservative side of the spectrum, dispute existing research and offer a different narrative that questions or even contradicts long-standing and replicated scientific findings.[126] This skepticism has caused certain segments of the population to reject evidence of climate change or human contributions to it and has led some policymakers to hesitate to take actions recommended by the scientific community.[127] Not implementing policies that respond to projected changes in climate effects could have far-reaching consequences, including the more rapid advance of

---

[123] David Freedman, "The Truth About Genetically Modified Food," *Scientific American*, September 1, 2013.

[124] Salzberg, 2016. As elsewhere, we focus specifically here on the issue of consumption because this is where public opinion data are more extensive and robust.

[125] Freedman, 2013.

[126] Naomi Oreskes, "The Scientific Consensus on Climate Change," *Science*, Vol. 306, No. 5702, 2004; Thomas F. Stocker and Dahe Qin, eds., *Climate Change 2013: The Physical Science Basis*, Working Group I Contribution to the Fifth Assessment Report of the Intergovernmental Panel on Climate Change, New York: Cambridge University Press, 2013.

[127] Funk and Kennedy, 2016b.

global warming, an increase in extreme weather events, rising sea levels, and other environmental changes. Such a delay could also have serious economic consequences. Precise estimates vary but are significant across the board. In 2015, Citigroup estimated that climate change, if unmitigated, could cost $44 trillion in lost gross domestic product (GDP) to the worldwide economy by 2060. Brookings projected that the figure could reach up to 20 percent of world GDP by 2100.[128]

A final example concerns attacks on the science and processes used by the Food and Drug Administration (FDA) to regulate the release of new pharmaceutical products and drugs. In this arena, disinformation can have serious consequences. Some critics suggest that the FDA's evaluation processes, research methods, and scientific analyses of new drugs and treatments are unnecessary, burdensome, or simply flawed. Others distrust the organization on the grounds that incentives and conflicts of interest prevent FDA regulators from allowing new drugs and technologies into the marketplace.[129]

However, analyses of FDA processes and evaluations of past FDA studies and decisions suggest that these critiques have little merit. One study found that the FDA typically makes decisions faster than regulators in Canada and Europe and that many of the drugs the FDA did not approve were rejected due to potentially serious medical consequences described in carefully completed FDA studies. Other drugs were revealed simply to be ineffective—findings that could be arrived at only through carefully executed evaluations.[130] There are cases in which FDA approvals have come more slowly compared with elsewhere, and there are cases

---

[128] Marshall Burke, "The Global Economic Costs from Climate Change May Be Worse Than Expected," Washington, D.C., Brookings Institution, December 9, 2015; Jason Channell, Elizabeth Curmi, Phuc Nguyen, Elaine Prior, Alastair R. Syme, Heath R. Jansen, Ebrahim Rahbari, Edward L. Morse, Seth M Kleinman, and Tim Kruger, *Energy Darwinism II: Why a Low Carbon Future Doesn't Have to Cost the Earth*, Citi GPS: Global Perspectives & Solutions, August 2015.

[129] Matthew Herper, "Would Trump's FDA Deregulation Create an Age of Miracles? Don't Bet on It," *Forbes*, March 1, 2107.

[130] Matthieu Larochelle, Nicholas S. Downing, Joseph S. Ross, and Frank S. David, "Assessing the Potential Clinical Impact of Reciprocal Drug Approval Legislation on Access to Novel Therapeutics in the USA: A Cohort Study," *BMJ Open*, Vol. 7, No. 2, 2017.

in which FDA decisions could be perceived as overly cautious. However, this does not appear to be the norm. These findings suggest that, far from being burdensome, unnecessary, or fundamentally flawed, work done by the FDA might actually protect consumers. While there are undoubtedly areas for improvement in the FDA process, eliminating FDA safeguards or lowering FDA standards based on misperceptions or disinformation about the role the organization plays could reduce the safety of new medical technologies and drugs and increase the risk assumed by doctors and patients who use them.

### Reducing Disinformation

Research focused on ways to reduce the effects of disinformation has been largely responsive in nature, focusing on how to detect and remove "fake news" and other types of false information, rather than proactive in identifying positive steps, such as developing incentives to promote journalistic standards and the use of facts, that could improve the information market. One line of research focuses on using technology interventions to identify disinformation and either flag it or remove it from the websites or social media feeds that host it.[131] Such companies as Facebook and Twitter are pursuing approaches along these lines. These approaches are complicated, however, by the sheer volume of information available on the internet. Information scientists working in labs outside of such companies as Facebook and Twitter have also been working to develop better means of tracking and removing misinformation from online platforms. It is still too early to evaluate whether these approaches will provide workable solutions in real-world environments. However, several examples provide insight into possible ways to overcome the challenges posed by online disinformation and misinformation. A 2016 study, for instance, described a platform that is able to collect, detect, and analyze online misinformation and also assess the accuracy of other fact-checking sites.[132] Another set of studies

---

[131] K. P. Krishna Kumar and Gopalan Geethakumari, "Detecting Misinformation in Online Social Networks Using Cognitive Psychology," *Human-Centric Computing and Information Sciences*, Vol. 4, No. 1, 2014, p. 14.

[132] Chengcheng Shao, Giovanni Luca Ciampaglia, Alesssandro Flammini, and Filippo Menczer, "Hoaxy: A Platform for Tacking Online Misinformation," *Proceedings of the 25th*

focuses on the use of algorithms to identify specific nodes or users that are proliferating misinformation as well as to maximize the efficacy of monitoring frameworks.[133] Additional work in this area could be valuable if it can provide more-efficient and more-effective ways to remove disinformation (and those who proliferate it) in a way that is precise and targeted and that prevents infringement on individual rights.

A second approach concerns legal and policy responses that would make the spread of "fake news" or libelous content illegal, as has been done in Europe.[134] However, implementing such legislation while protecting individual civil rights could prove challenging, especially given partisan disagreements about what constitutes "fake news." A third stream of work, which builds on research focused on reducing cognitive biases, recommends an inoculation approach: warning people that they might encounter disinformation, identifying sources that are likely to proliferate disinformation, providing simple and accurate messages to counter false information, and training consumers to recognize "fake news" when they encounter it. Inoculation approaches have shown some success in certain contexts, but it remains unclear whether the medical model is transferable, especially given the strength of individual cognitive biases.[135]

In whatever form it comes, then, disinformation is dangerous and a source of concern regarding public health, democracy, the environment, and the economy. However, there is limited systematic research on how much disinformation exists, how it has changed over time, and

---

*International Conference Companion on World Wide Web*, April 11–15, 2016.

[133] Nam P. Nguyen, Guanhua Yan, and My T. Thai, "Analysis of Misinformation Containment in Online Social Networks," *Computer Networks*, Vol. 57, No. 10, 2013; Nam P. Nguyen, Guanhua Yan, My T. Thai, and Stephan Eidenbenz, "Containment of Misinformation Spread in Online Social Networks," *Proceedings of the 4th Annual Association for Computing Machinery Web Science Conference*, New York: ACM, 2012.

[134] James Dobbins, "Reining in Internet Abuse (Without Abusing the First Amendment)," *Tulsa World*, March 27, 2017; Seth Fiegerman, "Facebook's Global Fight Against Fake News," CNN, May 9, 2017; Lazer et al., 2017.

[135] Teresa A. Myers, Edward Maibach, Ellen Peters, and Anthony Leiserowitz, "Simple Messages Help Set the Record Straight About Scientific Agreement on Human-Caused Climate Change: The Results of Two Experiments," *PloS One*, Vol. 10, No. 3, 2015.

how effective disinformation has been at changing attitudes on a range of policy issues. For the purpose of understanding Truth Decay, the development of a deeper understanding of how disinformation is processed and assessed, how it is weighted in decisionmaking processes, what types and sources are most influential, and how it spreads (e.g., word of mouth, social media, print media) is essential. Additional work to identify the full range of sources of disinformation—as well as their different motives, media, audiences, and messages—would significantly advance understanding of this issue among the public, government and public officials, and researchers. Specifically, a more precise understanding of the many different sources and forms of disinformation would facilitate identification of more-precise responses that target specific types and proliferators, perhaps leading to better results.

### Changes in the Information System: Areas for Future Research

Much has been written on ways in which changes to media practices, legislation, or new technology might ameliorate the extent to which the information system feeds Truth Decay. Proposals include better certification or vetting of news sources; alternative filtering and search algorithms that reduce the bias or skew of the results; computer programs that can detect flawed information before it permeates a social network (as discussed in the previous section);[136] better monitoring of social media networks by the networks themselves, or by the government, to identify and remove misinformation and disinformation; collaboration between journalists and the research community;[137] and promoting better media literacy among web users.[138]

Existing research, just described above, on the information system can help inform exploration and testing of these possible responses. However, many unanswered questions remain. Some of the most significant and important for understanding Truth Decay concern changes in the volume, speed, and types of information over time. There is a

---

[136] Kumar and Geethakumari, 2014.

[137] Lazer et al., 2017.

[138] Philip J. Calvert, "Scholarly Misconduct and Misinformation on the World Wide Web," *The Electronic Library*, Vol. 19, No. 4, 2001.

common perception that more information and more disinformation are available now than in the past, and information appears to travel much faster now and to a wider audience. Episodic, unsystematic evidence to support these perceptions exists but rigorous empirical data are limited. Understanding how much the volume of information has changed, what types of information have increased the most, and how much faster information spreads is essential to precisely identifying the challenges presented by new communication channels and these challenges' importance to Truth Decay. When it comes to understanding changes in disinformation, in particular, a more precise map of the information system that identifies types of disinformation, senders, their intent, audiences, and the form or medium will be required. This type of mapping would allow researchers to pinpoint the sources, senders, or audiences that contribute most directly to an increase in disinformation. Similarly, understanding how media content has changed—in terms of topics and the relative amount of opinion and fact—will also be important for designing responses to Truth Decay, for understanding the extent to which Truth Decay has occurred or is occurring, and for identifying areas where it is particularly severe or damaging.

Another set of important but unanswered questions focuses more closely on mechanisms. For example, how does an increase in the speed and volume of information affect the quality of that information? Additional research into how media exposure contributes to polarization will be valuable for understanding relationships between the drivers of Truth Decay. Additional research on how information spreads through social networks (both online and offline) and how filters and search algorithms can shape beliefs and strengthen biases could also be valuable. Finally, understanding the broader implications (both benefits and costs) of democratized access to information and the ability to be a source of information are also an important area that deserves future study. The research agenda in Chapter Six proposes additional avenues for research into the information system.

## Competing Demands on the Educational System

As the information system changes and evolves, the U.S. educational system faces increasing demands from a number of sources, including the responsibility to prepare students to confront a more complicated and challenging information system, to evaluate information and sources, and to distinguish between opinion and fact. This responsibility is added to a growing list of new and preexisting demands: standardized tests, extracurricular activities, before- and after-school care, and other services. At the same time, schools are facing budget constraints. The fiscal constraints and demands placed on the educational system and the resulting gap between the rapidly evolving challenges of the new information system and the curricula offered to students in most public schools constitute the third key driver of Truth Decay. This gap drives and perpetuates Truth Decay by contributing centrally to the development of a citizenry that is susceptible to consuming and disseminating disinformation, misinformation, and information that blur the line between fact and opinion. Specifically, without the training that they need to carefully evaluate sources, to identify and check their own biases, and to separate opinion and fact, students matriculating out of schools that teach kindergarten through 12th grade (K–12)—which is the focus in this report—or universities may be highly vulnerable to false and misleading information and easy targets for intentional disinformation campaigns and propaganda. Furthermore, once consuming this information themselves, these users are more likely to pass the information along to others, perpetuating the challenges that Truth Decay poses and contributing to a context in which Truth Decay flourishes.

To be clear, we do not intend to imply that the educational system is to blame for Truth Decay. In recent years, school districts across the country have begun working to develop media literacy programs (that teach students how to evaluate information and the credibility of sources, without telling them what to believe) and to reintroduce civics classes to address some of the challenges described here. For example, the Common Core State Standards include new requirements that address the changing nature of literacy in the internet age and that place a greater emphasis on higher-level critical-thinking skills.[139] However, the adoption of these standards is incomplete and uneven, and teachers report continuing obstacles to incorporating some of these changes into curricula.[140] Furthermore, although these changes move toward solutions to Truth Decay, they have not occurred at the same time or at the same speed as many of the changes in the information system, such as the rise of social media and the explosion in the number and diversity of sources of information. It is this lag and this gap between the challenge and student preparation that we argue has been a driver of Truth Decay because, as mentioned, it contributes to the creation of an electorate that is susceptible to bias, disinformation, and misinformation, and is also liable to perpetuate this information and the challenges that come along with Truth Decay.

The lag between the changes in the information system and the educational system's response might, in part, be a reflection of the "stickiness" of institutions—the fact that it takes time for an institution or organization to identify problems and implement responses.[141] There is research that suggests that schools might change especially slowly because of the characteristics of the educational system and its change process. First, efforts to alter school policies and approaches have often been incremental, focusing on marginal changes around the edges that end up having narrow effects. Second, these efforts are often cyclical, so that ideas for innovations and alterations to existing policies come up repeatedly. Third, even changes that are implemented can have very different effects on different types and levels of education and

---

[139] Sally Valentino Drew, "Open Up the Ceiling on Common Core State Standards: Preparing Students for 21st Century Literacy—Now," *Journal of Adolescent & Adult Literacy*, Vol. 56, No. 4, December 2012/January 2013.

[140] Amy Hutchinson and David Reinking, "Teachers' Perceptions of Integrating Information and Communication Technologies into Literacy Instruction: A National Survey in the United States," *Reading Research Quarterly*, Vol. 46, No. 4, 2011.

[141] James Mahoney and Kathleen Thelen, "A Theory of Gradual Institutional Change," in James Mahoney and Kathleen Thelen, eds., *Explaining Institutional Change: Ambiguity, Agency, and Power*, New York: Cambridge University Press, 2010.

across state lines.[142] Finally, the fact that most elementary, middle, and high schools are governed at the local level might also slow the pace of change, even when the need for updated policies is agreed upon by all relevant stakeholders.

There is also evidence, described in more detail in this section, that there were specific aspects of the prevailing curriculum in the 2000s and early 2010s that might have further slowed the response of the educational system to the changing external demands. In this section, we focus on two areas that our analysis suggests could be the most directly related to the ways in which competing demands on the educational system contribute to Truth Decay: the crowding out of civics education and the reduced time spent on training students in critical-thinking skills.[143] We focus on schools (primarily K–12 schools) in this section because they provide the most direct route for educating large portions of the electorate during a particularly formative period. However, civic and media literacy is equally absent from college curricula in most cases. Furthermore, educating adults in these areas and ensuring that they too have the ability to critically evaluate information is also crucially important, especially in the near term, and programs to teach media literacy and civic engagement to adults are equally lacking. A solution to Truth Decay will need to better prepare both youths and adults to confront the information system they face by analyzing, critically assessing, and digesting news and social media as they receive it. We return to this issue of responses in Chapter Six.

## Benefits of Civics Education and Training in Critical Thinking

Research suggests that both civics education and training in critical thinking confer significant benefits on students, benefits that could prove to be powerful tools against Truth Decay. An insufficient emphasis on civics education might feed Truth Decay in two ways. First, students who do not have sufficient understanding of political processes,

---

[142] David Tyack and Larry Cuban, *Tinkering Toward Utopia: A Century of Public School Reform*, Cambridge, Mass.: Harvard University Press, 1997.

[143] As noted earlier, we emphasize that schools are working to address both problems but have not yet closed the gap.

players, and institutions in the United States might be less able to effectively evaluate political reporting or the statements of political candidates and so could struggle to develop informed political attitudes and could be susceptible to influence by agents promoting Truth Decay. Second, those who do not understand the institutions of democracy and value their benefits could be less likely to trust those institutions. Importantly, the value of civics education, although it accrues across a student's lifetime, appears to be greatest when the student is in high school or even college.[144]

There is evidence to suggest that both mechanisms might be relevant. For example, as noted earlier, studies show that, where it is provided, civics education can be effective in increasing students' political knowledge and awareness, especially when that training encourages students to openly question and discuss ideas, including current and controversial events.[145] Voters with greater political understanding are likely to base their vote on national interests rather than personal ones and to be more open-minded to diverse ideas.[146] In addition, improved political awareness and civic knowledge can increase trust in democratic institutions.[147] Furthermore, research suggests that students who are taught media literacy—one possible area of focus within a

---

[144] Richard G. Niemi and Jane Junn, *Civic Education: What Makes Students Learn*, New Haven, Conn.: Yale University Press, 1998.

[145] Bonnie Bittman and William Russell III, "A Multiple Regression of Civics Education Scores," *Research in Social Sciences and Technology*, Vol. 1, No. 2, 2016; Lauren Feldman, Josh Pasek, Daniel Romer, and Kathleen Hall Jamieson, "Identifying Best Practices in Civic Education: Lessons from the Student Voices Program," *American Journal of Education*, Vol. 114, No. 1, 2007; Jason Gainous and Allison Martens, "Civics Education: Liberals Do It Better," *Journal of Political Ideologies*, Vol. 21, No. 3, 2016; Joseph E. Kahne and Susan E. Sporte, "Developing Citizens: The Impact of Civic Learning Opportunities on Students' Commitment to Civic Participation," *American Educational Research Journal*, Vol. 45, No. 3, 2008; Peter Levine and Kei Kawashima-Ginsberg, *Civics Education and Deeper Learning*, Boston: Jobs for the Future, February 2015; National Task Force on Civic Learning and Democratic Engagement, *A Crucible Moment: College Learning and Democracy's Future*, Washington, D.C., 2012; Niemi and Junn, 2008.

[146] Michael X. Delli Carpini and Scott Keeter, *What Americans Know About Politics and Why It Matters*, New Haven, Conn.: Yale University Press, 1996.

[147] Delli Carpini and Ketter, 1996.

civics education course—are more likely to be able to identify false media claims than those who have not taken such a course.[148] Given contemporary concerns about and the prevalence of "fake news," this finding underscores the relevance and value of this type of education in the context of Truth Decay. Improved civic knowledge throughout the electorate, fostered through civics education and outreach, can also lead to more-informed voter beliefs and decisions about public issues and policies as well as an electorate that holds more-consistent views and opinions over time.[149] Not adequately teaching these and related subjects at the K–12 and university levels, then, may be one way in which existing gaps in the educational system might contribute to Truth Decay.

Research similarly suggests that students who receive training in critical thinking tend to have better academic and longer-term economic outcomes and to gain skills that could reduce the efficacy of disinformation and aid in the fight against Truth Decay.[150] This research also emphasizes that critical thinking is a skill that must be developed and intentionally built and is not something that students will develop on their own. According to one study, students who are trained to conduct higher-level critical thinking tasks as part of the course curriculum learn material more deeply and completely and are better able to engage with it and apply it than those who are trained only to memorize and supply basic facts and responses.[151] Activities and courses constructed to emphasize critical thinking are similarly important because they train students to analyze, critique, and apply the information they

---

[148] Joseph Kahne and Benjamin Bowyer, "Educating for Democracy in a Partisan Age: Confronting the Challenges of Motivated Reasoning and Misinformation," *American Educational Research Journal*, Vol. 54, No. 1, February 2017.

[149] Delli Carpini and Keeter, 1997.

[150] Mamoru Ishikawa and Daniel Ryan, "Schooling, Basic Skills and Economic Outcomes," *Economics of Education Review*, Vol. 21, No. 3, 2002.

[151] Jamie Jensen, Mark McDaniel, Steven Woodward, and Tyler Kummer, "Teaching to the Test . . . or Testing to Teach: Exams Requiring Higher Order Thinking Skills Encourage Greater Conceptual Understanding," *Education Psychology Review*, June 2014.

have learned, rather than just repeating or memorizing it.[152] Critical thinking can be woven into any subject matter or course by asking students not just to memorize or repeat information but rather to engage with information, assess it, analyze it, and apply it to different contexts and situations. As the information system changes and the volume and speed of information increase dramatically, the ability to filter and evaluate information—a skill imparted by classes that include a component on critical thinking—becomes increasingly vital. Similarly, an increase in the diversity and number of sources increase the importance of understanding what it means to be an "educated and engaged consumer of news," including understanding which and how many sources to consult. If this type of training is not a foundational part of elementary and secondary school education, there is a risk that students will graduate from high school without the skills they need to navigate today's challenging information system. This might increase students' susceptibility to disinformation or to the influences of their own biases or the biases of others. In addition to consuming and accepting false, misleading, or opinion-based news as fact, they might also share this information with others, thus contributing to a context in which Truth Decay flourishes.

## The Current Status of Civics Education and Critical Thinking Training

### Civics Education and Media Literacy

Despite the proven benefits and ability of a civics education to inculcate students with an understanding of how to consume different types of media and to actively participate as citizens in a democracy, the quality and priority given to civics—and, in some cases, to training focused explicitly on critical thinking—declined in the early 2000s in ways that appear to have fed Truth Decay. For example, although a 2014 assessment found that civics knowledge among eighth-graders had increased since 1998 (though there had been no change since 2010), other analyses and discussions with teachers conducted as part of the study suggested that pressures created by competing demands have led to a sharp

---

[152] Jensen et al., 2014.

drop in the time, resources, and importance assigned to civics education.[153] In many cases, civics is simply folded into social studies or history classes, where it loses prominence and receives minimal focus. Furthermore, recent legislation, such as No Child Left Behind and subsequent initiatives (including the Common Core State Standards and the "Race to the Top" Initiative implemented in 2009 and 2010), has led to an increased use of testing to evaluate students and teachers. This has had the effect, intentionally or unintentionally, of promoting reading and math education and in some cases crowding out social studies (where most civics courses are currently taught) and other subjects. In a 2012 survey, two-thirds of public school teachers reported that social studies, science, and the arts had been crowded out by a focus on standardized testing.[154] Although changes in more recent years have restored some attention to social studies and civics-oriented classes, it will likely take additional time and sustained commitment to fully address the imbalance. However, although progress in civics education has occurred slowly, changes in the information system have moved so rapidly that even responsive schools might not have been able to keep up. In the meantime, however, there is a cohort of students who are entering adult life and becoming politically active but might not have received the training needed to effectively navigate today's information system or to understand what is required of them as citizens. As noted, this lack of training might make students emerging (or recently graduated) from schools more susceptible to bias, disinformation, and even intentional agents of Truth Decay, discussed in more detail later.

---

[153] S. G. Grant, "High-Stakes Testing: How Are Social Studies Teachers Responding?" *Social Education*, Vol. 71, No. 5, September 2007; Wayne Journell, "The Influence of High-Stakes Testing on High School Teachers' Willingness to Incorporate Current Political Events into the Curriculum," *High School Journal*, Vol. 93, No. 3, Spring 2010; National Center for Education Statistics, "Are the Nation's Eighth-Graders Making Progress in Civics?" infographic, The Nation's Report Card, U.S. Department of Education, NCES-2015-112c, 2014; Judith L. Pace, "The Complex and Unequal Impact of High Stakes Accountability on Untested Social Studies," *Theory & Research in Social Education*, Vol. 39, No. 1, 2011.

[154] Farkas Duffett Research Group, *Learning Less: Public School Teachers Describe a Narrowing Curriculum*, Washington, D.C.: Common Core, 2012.

One marker of the poor state of civics education and its possible implications for Truth Decay is the low political knowledge scores of Americans, a result that is not new but is nonetheless an indicator of the fact that students emerge from school lacking civic literacy and displaying little interest in seeking out and retaining relevant political information. Tests of political knowledge reveal consistently abysmal scores. For example, a 2007 Pew Research Center study showed that 66 percent of respondents could name their state's governor and 49 percent could name the Speaker of the House and Senate Majority Leader.[155] This was not an all-time low but rather the typical level across several years of surveys.[156] Low levels of political knowledge among the general public are not new, but they are a reminder of how badly better civics training and education is needed.

An often-overlooked aspect of media literacy and civic engagement is the ability to understand and interpret statistics and probability, which are used in public opinion polls and media coverage on almost every topic, ranging from health care and unemployment to immigration and foreign policy. The ability to interpret and evaluate statistics—a sort of "quantitative literacy"—could be as necessary to being an informed and engaged citizen in today's society as being able to analyze and evaluate different news sources. Without an ability to understand and interpret statistics, newly graduated students (as well as those still in school) may be easily swayed by false and misleading information and may pass it along to others. Shortcomings in statistics education, then, might be another way in which gaps in the existing educational system can, over time, create an electorate that is ripe for Truth Decay and its four trends.

In general, statistics and probability appear to have been increasingly incorporated into mathematics curricula at a growing number of schools. Data analysis and statistics have been identified as core areas of mathematics instruction by the National Council of Teachers of Mathematics for nearly 20 years, and these topics remain central compo-

---

[155] Pew Research Center, "Public Knowledge of Current Affairs Little Changed by News and Information Revolutions," webpage, April 15, 2007.

[156] Pew Research Center, 2007.

nents of mathematics education today.[157] Although statistics education might be sufficient in its own right, it is possible that additional effort is needed to integrate this training with media literacy or to update the current curriculum so that it directly addresses the reliability and interpretation of new forms of data rapidly emerging in the information system. Specifically, this would entail teaching students not only to calculate statistics but also to interpret them in context and to identify when they are misused or misleading.

There are some programs that aim to fill existing gaps between the seeming necessity of civics education and its current status in many school districts. In response to the decline in civics-focused education and training for critical thinking, a number of efforts are seeking to create and promote programs focused on these subjects for use in schools across the country. For example, former Supreme Court Justice Sandra Day O'Connor has created a civics education course called iCivics, a program that teaches students how democracy works by offering games and role-playing exercises in which students take on the role of a judge, a senator, or a community activist.[158] Evaluations of the program have shown that it is effective in increasing civic knowledge and community engagement.[159] By 2010, schools in all 50 states were using the iCivics program and the program recently added a Spanish version.[160] The Media Literacy Project was founded in 1993 to teach students about critically evaluating information and consuming media. The program aims to teach students how to analyze and assess information rather than simply accepting it; to understand marketing, spin, and media manipulation strategies; and to push for

[157] Christine Franklin, Gary Kader, Denise Mewborn, Jerry Moreno, Roxy Peck, Mike Perry, and Richard Schaeffer, *Guidelines for Assessment and Instruction in Statistics Education Report: A Pre-K–12 Framework*, Alexandria, Va.: American Statistical Association, 2007.

[158] iCivics, "Our Story," webpage, undated.

[159] Brooke Blevins and Karon LeCompte, "Going Beyond the Games with iCivics. A Response to 'The Challenges of Gaming for Democratic Education: The Case of iCivics,'" *Democracy and Education*, Vol. 24, No. 2, 2016, Article 9.

[160] iCivics, "iCivics Celebrates Gaming Milestone," webpage, October 21, 2010; Drew Gerber, "Spanish-Language Video Game Aims to Teach Students About Civil Rights," *Washington Post*, November 24, 2017.

access and transparency in journalism. The program was intended to provide youths and adults with the ability to evaluate sources, recognize bias, identify media marketing strategies, and create and share their own media messages. The organization was most active in the period between 2010 and 2014, but it ended in June 2016 because of a lack of resources.[161] The News Literacy Project is another example aimed at middle- and high-school students that aims to teach students how to evaluate sources and information through a four-week module taught as part of English or social studies classes. The unit includes classroom lessons, sessions taught by journalist volunteers, and other interactive activities.[162] In addition, Stony Brook University has developed a six-week online course intended to help teach media consumers how to distinguish between trustworthy sources and sources that may be biased or misleading.[163]

Changes to the Common Core also aim to address the gaps identified here as facilitating and perpetuating the spread of Truth Decay. For example, the Common Core State Standards include new requirements that address media and digital (online) literacy. According to these updated standards, students are expected to be able to integrate diverse sources and forms of media, evaluate the quality and accuracy of each source, and use technology to collaborate, interact, and publish information.[164] These new standards clearly target the types of skills students need to navigate a rapidly changing information environment. However, subsequent research and teacher surveys suggest that these new standards have thus far been unevenly implemented. Many teachers recognize the importance of these standards but also report a lack of resources (i.e., money or time) needed for full implementation. For example, several studies found that some administrators have resisted

---

[161] Media Literacy Project, "About Us," webpage, undated-a; Media Literacy Project, "What We Do," webpage, undated-b.

[162] News Literacy Project, "Program," webpage, undated.

[163] Stony Brook University Happenings, "'Making Sense of the News: News Literacy Lessons for Digital Citizens' Online Course from the Center for News Literacy," webpage, December 2016.

[164] Drew, 2012/2013.

including digital literacy in school curricula because they perceive digital media as being inferior to conventional media or even harmful to student literacy in a more-traditional sense.[165] As another example, a survey of U.S. teachers involved in literacy education who were asked to identify obstacles to implementation of digital literacy courses cited lack of time as the most significant obstacle, followed by lack of access to technology, lack of professional development training to enable them to instruct the material, lack of technical support, and lack of incentives.[166] Finally, critics argue that the new standards do not go far enough in addressing some of the gaps between the current curricula used in most schools and the challenges presented by the information environment and thus may continue to produce young adults who are highly susceptible to Truth Decay and the disinformation and blurring of the line between opinion and fact that come with it.[167]

As noted, a lack of attention to civic education and media literacy can also affect adults. The absence of effective community outreach and adult or continuing education programs at the national level in these areas is as much a driver of Truth Decay as the gap between school curricula and the demands of the information system. Just as students without the proper training may be vulnerable to consuming and disseminating misinformation, adults who are unable to critically evaluate sources, to seek out unbiased sources of information, or able to distinguish between fact and opinion will be equally likely to become victims of opinion sold as fact or disinformation spread intentionally and equally likely to spread this information to others, perpetuating and worsening the challenges posed by Truth Decay. Attacking this problem in elementary, middle, and high schools may be easier than targeting adults, who would need to come voluntarily and who might already have well-formed biases that would prevent them from fully absorbing any program that aims to increase civic and media literacy. However, it might be possible to use community outreach programs (offered through libraries or operated through schools but also targeted

---

[165] Drew, 2012/2013.

[166] Hutchinson and Reinking, 2011.

[167] Drew, 2012/2013.

at parents) to promote media and civic literacy among adults who are out of school or even in a family-based forum where children and adults could learn skills together. Were it created, this type of infrastructure could help relieve some of the pressure on schools, as it would provide another form of outreach targeted at older generations. This type of program might be difficult to implement or scale, but it is an approach worth exploring.

### Critical Thinking

Trends in training for critical thinking also suggest the existence of some gaps and shortcomings relevant to Truth Decay. Research based on surveys and interviews with public school teachers reveal a decline in emphasis on critical thinking and in support for lessons that encourage students to engage with the material they are learning.[168] These same teachers cite an increasing and single-minded focus on test scores, efficiency, and achievement as the reason less time is spent on units that incorporate critical thinking: More time is spent teaching test-taking strategies, which leaves less time available for teaching higher-level critical-thinking skills.[169]

To be clear, a reduction in the emphasis placed on social studies education or critical thinking activities in favor of math and science is certainly not required by No Child Left Behind or other initiatives. Instead, it might be that the teachers surveyed perceive that they are simply unable to meet the requirements of this legislation or subsequent initiatives without cutting back elsewhere. In 2008, Wagner argued that, based on his research on the educational system, some schools and teachers are focused on teaching critical thinking but the majority did an insufficient job of imparting this skill to students and of adapting quickly enough to the changing external job and information markets.[170]

---

[168] Joel Westheimer, "No Child Left Thinking," *Colleagues*, Vol. 12, No. 1, 2015.

[169] Barbara Newell, *A Quantitative Research Study on the Effects and Perceptions of the No Child Left Behind Legislation*, dissertation, University of Phoenix, 2014; Westheimer, 2015.

[170] Tony Wagner, *The Global Achievement Gap: Why Even Our Best Schools Don't Teach the New Survival Skills Our Children Need—and What We Can Do About It*, New York: Basic Books, 2008.

Even if this is not a new concern, there are reasons why a lack of focus on critical thinking in schools might be particularly worrisome now, viewed through the lens of Truth Decay. Specifically, critical-thinking skills are necessary to distinguish fact from opinion and to screen out misleading information, bias, and low-quality sources. These skills become more important as the information system grows more complex. A lack of training in these areas could increase the vulnerability of graduating students and recently graduated young adults to misleading information, intentional disinformation, or opinion and bias and may perpetuate Truth Decay as students consume and disseminate this information.

One way to assess how well critical-thinking skills are being taught is to consider trends in science education, and particularly those focused on teaching the scientific method, which is a type of critical thinking. A number of studies from the late 1990s and early 2000s questioned whether science education standards in the United States (and particularly the emphasis of these standards on rigorous, inquiry-based learning and knowledge of basic scientific facts) were sufficient. A 2012 study commissioned by the Thomas B. Fordham Institute found that only 13 states earned an "A" or "B" grade for their science standards, and that 17 earned a "D" or an "F."[171] The study criticized schools for not combining clearly defined and objective standards for basic facts and information that students must learn with inquiry-based activities that include opportunities for students to apply the scientific method in hands-on learning. Researchers noted that one of the biggest shortcomings was teachers' tendency to deemphasize direct instruction of important topics, methods, and processes and instead focus on teaching science "through discovery."[172] A 2015 evaluation of the current status of science education identified some of the shortcomings of science curricula in the areas of promoting critical thinking and

---

[171] Paul Gross, Lawrence Lerner, Ursula Goodenough, John Lynch, Martha Schwartz, and Richard Schwartz, *The State of State Science Standards 2012*, Washington, D.C.: Thomas B. Fordham Institute, 2012.

[172] Gross et al., 2012.

the importance of facts and data.[173] For example, the authors found that only about half of teachers surveyed in 2012 "have students represent and/or analyze data using tables, charts, or graphs" at least once a week, and that only 17 percent reported that they "require students to supply evidence in support of their claims" during all or most lessons.[174] Teachers have also indicated that they place a heavy emphasis on lesson plans that involve the teacher explaining concepts to the class or the students completing workbook problems or questions, rather than a more-interactive approach that emphasizes critical-thinking skills.[175] A lack of sufficient training in the scientific method and a limited focus on the use of facts and data do not mean that critical thinking is not covered in other courses, but might be indicative of one way in which gaps in the curricula used in some schools contribute to the creation of an electorate and civic environment that feeds and perpetuates Truth Decay.

There have been efforts to address this gap between the critical-thinking skills that students need to navigate the information system and those that were included in school curricula in the early and mid-2000s. The Common Core Standards Initiative, for instance, which was launched in the late 2000s, "focuses on developing the critical-thinking, problem-solving, and analytical skills students will need to be successful."[176] The original standards were adopted by 42 states and the District of Columbia, suggesting a renewed commitment to imparting these skills to students in the coming years.[177] As already mentioned, there have also been efforts focused explicitly on teaching the scientific method. Recently, the Next Generation Science Standards were developed to advance the teaching of the scien-

---

[173] Suzanne Wilson, Heidi Schweingruber, and Natalie Nielsen, eds., *Science Teachers' Learning: Enhancing Opportunities, Creating Supportive Contexts*, Washington, D.C.: National Academies of Sciences, Engineering, and Medicine, 2015.

[174] Eric R. Banilower, P. Sean Smith, Iris R. Weiss, Kristen M. Malzahn, Kiira M. Campbell, and Aaron M. Weis, *Report of the 2012 National Survey of Science and Mathematics Education*, Chapel Hill, N.C.: Horizon Research, 2013.

[175] Banilower et al., 2013.

[176] Common Core Standards Initiative, "What Parents Should Know," webpage, undated-b.

[177] Common Core Standards Initiative, "Standards in Your State," webpage, undated-a.

tific method and address some of the challenges just described, the principles of scientific inquiry and scientific literacy, and more-specific methodologies (such as the use of case studies and primary investigation). About 40 states have shown interest in the Next Generation Science Standards, but only 18 had adopted them as of December 2016 (representing about 35 percent of students in the United States).[178]

Common Core standards and other changes in education policy have moved toward a more rigorous emphasis on teaching the critical-thinking skills required to prepare and train students for the challenges presented by the existing information system and to reduce susceptibility to Truth Decay. For instance, one study found that teachers reported that Common Core Performance Standards imparted critical-thinking skills to students more effectively than did the standards dictated in the original No Child Left Behind legislation.[179] However, it is worth noting again that the adoption of these standards has not been universal, and it is still somewhat unclear the degree to which states and school districts have succeeded at revising curricula and school course loads to reflect the new standards—or at building new priorities that truly inculcate the teaching of critical thinking as a core objective that is incorporated into all courses. In 2015, large numbers of students in New York and elsewhere opted out of Common Core–related tests, and although adoption of the Common Core remains widespread (42 states are members of the initiative), some states have been abandoning the standards.[180] Adoption of the science standards is far from universal, as noted earlier. Furthermore, recent surveys show that some teachers report dissatisfaction with certain aspects of the Common Core Standards, including the areas of emphasis, the

---

[178] Next Generation Science Standards, *Next Generation Science Standards: Executive Summary*, June 2013; National Science Teachers Association, "About the Next Generation Science Standards," webpage, undated.

[179] Sandra Cochrane and Joshua Cochrane, "Teacher Perceptions of the Common Core Performance Standards," *Georgia Education Researcher*, Vol. 12, No. 1, June 30, 2015.

[180] Emmanuel Felton, "Are the Common Core Tests Turning Out to Be a Big Success or a Resounding Failure?" The Hechinger Report, April 2015.

number of standards teachers are required to cover, and the training they themselves receive to teach components of the Common Core.[181]

Finally, there is the issue of testing. Although there are no specific "Common Core required tests," most states have developed or worked with contractors to develop assessments to evaluate the extent to which students have reached desired levels of competency in various areas. Administering these tests themselves might take limited time, and the tests might yield benefits in terms of evaluating student readiness, but the time spent preparing students to take the assessments can crowd out other subjects and activities (including such items as civics, social studies, and science). Although there is still debate on the precise effects of standardized testing on critical-thinking skills, the heavy focus on testing and memorization in many states might also reduce time spent on certain types of activities and contribute to a narrowing of curricula toward specific topics and question styles.[182] Some standardized tests, such as Advanced Placement exams or the California Critical Thinking Skills Test (aimed at graduate and undergraduate students and executive-level adults), include components that require application of concepts and analysis.[183] However, even as assessments are being revised to better capture critical-thinking skills, many tests offered at lower grade levels are heavily weighted toward memorization and repetition.[184] Determining the appropriate balance between these two types of learning—memorization and higher-order thinking— might be an important agenda item for educators and administra-

---

[181] Gary Troia and Steve Graham, "Common Core Writing and Language Standards and Aligned State Assessments: A National Survey of Teacher Beliefs and Attitudes" *Reading and Writing*, Vol. 29, No. 9, November 2016.

[182] Laura S. Hamilton, Brian M. Stecher, Julie A. Marsh, Jennifer Sloan McCombs, Abby Robyn, Jennifer Russell, Scott Naftel, and Heather Barney, *Standards Based Accountability Under No Child Left Behind: Experiences of Teachers and Administrators in Three States*, Santa Monica, Calif.: RAND Corporation, MG-589-NSF, 2007; Linda Valli and Robert Croninger, "High Quality Teaching of Foundational Skills in Mathematics and Reading," Chicago: Data Research and Development Center, undated.

[183] Insight Assessment, "California Critical Thinking Skills Test (CCTST)," webpage, undated.

[184] Jacobs, 2007; Valli and Croninger, undated.

tors going forward. Finally, schools, like other organizations, change slowly, which means that real institutional change can take some time to become manifest. Unfortunately, the information system has been changing and will continue to change quickly, and the gap between the training that students receive to process and evaluate information and the demands these students will face beyond school could continue to widen, at least in the near term. Attention to addressing and closing this gap could be an important way to fight Truth Decay.

## Summary

The gap between the requirements of the new information system and the training provided by schools in such areas as civic and media literacy and critical thinking means that students and young adults are not able to detect, account for, and correct the blurring of the line between opinion and fact that characterizes Truth Decay, and this lack of skill could affect their interpretation and use of information. The gap between the requirements of the information system and current school curricula drives and perpetuates Truth Decay by contributing to the creation of an electorate that is highly susceptible to mis- and disinformation and to information that blurs the line between fact and opinion (or fact and falsehood) and by contributing to the creation of a context in which this information is shared and in which Truth Decay flourishes. Unless students (and adults) are able to deeply question and assess any piece of information they encounter, they are susceptible to believing or spreading false information and disinformation and are more likely to be influenced and swayed by their own emotions or the attitudes of friends in forming beliefs and making decisions. As the number and diversity of sources and the volume and speed of information increase, the ability to critically evaluate information, apply information from one area to another, and engage and analyze new information becomes more central and important to belief and opinion formation. Critical thinking and media literacy are required to complete each of those tasks—without these skills, students will leave school ill equipped to process the massive amount of information that confronts them each day through social media, television, and newspapers. This creates an environment in which Truth Decay thrives: People struggle to distinguish fact from opinion, lack trust in key institutions, and are more easily swayed by disinformation, personal opinions, and social influences, and people are more likely to share this information, passing biases on to others. Trends over the past five years are promising in terms of attention to the importance of civics education and training in critical thinking, but this effort will need to not only continue but keep pace with the continually evolving media and information system in order to both rein in and counteract Truth Decay.

In suggesting that school curricula need a greater focus on civics, media literacy, and critical thinking, we understand that placing new demands on an already-overburdened educational system could create still more challenges for teachers and administrators. However, this additional emphasis on civics, media literacy, and critical thinking could be effectively integrated into existing courses and so might involve a minimal number of new requirements or demands. For example, civics instruction could easily be integrated into social studies, history, and even English classes (through assigned reading). Media literacy objectives could be incorporated into math classes in the form of probability and statistics training, as well as in research projects conducted for social studies, history, English, or other courses. Critical thinking, which research suggests can be taught more effectively when integrated into coursework than when assigned as a stand-alone topic, can similarly be folded into science (as noted), math, reading comprehension, and other classes.[185] In this way, these important topics could be addressed mostly within the existing curriculum, with some small modifications.[186] Most importantly, however, educators—a key element in the process of designing and implementing new material, modules, or teaching techniques— should be involved in the design of future revisions to curricula to better address the demands of the contemporary information and political system.

---

[185] David Perkins, *Making Learning Whole*, San Francisco: Josey Bass, 2009.

[186] As already noted, many schools are moving in this direction.

Finally, instruction in civics, media literacy, and critical thinking need not occur only through classroom-based training. It can also be accomplished through political discussions held in schools, extracurricular activities (such as debate teams), and community service– oriented programs that teach by doing, all of which improve awareness and understanding of civic responsibilities and political institutions.[187] Such activities might be ways to teach and build civic engagement and critical thinking in contexts that avoid partisanship and political competition.

## Competing Demands on the Educational System: Areas for Future Research

Educating youths and adults could be a powerful tool to counter Truth Decay. An increased emphasis on critical thinking, courses that teach students to process and evaluate the large volume of information they encounter every day, classes that inform students about their own cognitive biases and how to reduce them, and programs that instill in students the responsibility for engaging directly in democracy could all be valuable tools in restoring civil discourse and trust in institutions. However, there are many questions in this area. First, data are limited regarding the quality and prevalence of civics programs for youths and adults at the local level. It would be useful to know how these types of programs vary across states and across demographic groups. Similar data on the ways in which students are taught critical-thinking skills,

---

[187] Alexander W. Astin and Linda J. Sax, "How Undergraduates Are Affected by Service Participation," *Journal of College Student Development*, Vol. 39, No. 3, 1998; Pamela Johnston Conover and Donald D. Searing, "A Political Socialization Perspective," in Lorraine M. McDonnell, P. Michael Timpane, and Roger Benjamin, eds., *Rediscovering the Democratic Purposes of Education*, Lawrence, Kan.: University Press of Kansas, 2000; Maryann Jacobi Gray, Elizabeth Heneghan Ondaatje, Ronald D. Fricker, Sandy A. Geschwind, Charles A. Goldman, Tessa Kaganoff, Abby Robyn, Melora Sundt, Lori Vogelgesang, and Stephen P. Klein, *Combining Service and Learning in Higher Education: Evaluation of the Learn and Serve America, Higher Education Program*, Santa Monica, Calif.: RAND Corporation, MR-998-EDU, 1999; Alan Melchior, Joseph Frees, Lisa LaCava, Chris Kingsley, Jennifer Nahas, Jennifer Power, Gus Baker, John Blomquist, Anne St. George, Scott Hebert, JoAnn Jastrzab, Chuck Helfer, and Lance Potter, *Summary Report: National Evaluation of Learn and Serve America*, Education Resources Information Center Clearinghouse, U.S. Department of Education, 1999; Niemi and Junn, 1998.

at all levels of schooling, could allow practitioners and policymakers to identify areas with the biggest gaps in civics and critical-thinking programs. Evaluations that assess the effectiveness of existing programs and less-traditional interventions, such as iCivics, would also be informative. Experimental programs that develop new educational interventions, in both schools and local communities, could be productive, especially if these programs offer insight into the types of outreach, courses, or activities that are most likely to prepare people of all ages to face today's challenging information system.

Research that investigates how to expand educational programs in schools and how to fund and scale these efforts should also consider how to educate entire communities—for example, through programs offered at civic centers, churches and synagogues (or other places of worship), or libraries. This is particularly important in the near term: Educating children will help reduce the challenges of Truth Decay in the longer run, but tackling these issues in the immediate future will require a commitment to improving the analytical skills of everyone else. The research agenda in Chapter Six proposes additional avenues for research of the educational system.

## Polarization

The final driver of Truth Decay is polarization, both political and socio-demographic. Polarization is perhaps one of the more complex drivers of Truth Decay because it both causes and is exacerbated by Truth Decay. Polarization drives increasing disagreement about facts and interpretations of those facts and the blurring of the line between opinion and fact by creating two or more opposing sides, each with its own perspectives and beliefs. These polarized groups can become insular in their thinking and communication (for example, in echo chambers formed on social media). In such a closed environment, it is easy for each group to develop its own interpretation of facts and information and for false information to proliferate and become ingrained. At the governing level, polarization creates incentives for elected officials to serve as agents of Truth Decay, intentionally blurring the line between opinion and fact to advance specific interests. Polarization can also affect trust and confidence in government at the electoral level—minority-party voters are especially likely to distrust institutions (and information from those institutions) controlled by the opposite party. Finally, in a polarized environment, each side might have incentives to use disinformation to solidify support within its own base, thus contributing to the blurring of the line between opinion and fact. At the same time, Truth Decay contributes to polarization. As each side develops its own interpretation of facts, the opposing sides can move further and further apart in their beliefs about key issues and even in their perceptions of each other.

Polarization also has serious consequences for the health of democracy, economics, and diplomatic relations. Perhaps most seriously from the perspective of American democracy, polarization also leads to the political inaction and dysfunction at all levels of government and contributes to the erosion of civil discourse.[188] Polarization can also contribute to uncertainty about the meaning and likely enforcement of government policies by increasing the likelihood of large policy shifts as government control swings from one party to the other.[189] Polarization can also reduce the efficiency and quality of legislative processes and undermine both trust in government and the efficacy of checks and balances more generally.[190]

## Political Polarization
### Political Polarization Among Political Representatives
By most measures, political polarization in the current U.S. political system has reached historically high levels. Divides are especially visible among elected officials but are becoming clearer among the mass elec-

---

[188] We provide metrics of this inaction and its costs in Chapter Five.

[189] Scott Baker, Nicholas Bloom, Brandice Canes-Wrone, Steven Davis, and Jonathan Rodden, "Why Has U.S. Policy Uncertainty Risen Since 1960?" Cambridge, Mass.: National Bureau of Economic Research, NBER Working Paper 19826, January 2014.

[190] Michael Barber and Nolan McCarty, "Causes and Consequences of Polarization," in Jane Mansbridge and Cathie Jo Martin, eds., *Negotiating Agreement in Politics*, Washington, D.C.: American Political Science Association, 2013; Diana Epstein and John D. Graham, *Polarized Politics and Policy Consequences*, Santa Monica, Calif.: RAND Corporation, OP-197-PV/EMR, 2007.

torate as well. One metric used to track distance between Republican and Democratic lawmakers measures the distance in the ideological positions of the votes of congressional Republicans and Democrats in both the House and Senate.[191] Figure 4.3 shows a consistent increase in the extent of polarization between congressional Republicans and their Democratic counterparts (at least as assessed by this metric) since the 1940s. Although this trend is not new, it also shows no signs of leveling off. More importantly from the perspective of this report, polarization has been growing at an increasing rate since about 2000 (especially in

**Figure 4.3**
**Distance Between the Parties Along the Liberal-Conservative Dimension, 1879–2013**

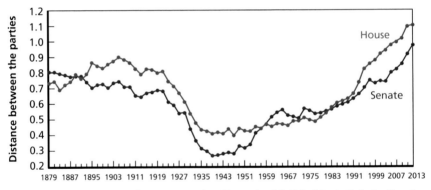

SOURCE: James Moody and Peter J. Mucha, "Portrait of Political Party Polarization," *Network Science*, Vol. 1, No. 1, 2013.
NOTES: *Distance between the parties* refers to the ideological distance between the two political parties across all assessed congressional votes on a liberal to conservative scale and is measured using the DW-NOMINATE metric, which assesses the ideological position of political decisions on that ideological scale. Greater distance between parties equates to greater polarization (see Poole and Rosenthal, 1985). Each point on the line in the figure represents a measure of the distance between the parties. The red and blue lines connecting those points reflect the trends in the U.S. House and Senate, respectively.
RAND RR2314-4.3

---

[191] This measure is calculated by rating the votes of senators and representatives on a scale from liberal to conservative and then aggregating individual scores for each party to assess the distance between the two parties in terms of ideological positions. See Keith Poole and Howard Rosenthal, "A Spatial Model for Legislative Roll Call Analysis," *American Journal of Political Science*, Vol. 29, No. 2, 1985.

the Senate), meaning that it is getting more severe more quickly than in the past. Another measure reveals that, as of 2017, 23 percent of states have split representation (i.e., two senators from different parties).[192] Figure 4.4 shows the percentage of states in each Congress since 1913 that have had split representation and illustrates that the number of mixed-party Senate delegations has been at its current low level three other times in that period: 1913–1915, 1939–1941, and 1955–1957. Note that, as recently as 2000, the rate of mixed-party Senate delegations reached 38 percent.

Research into the causes of this increase in political polarization in U.S. government finds that, until the 1970s, most of the increase in polarization was driven by member replacements—when incumbents lose elections to challengers from another party. Since then, however, the

**Figure 4.4**
**Percentage of States with Mixed-Party Senate Delegations, 1913–2017**

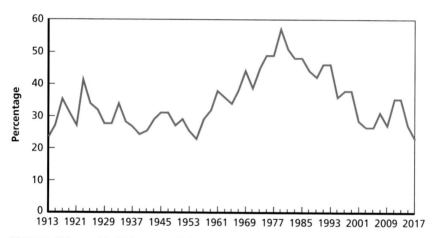

SOURCE: "Biographical Directory of the United States Congress, 1774–Present," Bioguide.Congress.Gov, undated.
RAND RR2314-4.4

---

[192] Even with 50 states, the percentage of states with split Senate delegations may be an odd number due to the fact that senators move in and out of office during the course of an average congressional term due to events such as retirements, illnesses, appointment to cabinet or other posts, special elections, etc. The presence of third-party candidates can further complicate the calculation of Senate splits. Finally, in some cases, senators might switch parties.

increase in polarization has been caused both by member replacement, particularly the ouster of moderate Southern Democrats in favor of conservative Republicans, and by *member adaptation*—when individual members' positions become increasingly extreme over time.[193] This adaptation, which explains much of the increase in polarization since 1996, appears to be driven by both heightened interparty (in swing states) and intraparty (in primary elections) competition and changing constituent attitudes (which might reflect changes in attitudes among an unchanging group of voters or might be a result of redistricting that changes the voter mix included in a district). In other words, the attitudes and votes of individual lawmakers might shift in response to constituents or to pressure created within Congress itself.[194] Congressional stagnation— the fact that political incumbents in the House and the Senate continue to be reelected at high rates and retire at lower ones—is another characteristic of recent elections (Figure 4.5). Although high rates of reelection and low retirement rates are not new, there has been a slight upward trend in incumbent reelection (over the past decade) and a decrease in incumbent retirement (over the past quarter-century). This can entrench and even exacerbate polarization, as members are not replaced for long periods and become increasingly extreme in their views.[195]

### Political Polarization at the Popular Level

Political polarization has also occurred outside of Congress and is apparent in broader society. The consistency of partisan voting among Republicans and Democrats is at an all-time high, meaning that a given voter is increasingly likely to vote only for Democrats or only for

---

[193] Jamie L. Carson, Michael H. Crespin, Charles J. Finocchiaro, and David W. Rohde, "Redistricting and Party Polarization in the U.S. House of Representatives," *American Politics Research*, Vol. 35, No. 6, 2007; Sean M. Theriault, "Party Polarization in the U.S. Congress: Member Replacement and Member Adaptation," *Party Politics*, Vol. 12, No. 4, 2006.

[194] Adam Bonica, "The Punctuated Origins of Senate Polarization," *Legislative Quarterly*, Vol. 39, No. 1, February 2014.

[195] John N. Friedman and Richard T. Holden, "The Rising Incumbent Reelection Rate: What's Gerrymandering Got to Do with It?" *Journal of Politics*, Vol. 71, No. 2, 2009; Kyle Kondik and Geoffrey Skelley, "Incumbent Reelection Rates Higher Than Average in 2016," *Rassmussen Reports*, December 15, 2016.

**Figure 4.5**
**Incumbent Reelection and Retirement Rates, 1946–2014**

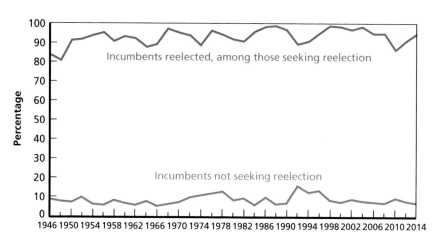

SOURCE: Brookings Institution, "Report: Vital Statistics on Congress—Data on the U.S. Congress, Updated January 2017," webpage, January 9, 2017.
RAND RR2314-4.5

Republicans in election after election. Over the past 20 years, the percentage of voters expressing views that are consistently liberal or conservative has more than doubled, from 10 percent to 21 percent.[196] Political polarization is exacerbated by *geographic polarization*—people who share similar political views tend to live close to each other, rather than being distributed throughout the population.[197] Analysis of voting returns for the 2016 presidential election show that, out of 3,113 counties in the nation, fewer than 10 percent had a single-digit margin of electoral victory in the presidential election; in 1992, more than one-third of counties fit this description.[198] As Figure 4.6 shows, the number of landslide counties, where the margin of elec-

---

[196] Pew Research Center, "Political Polarization in the American Public," webpage, June 12, 2014.

[197] The causes of geographic or demographic polarization are described in more detail later in this section.

[198] David Wasserman, "Purple America Has All But Disappeared," FiveThirtyEight Blog, March 8, 2017b.

**Figure 4.6**
**Number of Landslide Counties in Presidential General Elections, 1976–2012**

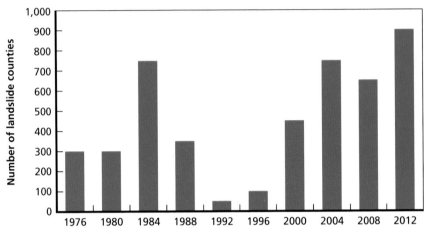

SOURCE: Pew Research Center, "Politically Competitive Counties Have Become Even Less Common," webpage, June 29, 2016b.
RAND *RR2314-4.6*

toral victory is more than 50 percent, has also increased dramatically over the past 25 years, as has the share of voters who live in extremely polarized counties. Looking at the period from 1976 to 2012 shows the median number of landslide counties as 450 and the average as 472. In 2016, 1,196 counties were decided by margins greater than 50 percent—about 2.5 times as many as the average over the preceding 20 years.[199] There are a number of reasons for this change, including politically motivated redistricting and sorting between parties, both of which have contributed to the homogeneity in political districts that is driving this trend in landslide elections.[200] Both of these issues are addressed later in this chapter.

---

[199] Wasserman, 2017b.

[200] *Party sorting* refers to a process of partisan conversions that has made each of the two political parties increasingly homogenous, even as the underlying views of average Americans have changed less dramatically. While both the Democratic and Republican parties had conservative and liberal factions in the past, party elites on both sides have become more extreme and differences between party platforms more pronounced, and voters have been able to better align themselves with the party that most closely fits their attitudes and views.

In addition to the measures already shown, political polarization can also be observed in trends in the beliefs and attitudes of people on each side of the political spectrum, both within the government and among the electorate. For example, since 1970, party elites have grown farther apart regarding environmental spending, and attitudes among the public have followed suit, becoming increasingly polarized along party lines.[201] At the level of the electorate, polls show that Republicans and Democrats have very different views on several key issues:

- A May 2017 Quinnipiac University poll reported that 49 percent of Republicans approved of the American Health Care Act while approval among Democrats was well below 10 percent.[202]
- A 2017 Pew Research Center survey found that about 90 percent of Democrats expressed support for the media acting as a government "watchdog," compared with about 40 percent of Republicans. (This is a sharp change from 2011, when about 60 percent of respondents on both sides of the political aisle expressed this view.[203])
- A December 2016 survey showed that 58 percent of Republican respondents reported that environmental regulations are too costly and hurt jobs and the economy, a position held by 17 percent of Democrats.[204]

---

This realignment has led some voters to switch parties, thus eliminating more moderate voters in each party. The end result is parties that are more homogenized and the appearance of more severe interparty divides even where underlying attitudes of individual voters have changed less dramatically. See Matthew Levendusky, *The Partisan Sort: How Liberals Became Democrats and Conservatives Became Republicans*, Chicago: University of Chicago Press, 2009.

[201] Aaron McCright, Chenyang Xiao, and Riley Dunlap, "Political Polarization on Support for Government Spending on Environmental Protection in the USA, 1974–2012," *Social Science Research*, Vol. 48, 2014.

[202] Quinnipiac University Poll, "GOP Health Plan Backers Could Feel Pain at the Polls, Quinnipiac University National Poll Finds; Only 20 Percent of U.S. Voters Support Plan," May 25, 2017b.

[203] Michael Barthel and Amy Mitchell, "Americans' Attitudes About the News Media Deeply Divided Along Partisan Lines," Pew Research Center, May 10, 2017.

[204] Monica Anderson, "For Earth Day, Here's How Americans View Environmental Issues," Pew Research Center, April 20, 2017.

Although there has never been a consensus on these issues—health care, views of the media's role, and environmental regulations—disagreement appears to be deepening at an increasing rate. It is not just that Americans live in a divided political society but that this divide is becoming increasingly deep and increasingly difficult to counter.

Data and metrics presented thus far suggest a strongly polarized electorate, but it is important to understand the sources of this divide. A closer look at a number of additional metrics suggest that the widening divide between Republicans and Democrats at the popular level could be due to party sorting rather than an actual shift in attitudes. For example, the number of people who identify as independents or who place themselves at or near the midpoint on the political spectrum has not decreased.[205] Furthermore, public opinion polls reveal a number of areas of consensus across party lines, including the value of democracy and the importance of Medicare and Medicaid.[206] One explanation for the apparent contradiction between (1) data on the number of landslide counties and the sharp partisan divides and (2) data that suggest areas of agreement and stability in the number of independent voters could be party sorting. The concept of *party sorting* suggests that, rather than changing their attitudes, people are shifting and sorting themselves into two more-homogenous parties consisting of people who used to be mixed across party lines. Thus, median voter attitude on either side of the partisan divide might appear to have become more extreme although attitudes of the electorate have not changed at the aggregate level.[207]

This explanation lends nuance to an understanding of how polarization could be affecting the broader electorate. Opinions might not be growing more extreme, but the distance is increasing between parties in terms of both their platforms and the mean preferences of their members. However, this is still a form of polarization at the systemic, electorate level. Americans on both sides of the political

---

[205] Matthew Gentzkow, "Polarization in 2016," Stanford, Calif.: Stanford University, Toulouse Network for Information Technology Whitepaper, 2016.

[206] Lee Drutman, "Political Divisions in 2016 and Beyond," Voter Study Group, June 2017.

[207] Morris Fiorina, "Americans Have Not Become More Politically Polarized," *Washington Post*, June 23, 2014; Levendusky, 2009.

spectrum are increasingly farther apart on a wide range of political and social issues, increasing the finality, severity, and consequences of this division. It seems that many areas of disagreement involve issues about which people care deeply and feel strongly: immigration, economic inequality, moral issues, and government intervention. When it comes to polarization, the cross-party chasm appears to have the most-significant implications for Truth Decay. As the party divide widens, communication across the gap becomes increasingly difficult and the sharing of ideas and opinions ceases. This creates echo chambers on each side: Each group has its own narrative and worldview, both of which might be incomplete or contain inaccuracies but thrive because they go unchallenged within the party.

### Explaining the Increase in Political Polarization

There are many possible explanations for why political polarization seems to be increasing at such a precipitous rate. Several of the factors contributing to the increase in polarization also affect or drive aspects of Truth Decay. First, cognitive biases and other mental heuristics strengthen partisan affiliations over time as individuals seek information that matches their worldviews and protects their self-identity, a tendency we described earlier.[208] Those who hold a liberal worldview and identify as a Democrat will seek information that is favorable to Democrats and that confirms the correctness of Democratic political views. Similarly, those who hold a more conservative worldview will seek information that is more favorable to Republicans and that confirms the correctness of Republican political views. Over time, this trend could cause the two parties to move further apart, worsening polarization. As noted elsewhere, confirmation bias can contribute to the persistence of false or misleading beliefs and information.

Heuristics might also play a role because individuals might rely on partisan identification when assessing candidates or policies. Although the human tendency to use heuristics and biases has not changed, the increasing complexity of the information system might cause people

---

[208] Dan M. Kahan and Donald Braman, "Cultural Cognition and Public Policy," *Yale Law & Policy Review*, Vol. 24, No. 1, 2006.

to rely more heavily on heuristics, such as partisan affiliation, when making important political decisions or forming attitudes and beliefs about policy issues. At an aggregate level, this individual tendency to rely more heavily on partisan cues could deepen the partisan divide.

Second, the previously discussed changes in the media environment—especially the power of social media and its filters, as well as search engine algorithms—limit the diversity of the information that a person consumes, create partisan echo chambers, and further entrench partisan identity and polarization. The increasingly partisan nature of some media outlets could have a similar effect, contributing to the formation of rival partisan narratives, blurring the line between opinion and fact, and solidifying partisan identity. (The media is one target of blame for exacerbating polarization, and although there is some support for this argument, little causal empirical evidence has documented the press's ability to increase the level of political polarization around a given issue or debate.[209]) Even education can play a role in entrenching partisanship, especially if partisan interpretations of current or historical events or scientific findings are presented as part of the curriculum.

The characteristics of U.S. political institutions and processes are another driver of political polarization. First, gerrymandering and redistricting initiatives undertaken at the state level by politicians seeking to solidify their own political positions and those of their party can create artificial geographic boundaries intended to disadvantage opposition parties in elections. This often leads to the creation of homogenous political districts, with supporters of opposition parties squeezed into as few districts as possible or split across districts in small numbers to minimize political influence. The outcome adds a geographic component to political polarization, with a very strong majority of Democrats in one district and a very strong majority of Republicans in another. This reduces interparty competition, essentially embedding political partisanship in state legislatures and the U.S. House of Representatives.[210] Research confirms that redistricting has drastically reduced the number of competi-

---

[209] Prior, 2013.

[210] J. Gerald Hebert and Marina K. Jenkins, "The Need for State Redistricting Reform to Rein in Partisan Gerrymandering," *Yale Law & Policy Review*, Vol. 29, No. 2, 2010.

tive political districts at the national level.[211] In fact, a number of studies offer clear evidence that geographic clustering, caused by redistricting and other factors discussed later in this section, is a strong driver of political polarization.[212] Although redistricting and its use to improve the electoral outcomes of political opportunists are not new, the political exploitation of redistricting has become more common in recent years—and more effective in segregating voters from different locations on the political spectrum. Specifically, new analytic mapping technologies and better data have allowed politicians to optimize redistricting strategies, resulting in increasingly precise segregation of political districts.[213] This, in turn, has magnified the effect of redistricting on polarization and caused divisions to increase over the past ten years.

Another driver of polarization is the influence of private campaign donors and large organizational donors, such as lobbyists, unions, corporate interests, and others. Wealthy donors have long influenced electoral politics and policy outcomes with large donations supporting specific candidates and positions. This influence has increased over the past 15 years. The McCain-Feingold Act,[214] campaign finance legislation passed in 2002, was intended to regulate donations to political parties, but many of the regulations it put in place have been eroded or eliminated since then, restoring the influence and power of wealthy donors in shaping the political landscape. Limits on corporate donations were loosened in 2007 and eliminated in 2010 after the Supreme

---

[211] Micah Altman and Michael McDonald, "Redistricting and Polarization," in James Thuber and Antoine Yoshinaka, eds., *American Gridlock: The Sources, Character, and Impact of Political Polarization*, New York: Cambridge University Press, 2015.

[212] Jesse Sussell and James A. Thomson, *Are Changing Constituencies Driving Rising Polarization in the U.S. House of Representatives?* Santa Monica, Calif.: RAND Corporation, RR-896-RC, 2015.

[213] Jeffrey C. Esparza, "The Personal Computer vs. the Voting Rights Act: How Modern Mapping Technology and Ethically Polarized Voting Work Together to Segregate Voters," *UMKC Law Review*, Vol. 84, No. 1, Fall 2015; Benjamin Forest, "The Changing Demographic, Legal, and Technological Contexts of Political Representation," *Proceedings of the National Academy of Sciences*, Vol. 102, No. 43, 2005; Raymond J. La Raja, "Campaign Finance and Partisan Polarization in the United States Congress," *Duke Journal of Constitutional Law & Public Policy*, Vol. 9, No. 2, 2014.

[214] Public Law 107–155, Bipartisan Campaign Reform Act of 2002, March 27, 2002.

Court decision in *Citizens United v Federal Election Commission*, which made it possible for lobbyists, nonprofits, and other organizations to spend unlimited funds on election activities.[215] Since then, these groups have become more engaged in the game of political influence, and their influence on political positions, platforms, and outcomes has also grown, once again pulling both parties away from the center and toward positions that are more ideologically extreme and polarized and that benefit small segments of the population rather than the entire electorate.[216] With money comes influence, and large donors are able to pull candidates toward policy preferences that might or might not match those of the majority.[217] The disproportionate influence of large campaign donors and lobbyist organizations might drive Truth Decay to the extent that it undermines trust in government (or other institutions) and erodes the political efficacy of the broader public. Although some research suggests that political efficacy is higher when public disclosure laws and caps on contributions are in place, there is little work exploring the causal mechanisms that might drive this relationship.[218] The relationships among campaign finance, polarization, trust in government, and political efficacy reflect an area where additional research is needed and where additional insights could prove valuable in better understanding Truth Decay.

---

[215] *Citizens United v. Federal Election Commission*, 558 U.S. 08-205, 2009. For context, see Thomas Stratmann, "Campaign Finance: A Review and Assessment of the State of the Literature," *Oxford Handbook of Public Choice*, April 20, 2017.

[216] Raymond J. La Raja and Brian F. Schaffner, "The Effects of Campaign Finance Spending Bans on Electoral Outcomes: Evidence from the States About the Potential Impact of Citizens United v. FEC," *Electoral Studies*, Vol. 33, No. 1, 2014.

[217] Brittany H. Bramlett, James G. Gimpel, and Frances E. Lee, "The Political Ecology of Opinion in Big-Donor Neighborhoods," *Political Behavior*, Vol. 33, No. 4, 2011; Eric Heberlig, Marc Hetherington, and Bruce Larson, "The Price of Leadership: Campaign Money and the Polarization of Congressional Parties," *Journal of Politics*, Vol. 68, No. 4, 2006; Raymond J. La Raja and Brian F. Schaffner, *Campaign Finance and Political Polarization: When Purists Prevail*, Ann Arbor, Mich.: University of Michigan Press, 2015.

[218] David M. Primo and Jeffrey Milyo, "Campaign Finance Laws and Political Efficacy: Evidence from the States," *Election Law Journal: Rules, Politics, and Policy*, Vol. 5, No. 1, February 2006.

Finally, the primary system has a similar polarizing effect on political candidates and party platforms. In primary elections, candidates must appeal to the more-extreme members of political parties, who are most likely to show up for primaries and elections when turnout is very low and thus dominate the primary process. This means candidates have little incentive to appeal to moderate voters. Furthermore, in states or districts that contain a strong majority of Democrats or Republicans, the winner of the primary might never face a strong need to appeal to moderate or independent voters. The result is that in some cases (but certainly not all) the candidates who end up winning general elections have more-extreme views than mainstream voters and operate accordingly once in office.[219] This catering to the extremes in primaries is one driver of polarization that does not seem to have changed: Although the process has contributed to polarization, it is not clear that it has contributed to the *increase* in polarization focused on in this discussion. However, many of the other changes discussed in this section—e.g., gerrymandering, financing—have created a situation in which primary candidates can (and sometimes have to be) more extreme to win.

Given the number of drivers of political polarization operating in today's political system, it is not surprising that the partisan divide seems to be worsening, that Truth Decay is flourishing, and that trust in political institutions has reached all-time lows. As parties become increasingly polarized, and as candidate views become increasingly extreme and unrepresentative of the wider electorate, it seems natural that voter confidence and trust in government will decline.

## Sociodemographic and Economic Polarization
### Demographic Polarization

Like political polarization, sociodemographic and economic polarization are severe—and are perhaps even more troubling in terms of Truth

---

[219] Anthony Downs, *An Economic Theory of Democracy*, New York: Harper & Row, 1957; Eric McGhee, Seth Masket, Boris Shor, Steven Rogers, and Nolan McCarty, "A Primary Cause of Partisanship? Nomination Systems and Legislator Ideology," *American Journal of Political Science*, Vol. 58, No. 2, 2014.

Decay because of their contribution to the formation of echo chambers that blur the line between opinion and fact, erode areas of agreement about facts and analytical interpretations of those facts, and even reduce trust in certain institutions. By *sociodemographic polarization*, we refer to the gradual segregation of the United States that has occurred as people move to live near people with whom they share traits of race, age, economic background, occupation, beliefs, and partisanship—and, as a result, political attitudes in specific regions become increasingly homogenous.[220] In 2009, Bishop averred that Americans increasingly choose to live and surround themselves with people who have similar political and cultural views, resulting in the formation of a series of internally homogenous political districts. He argues that this is not the result of intentional decisions to live among either Democrats or Republicans; instead it is because the things that people do consider when making decisions about where to live—cultural or demographic characteristics and economic opportunities—are directly associated with political worldviews.[221] Geographic polarization is evident in the increase in landslide election outcomes and the lack of diversity in the partisanship of state and local representatives, which we discussed earlier.[222]

Other authors have found support for this hypothesis. Bishop relied on presidential election returns; other authors have relied on party registration data. One such study, which focused on California, found an increase in demographic segregation between Democrats and Republicans between 1992 and 2010 on ten of the 12 segregation measures considered. According to the study, the increase in segregation varied, depending on the measure, from 3 percent to 23 percent, a sizable increase.[223] Bishop and others have argued that demographic sort-

---

[220] Bill Bishop, *The Big Sort: Why the Clustering of Like-Minded America Is Tearing Us Apart*, Wilmington, Del.: Mariner Books, 2009.

[221] Bishop, 2009.

[222] Corey Lang and Shanna Pearson-Merkowitz, "Partisan Sorting in the United States, 1972–2012: New Evidence from a Dynamic Analysis," *Political Geography*, Vol. 48, 2015.

[223] Jesse Sussell, "New Support for the Big Sort Hypothesis: An Assessment of Partisan Geographic Sorting in California, 1992–2010," *PS: Political Science & Politics*, Vol. 46, No. 4, 2013.

ing is a challenge to American democracy because it prevents diversity of ideology at the local level and forestalls the types of political discussion and debate that are necessary for a vibrant marketplace of ideas.[224] However, other research has challenged this thesis, arguing that evidence of demographic sorting is weaker than Bishop's analysis suggests. These authors suggest that the trends he observes are less a matter of increasing demographic polarization and more related to an increase in the number of Republican and independent registrants and a decrease in the number of registered Democrats in a specific set of counties and states. However, even these critics do not suggest that demographic sorting has not occurred. Rather, they dispute the extent of this sorting and the mechanisms driving it.[225]

Regardless of the specific mechanisms that drive it, geographic polarization is also worrisome in terms of Truth Decay because it deepens the intergroup divide and makes it easier for each side of the group to develop its own narrative, its own set of interpretations, and its own set of experiences, all of which diminish the value of objective facts. Geographic polarization effectively creates a large echo chamber in which facts are pushed aside in favor of beliefs and opinions and in which disinformation can spread quickly. Geographic clustering might also be a driver of political polarization. In fact, Sussell and Thomson estimate that 30 percent of the increase in polarization in the House of Representatives between the 93rd (1973) and 112th (2011) Congresses is because of geographic clustering of the electorate along such dimensions as marriage rates, race, education, and urbanicity.[226] In these ways, geographic polarization can speed the advance of Truth Decay while almost institutionalizing it in local communities.

### Social and Economic Polarization

Polarization also extends to social and economic domains beyond geography. People are increasingly likely to work, socialize, and attend church

---

[224] Bishop, 2009.

[225] Samuel J. Abrams and Morris P. Fiorina, "'The Big Sort' That Wasn't: A Skeptical Reexamination," *PS: Political Science & Politics*, Vol. 45, No. 2, 2012.

[226] Sussell and Thomson, 2015.

with people who look like them, all of which leads to polarized social groups of people who rarely interact across group lines.[227] A 2015 study found that, as partisan identity and partisan-based geographic segregation strengthen—both trends that have been present in the United States over the past decade—social polarization, including anger, bias, and activism across party lines, also becomes more severe. This means that political and geographic polarization can feed more basic social polarization and partisan cleavages that extend outside of politics and interfere with discussions and relationships across party lines. The study suggests that social polarization in the United States has increased, and this increase can be measured by a simultaneous increase in the amount of hostility felt by members of one party toward the other, the amount of partisan activism in which a person engages (e.g., attending a rally, trying to influence votes of others), and a person's bias toward representatives of his or her own party.[228] Those who suggest that polarization in the United States today is not severe often point to areas of broad agreement across party lines. However, if the areas of disagreement concern issues of core importance to individual voters, then divisiveness on these issues could be enough to overwhelm areas of agreement. Additional research to identify the areas of strongest agreement and disagreement within the U.S. electorate would provide greater insight into the extent and depth of polarization and could provide insights into areas where partisan divides can be most easily bridged.

As income inequality increases, polarization also becomes economic. In terms of opportunities, experiences, and policy preferences, the distance between the very well-off and those who are struggling has increased over the past two decades, and this divide might have contributed to the rise of competing narratives and perceptions about economic opportunity across class lines.[229] Interaction between the

---

[227] Bishop, 2009.

[228] Lilliana Mason, "'I Disrespectfully Agree': The Differential Effects of Partisan Sorting on Social and Issue Polarization," *American Journal of Political Science*, Vol. 59, No. 1, 2015.

[229] Divisions along class lines might not replace those that exist along racial or gender lines—rather, they might add yet another dimension to the formation of multiple competing narratives that appear to be emerging in contemporary society.

very rich and the very poor is rare, which, combined with a continued rise in inequality, broadens the chasm between the two groups.[230]
Income inequality has been increasing in the United States by almost
any measure considered. Using capitalized income tax data, an
analysis of inequality since 1913 shows that, although income
inequality fell between 1929 and 1978, it has increased consistently
since then, reaching levels as high as those seen in the late 1920s
in recent years, and continuing to rise.[231] This growing inequality is
driven almost entirely by an increase in the share of wealth held by
the top 0.1 percent of people in the United States, up from 7 percent
in 1979 to 22 percent in 2012.[232] The 2008 recession accelerated
income inequality because it had differential effects on the very
rich and the middle and lower classes, hurting the latter considerably more. In addition, the recovery has benefited those at the top of
income distribution more than those near the bottom.[233] Economic
polarization is closely related to geographic sorting (those who are
wealthy tend to live in highly concentrated areas) and to partisan
identity and political polarization (economic well-being often influences political views and preferences).

Other research suggests that economic polarization is relatively
embedded and can have a cross-generational impact. Despite the
traditional narrative of the "self-made man" and a person's ability
to climb the economic ladder, research finds that economic mobility in the United States is actually quite limited, especially in areas
with high levels of geographic segregation and income inequality.
This research shows, for instance, that a resident of Charlotte, North

---

[230] John Voorhies, Nolan McCarty, and Boris Shor, "Unequal Incomes, Ideology, and Gridlock: How Rising Inequality Increases Political Polarization," working paper, August 2015.

[231] Emmanuel Saez and Gabriel Zucman, "Wealth Inequality in the United States Since
1913: Evidence from Capitalized Income Tax Data," *Quarterly Journal of Economics*, Vol. 131,
No. 2, 2016.

[232] Saez and Zucman, 2016.

[233] Emmanuel Saez, "Striking It Richer: The Evolution of Top Incomes in the United States
(Update with 2007 Estimates)," Berkeley, Calif.: University of California, Department of
Economics, 2009.

Carolina, who starts in the bottom quintile of income distribution has just a 4.4-percent probability of reaching the top quintile, and a similarly situated resident of San Jose, California, has a probability of 12.9 percent of reaching the top quintile.[234] Neither suggests a remarkably high level of economic mobility or high odds for a reversal in the level of economic polarization observed in society today.

## The Effect of Polarization on Truth Decay

Polarization along geographic, social, political, and economic dimensions is especially relevant to Truth Decay when all four realms are reinforcing and overlapping. Polarization in all forms contributes to the creation of echo chambers, in which people are rarely exposed to new ideas and become increasingly insulated from, and even fearful of, anything that is new or different. In this environment, cognitive biases might prevail, facts might become less relevant, and sources of formal authority can be cast aside if perceived as outside the group. Although we have discussed them separately, all forms of polarization are intimately connected to each other. Specifically, political polarization might worsen geographic segregation if people move to live near individuals with similar political views. At the same time, geographic sorting may contribute to political polarization if the political attitudes of a group become increasingly homogenous or insular over time. Geographic sorting also worsens social polarization and exacerbates the effects of economic polarization if people in a given region or district face similar economic realities. The fact that these dimensions of polarization are also often overlapping and reinforcing is also problematic, as the result is a divided society that leaves fewer areas or incentives for cross-group communication or compromise and in which specialized subgroups might have very different policy preferences. As noted elsewhere, one of the most damaging consequences of polarization is its ability to create echo chambers and to divide society to the extent where each side has its own narrative and even its own version of the facts. Polarization also contributes to political paralysis, the loss

[234] Raj Chetty, Nathaniel Hendren, Patrick Kline, and Emmanuel Saez, "Where Is the Land of Opportunity? The Geography of Intergenerational Mobility in the United States," *Quarterly Journal of Economics*, Vol. 129, No. 4, 2014.

of government efficacy, the erosion of public discourse, and the creation of uncertainty and anxiety. These are areas where additional research is needed to fully understand the effects of polarization. We address these again in Chapter Six.

## Polarization: Areas for Future Research

Current research on polarization focuses largely on explaining its causes, manifestations, and consequences, or on documenting its changes over time and its effects on party politics and the geographic distribution of the population. Despite all this work, empirical evidence is lacking in certain areas. For example, as we noted earlier, media outlets are criticized for significantly worsening polarization, but little causal empirical evidence documents the press's ability to increase the level of political polarization around a given issue or debate.[235] Similarly, there is mixed evidence on whether geographic sorting is driven primarily by shifting political attitudes among groups of people living in certain parts of the country, by active relocation and a form of self-selected segregation, or by institutional changes (e.g., redistricting). Additional research on ways to reduce polarization and on the drivers of geographic sorting and clustering is essential to understanding polarization and how it relates and contributes to the four trends that constitute Truth Decay, as well as to attempts to identify solutions.

The other surprising gap in research on polarization is the relatively small amount of literature focused on actively exploring ways that polarization can be reduced. Most work on this topic focuses on changes to institutions or political processes, but empirical evidence suggesting that these changes provide an effective solution is limited. For instance, studies that consider open primaries, which let non–party members vote in primary elections (in theory, this would moderate extreme candidates or reduce their likelihood of advancing), find that such a change has little effect on outcomes.[236] Studies of alternative approaches to redistricting might offer more opportunity for impact. Specifically, studies find that when the judicial branch or an indepen-

---

[235] Prior, 2013.

[236] McGhee et al., 2014.

dent commission makes redistricting decisions, the resulting changes have a limited effect on the degree of cross-party electoral competition, which might stem the increase in landslide counties and similar markers of polarization.[237] Another approach to lessening polarization, which has been explored in a more limited way, is regulating private campaign donations.[238]

Another body of work has looked at the power of cross-group communication. For example, when exploring ways to reduce interracial group divides and prejudice, several experiments have demonstrated that when two groups of people who hold opposite views or come from very different backgrounds are placed in a room together to discuss their perspectives, both groups often emerge with a better and more complete understanding of the views of those on the other side.[239] The idea that communication and direct contact can reduce polarization and overcome prejudice is a form of Allport's "intergroup contact hypothesis." Allport argued that intergroup contact would be most effective under four conditions: equal group status, a common set of goals, authority support, and intergroup cooperation.[240] Subsequent studies have confirmed this hypothesis, considered why it might be true and how it might work, and explored contexts in which it applies.[241] One analysis suggests that four processes might explain why intergroup contact reduces bias and prejudice: developing affective ties, learning about the other group, reconsidering the characteristics and beliefs of one's own group, and adopting

---

[237] Jamie L. Carson, Michael H. Crespin, and Ryan D. Williamson, "Reevaluating the Effects of Redistricting on Electoral Competition, 1972–2012," *State Politics & Policy Quarterly*, Vol. 14, No. 2, 2014.

[238] Nolan McCarty and Boris Shor, "Partisan Polarization in the United States: Diagnoses and Avenues for Reform," Cambridge, Mass.: Harvard University, working paper, 2015.

[239] See, for example, Thomas F. Pettigrew, "Generalized Intergroup Contact Effects on Prejudice," *Personality and Social Psychology Bulletin*, Vol. 23, No. 2, 1997; Thomas F. Pettigrew and Linda R. Tropp, "A Meta-Analytic Test of Intergroup Contact Theory," *Journal of Personality and Social Psychology*, Vol. 90, No. 5, 2006.

[240] Thomas F. Pettigrew, "Intergroup Contact Theory," *Annual Review of Psychology*, Vol. 49, No. 1, 1998.

[241] Pettigrew and Tropp, 2006, p. 751.

changed behavior.[242] Although Allport's theory was originally intended to apply primarily to racial and ethnic groups, subsequent work has found that the theory has applicability to other groups as well.[243] For instance, studies that expand this idea to the partisan context have found similar results—contact and communication across the partisan divide can help two groups begin to overcome some of their differences—but the result does not hold among all populations.[244] This suggests that communication and direct interaction are able to reduce polarization, but further research is needed to explore how this finding might be applied more widely to reduce political and economic polarization in the United States. Bridging divides might be difficult, but doing so could be necessary to reduce the negative consequences of Truth Decay or create a more productive political climate.

To move in that direction, additional research in a number of areas is necessary. Fortunately, there are already a large number of metrics that researchers can use to assess the severity of polarization along a number of dimensions. Existing work also provides a good sense of the key drivers of political polarization, although perhaps less so of sociodemographic polarization. There is not, however, strong causal evidence explaining whether partisan divides in U.S. political institutions create polarization in the electorate or whether the relationship operates more strongly in the opposite direction. Understanding this relationship could be important for identifying where to target responses to polarization. There is also limited work identifying whether institutional drivers of polarization—such as redistricting, the primary system, or social and demographic trends—are most directly to blame for the increase of polarization in the United States. Again, identifying the primary sources of extreme polarization is essential for designing effective solutions and could be the most productive focal point for

---

[242] Pettigrew, 1998.

[243] Pettigrew and Tropp, 2006; Thomas F. Pettigrew and Linda R. Tropp, *When Groups Meet: The Dynamics of Intergroup Contact*, New York: Psychology Press, 2011.

[244] Joshua J. Dyck and Shanna Pearson-Merkowitz, "To Know You Is Not Necessarily to Love You: The Partisan Mediators of Intergroup Contact," *Political Behavior*, Vol. 36, No. 3, 2014.

future research in this area. The research agenda in Chapter Six proposes additional avenues for research into polarization.

## The Question of Agency

A final question about Truth Decay, its four constituent trends, and its four drivers is one of agency: Is Truth Decay something that is outside of human control with this set of four external drivers, like a natural disaster, or is it caused by intentional actions on the part of specific people or organizations? The answer appears to lie somewhere between the two extremes. Some elements and drivers of Truth Decay seem to be a function of human nature or unintentional circumstance, rather than advertent action by specific people or entities. For instance, cognitive biases, such as the tendency to seek confirmatory information and to privilege personal experience over fact, were defined in this chapter as drivers of Truth Decay and can at least partly explain why disinformation is able to spread so easily, why the line between opinion and fact becomes blurred so easily, and why there is often resistance to and skepticism about even basic objective data that do not match common perceptions. Cognitive biases do seem to drive Truth Decay, but they appear to be programmed into human brains and are clearly not the result of intentional actions by an agent. Similarly, the way social media is set up may also contribute to Truth Decay. For instance, social media platforms, such as Twitter, make it easy to proliferate large volumes of information quickly and easily and allow anyone to become a source, which makes it both easier and possibly more likely that opinions, misinformation, and disinformation will spread widely. This can drive the blurring of the line between opinion and fact and the increasing relative volume, and resulting influence, of opinion and personal experience over fact. However, it would be inaccurate to say that original social media platforms were established to spread false information.[245]

---

[245] Some platforms seem more willing than others to tolerate the use of their sites for this purpose, however, as noted previously in this chapter.

But within the changes and circumstances that we have defined as drivers of Truth Decay, there are a large number of agents who actively and intentionally accelerate the problem and others who contribute to the problem less intentionally but in equally important ways. As a reminder, we define *drivers* as general conditions or changes that appear to be causing Truth Decay and *agents* as entities that accelerate the trends that constitute Truth Decay, intentionally or unintentionally, in order to advance political, economic, or other objectives. In this section, we discuss some of the institutions, groups, and events that seem to play a role in worsening and accelerating Truth Decay (or one of its trends) for their own gain—by providing misleading information to further their objectives, by spreading intentionally false information, by manipulating the context or framing of information in ways that distort underlying facts, or by withholding information to obscure objective facts and data. We discuss the specific drivers that enable these agents to accomplish these objectives, but we do not attempt to identify all groups or individuals who might act as agents of Truth Decay. Instead, we focus on four main types of actors: the media, academia and research organizations, political actors and the government, and foreign actors.[246] In reality, even agents not explicitly discussed in this section are likely to work through one of these four channels or institutions to accelerate Truth Decay by making use of social media to spread disinformation, disseminating opinion as fact through political lobbying organizations, or funding biased research that manipulates data to achieve a desired outcome.

## The Media

Many media corporations, in their pursuit of profit and efforts to produce programming that will attract viewers and benefit the bottom line, have contributed to Truth Decay in many ways. As we explored earlier in this chapter, the 24-hour news cycle and increasing competi-

---

[246] For further discussion of the ways in which facts and data might be manipulated by political actors, corporations, and other individuals and organizations see Charles Lewis, *935 Lies: The Future of Truth and the Decline of America's Moral Integrity*, New York: Perseus Books, June 2014.

tion in the news industry have motivated some media outlets to disseminate sensationalized and sometimes misleading information that attracts viewers and appeals to their preexisting beliefs. Some media organizations act with other motives as well, including partisan ones. As already discussed, some media outlets have become increasingly partisan over time and skew the information they present (both facts and opinions) to advance a particular political objective or to appeal to their increasingly partisan audiences.[247] These decisions, however, blur the line between opinion and fact and increase the relative volume, and resulting influence, of opinion and personal experience over fact, and might also contribute to the declining agreement about facts that is part of Truth Decay. There are many examples of instances in which media outlets were found to have disseminated information that was later determined to be false, either intentionally or through insufficiently rigorous research and reporting. In summer 2017, CNN retracted a story focused on Russian influence in the 2016 presidential election after that story was found to be incorrect; the incident resulted in the resignation of three high-ranking journalists and significant criticism from conservative entities.[248] A few months later, Fox News retracted a story about the death of Democratic campaign staffer Seth Rich, which it had promoted heavily on its website and television shows.[249] Media spin is not new and has long been a characteristic of the media market; these examples are not intended to suggest that all news coming out of either of the two outlets mentioned (or any others) always blur the line between opinion or often disseminate misinformation. Instead, the examples aim to illustrate the ways in which even major national media outlets sometimes contribute to Truth Decay, even unintentionally, by spreading false or misleading information or by insufficiently distinguishing between objective fact and opinion. In addition to misinformation and misleading information, some media outlets may use

---

[247] Groeling, 2008.

[248] Jacqueline Thomsen, "Three Resign from CNN After Russia Story Retraction," *The Hill*, June 26, 2017.

[249] Oliver Darcy, "Fox News' Now Retracted Seth Rich Story," CNN Money, August 10, 2017.

intentionally incorrect information to achieve economic and political objectives, to attract viewers, or to sway public attitudes.

## Academia and Research Organizations

Academia and research organizations, including those focused on the social sciences and those that work in such areas as health or other hard sciences, have also contributed to the trends that are part of Truth Decay. There is considerable discussion in the popular press and among research and academic communities about whether science is "broken." Those who suggest that it might indeed be broken argue that the tendency to publish certain types of findings over others or over nonfindings has undermined the quality and accuracy of scientific and research findings across academic disciplines and distorted the processes that undergird science as an institution in a fundamental way.[250] The pressure to publish has also led to the rise of predatory journals that charge authors fees for publication but have significantly lower standards than top-ranked journals and of pseudo-conventions that allow academics, regardless of whether they actually attend, to pad their résumés with conference presentations. Both predatory journals and pseudo-conventions erode academic standards and perpetuate and disseminate low-quality research.[251] Although these developments do not suggest that academic research and scientific findings are no longer worthy of public trust—these institutions have produced large bodies of knowledge that advance the common good—it does seem as though high-profile instances in which prominent research findings have been retracted because of intentional malfeasance, fabricated data, faulty methods, or other errors have contributed to a blurring of the line between opinion and fact, declining agreement about objective facts and data, and a decline of trust in institutions. Evidence that tobacco companies and big banks intentionally misled and deceived

---

[250] Daniel Engber, "Is Science Broken?" *Slate*, August 21, 2017.

[251] Gina Kolata, "Many Academics Are Eager to Publish in Worthless Journals," *New York Times*, October 30, 2017.

the public are two examples that might have undermined public trust in expert assessments.[252]

Errors and retractions are not unusual in academic journals across disciplines. A study focused on retraction rates in major scientific journals found the highest retraction rates among some of the most-respected journals, including *New England Journal of Medicine*, *Science*, and *Nature*, many the result of poor methodology, intentional data manipulation, or unintentional mistakes.[253] The higher retraction rate for these journals compared with others may reflect greater transparency and academic honesty, but it also might be an indicator of flaws in the article review process or of the prevalence of research errors or manipulation. The phenomenon also affects social science journals and articles. For example, the *Journal of Applied Psychology* has retracted studies in recent years because of data errors and misrepresentations. As another example, a widely publicized study by political scientists on the effect of different types of influencers on attitudes toward gay marriage was found in 2016 to be based on entirely fabricated data.[254] Beyond retractions, there is the tendency of many academic journals and the researchers who submit to them to suppress nonfindings and publish only results that are significant. However, this can encourage poor research practices, such as excessive use of data-mining (looking for significant results and manipulating statistical results), overfitting of statistical models that might contribute to omitted variable bias (biases created when the correct set of explanatory variables are not included), concern for statistical significance over substantive importance, or lack of consideration of the statistical power of a set of results (the likelihood of rejecting a null hypothesis that is in fact true—in other words, reporting an effect that is spurious). Each of these practices can lead to

---

[252] *United States v Philip Morris*, Civil Action No. 99-2496, 2004; Jim Puzzanghera and E. Scott Reckard, "Citigroup to Pay Record Fine in $7-Billion Mortgage Settlement," *Los Angeles Times*, July 14, 2014.

[253] Ferric C. Fang and Arturo Casadevall, "Retracted Science and the Retraction Index," *Infection and Immunology*, Vol. 79, No. 10, 2011.

[254] Authorea Team, "Do the Right Thing: 11 Courageous Retractions," webpage, undated; Maria Konnikova, "How a Gay Marriage Study Went Wrong," *The New Yorker*, May 22, 2015.

research findings that, although based on data, might be misleading or not reproducible by other scholars.[255] Importantly, much is made of how these practices affect findings in the hard sciences (e.g., chemistry, biology, environmental science), but the situation is the same in social sciences (e.g., economics, political science, sociology).[256] The net result of these practices and retractions, whether they are driven by incomplete peer review processes, fake data, or research error, might be to undermine public confidence in research and academic analysis—and even facts and data—more generally. Perhaps even more directly, biased or misleading research findings serve as a form of misinformation or disinformation that, as we have noted in this chapter, is an important driver of Truth Decay.

Partisan research organizations and research organizations funded by wealthy corporate or only private interests also contribute to the trends that constitute Truth Decay. An increasing number of "think tanks" and other research organizations either are unapologetically partisan or have a narrow, ideologically driven agenda (and, in some cases, research) that appears to be skewed by the interests of corporate or private donors. In his assessment of what he calls the "Ideas Industry," Drezner describes the rise of a new generation of think tanks in the 1960s and 1970s that were focused on political advocacy rather than scholarship and were funded by large donors with clear agendas.[257] The number of organizations sharing these characteristics has risen over the past several decades, the influence of private and corporate money has increased, and even more long-standing think tanks have begun to look for new funding streams.[258] Drezner notes that corporate support can affect not only the types of work that research organizations conduct but also the findings that are published

---

[255] John Ioannidis, "Why Most Published Research Findings Are False," *PLOS Med*, Vol. 2, No. 8, August 30, 2005.

[256] John Ioannidis, T. D. Stanley, and Hristos Doucouliagos, "The Power of Bias in Economics Research," *Economic Journal*, Vol. 127, No. 605, October 2017.

[257] Daniel Drezner, *The Ideas Industry*, Oxford and New York: Oxford University Press, 2017.

[258] Drezner, 2017.

and promoted.[259] He argues that many of these organizations compromise research ethics to preserve funding and are hesitant to release findings that are harmful to clients.[260] Even research organizations that intend to publish objective and unbiased research can end up with findings, or at least their presentation, affected by issues related to funding and client relationships. Other organizations make less effort to remain objective and operate almost as lobbying organizations. For example, ExxonMobil is being investigated by a group of attorneys general (led by New York and including a number of other states with Democratic political leadership) for allegedly working with a number of research groups to fund reports that question climate science, covering up the company's knowledge about how fossil fuels harm the environment, and misleading investors.[261] (ExxonMobil denies this claim, and the investigation and court proceedings are ongoing.[262]) Evidence suggests that the tobacco industry might have taken similar steps to undermine evidence linking smoking and secondhand smoke to cancer.[263] Organizations that rely on partisan donors often cannot stray from the ideological bent advanced by those donors.[264] Instead, these organizations publish reports that hold strongly to a partisan line, often using misleading data and analysis to reach the desired conclusion. Biased research agendas and misleading or skewed results contribute to Truth Decay by undermining trust in research organizations as providers of information and by blurring the line between opinion and fact through the promotion of faulty analysis and interpretation.

Sources of funding can also affect research conducted in a university, laboratory, or other research setting. One example is the phar-

---

[259] Drezner, 2017.

[260] Drezner, 2017.

[261] Eric Lipton and Brooke Williams, "How Think Tanks Amplify Corporate America's Influence," *New York Times*, August 7, 2016; "Texas Judge Kicks Exxon Climate Lawsuit to New York Court," Reuters Business News, March 29, 2017.

[262] ExxonMobil is a donor to the RAND Institute of Civil Justice.

[263] "Big Tobacco and Science: Uncovering the Truth," University of California, Davis, Health, webpage, undated.

[264]     Drezner, 2017.

maceutical industry. Sources of funding determine the types of drugs that are researched most intensively and the ones brought to market. Conflicts of interest driven by sources of funding also sway the results of trials intended to determine whether a drug is safe. Many drug trials are funded by the manufacturer, which has a vested interest in the success of those trials. In many cases, the researchers who conduct these studies have financial ties to the manufacturer. Although it is difficult to determine whether financial ties between researchers and manufacturers cause biased results, research does suggest that trials funded by industry tend to produce a greater number of positive results than those funded independently.[265] This suggests that monetary ties might cause bias that can affect the results of a research study. Although we use the example of pharmaceuticals, it is difficult to think of an area that might not be subject to this type of bias and to the risk of disseminating intentionally or unintentionally incorrect results. Biases and distortions of these sorts contribute to Truth Decay by making it harder to determine what is fact and by undermining trust in research and academic institutions more broadly.[266]

---

[265] Ben Goldacre, "Trial Sans Error: How Pharma-Funded Research Cherry Picks Positive Results [Excerpt]," *Scientific American*, February 13, 2013.

[266] In discussing the ways in which academia and other research organizations have contributed to the problem of Truth Decay, we wish to be transparent about RAND's policies and practices in such areas as research errors and the avoidance of both actual and apparent conflicts of interest. Each RAND manuscript is subjected to a rigorous peer-review process before publication designed to ensure that RAND standards of quality and objectivity are met. (See RAND Corporation, "Standards for High-Quality Research and Analysis," webpage, undated-c.) If and when errors are discovered after publication, RAND takes several steps. First, RAND is open and transparent about the fact that the error occurred. Second, if the error can be corrected, the publication is withdrawn and revised. If the error cannot be corrected (e.g., due to the nature of the data), the publication is withdrawn and formally retracted. Third, RAND conducts a lessons-learned assessment of how and why the error occurred to minimize the chances that a similar error will be made again. This assessment is conducted by members of RAND outside the original project team.

In 2011, for example, following an extensive internal review, RAND retracted a report about medical marijuana dispensaries and crime after reevaluating the data used in the study and determining that they were insufficient to address the research question asked. (See RAND Corporation, "RAND Retracts Report About Medical Marijuana Dispensaries and Crime," news release, October 24, 2011.)

In describing the ways in which academia, science, and the broader research community have contributed to Truth Decay, however, it is important to emphasize that despite the existence of errors, malfeasance, and bias, there are at least an equal number of examples of high-quality research that have greatly advanced prevailing understanding of important social, economic, and scientific principles in ways that have benefited society. Furthermore, there are self-regulating processes already under way within the broader research community, including efforts to support publication of nonfindings and to improve the peer review process to catch errors before publication. In fact, these ongoing efforts may have contributed to the growing number of retractions in leading academic journals. In this sense, retractions may be evidence of improvements in the research vetting and publication process that, if continued, could reduce the extent to which academic and research organizations contribute to Truth Decay.

**Political Actors and the Government**

Political actors and government as an institution also play a role. Unfulfilled promises and cases in which government organizations are found to be disseminating misleading or incorrect information contribute directly to declining trust in institutions and the more general blurring of the line between opinion and fact. For example, assurances by then-President Obama and others in his administration that, under the ACA, "if you like your health plan, you can keep it," did not reflect reality. Instead, millions were forced to change their health care plans when insurance companies stopped offering plans that did not meet the ACA's standards.[267] This unmet promise helped diminish support for the ACA and undermined the Barack Obama administration's credibility in the eyes of many. As another example, the consensus by the mid-2000s that Iraqi President Saddam Hussein never

---

RAND maintains numerous safeguards against both personal and organizational conflicts of interest, reserves the right to publish findings and recommendations in its contracts and grant agreements with clients and grantors, and discloses both the sources of funding for each publication and a list of all clients and grantors who have commissioned research at RAND. (See RAND Corporation, "How We're Funded," webpage, March 22, 2017.)

[267] D'Angelo Gore, "Keeping Your Health Plan," FactCheck.Org, November 11, 2013.

had the nuclear weapons that were one of the key justifications by the George W. Bush administration for the U.S. invasion of Iraq has had an enduring effect on public confidence in information coming out of the intelligence community, despite the fact that the problem in the lead-up to the 2003 invasion might have been less the intelligence itself and more how it was used.[268]

Individual politicians have also contributed to Truth Decay, blurring the line between opinion and fact and providing misleading information in order to improve their political fortunes or to achieve a given political outcome. Politicians across the political spectrum have always had a reputation for spinning facts to fit a desired story, and current political actors are no exception. In its "Politifact Scorecard," the fact-checking website Politifact rates the veracity of political figures based on how many of a selected set of public statements chosen by Politifact are true, mostly true, half true, mostly false, and false. A review of the scores for House and Senate leadership in both parties might reveal one possible (albeit partial) metric of the extent to which political actors misstate the truth. Among the selected set of public statements evaluated, Democratic and Republican leaders of the House and the Senate use false or mostly false statements 42 percent to 44 percent of the time, depending on the specific individual.[269] Whether this use of false or misleading statements is deliberate or not, the dissemination of false or mostly false information contributes to the progression of Truth Decay by blurring the line between opinion and fact, increasing the relative volume of opinion, and (because those making the statements are government officials) undermining trust in the government as a provider of information. There is no clear evidence to suggest that the average political figure is more or less truthful today than in previous decades. However, it is possible that these misstatements and misrepresentations

---

[268] Paul Pillar, "Intelligence, Policy, and the War in Iraq," *Foreign Affairs*, Vol. 85, No. 2, March/April 2006.

[269] Politifact, "Browse by Speaker," webpage, undated. Politifact deems some statements so incorrect that they are classified as "pants on fire." We include these as "false" statements in the above percentages. Politifact does not evaluate all statements but rather a select set of publicly relevant statements. Our evaluation focused on four positions: Majority Leader of the Senate, Speaker of the House, and the Minority Leaders of the House and Senate.

carry more weight now and have a greater influence on the attitudes of constituents because of changes in the information system, such as the rise of social media platforms (through which political actors can speak directly to constituents) and the 24-hour news cycle (which provides multiple opportunities for key political figures to share their views with a national audience). In this way, misleading statements by government organizations—or any false statement or spin by any political figure—can contribute to Truth Decay.

Finally, lobbying organizations and interest groups are another set of political actors that might contribute to Truth Decay. These groups typically lobby for or against a specific policy, and they are often willing to use misleading data or to blur the line between opinion and fact to achieve their desired outcome.[270] Lobbying organizations that use misleading or false data and information (intentionally or unintentionally) to sway public opinion contribute directly to Truth Decay by blurring the line between opinion and fact, undermining trust in institutions, and creating uncertainty about the veracity and reliability of facts, data, and analysis.

**Foreign Actors**

Finally, foreign actors appear to have contributed to the blurring of the line between opinion and fact and the increasing relative volume, and resulting influence, of opinion and personal experience over fact. The starkest example of this is Russian interference in the 2016 U.S. presidential election. An analysis released by the U.S. intelligence community reported that "Russia's state-run propaganda machine contributed to the influence campaign by serving as a platform for Kremlin messaging to Russian and international audiences."[271] The report notes that Russia used state-run or state-allied media outlets, such as RT and Sputnik, and a large number of individual agents and bots to spread targeted, false

---

[270] Jeffrey M. Berry, *Lobbying for the People: The Political Behavior of Public Interest Groups*, Princeton, N.J.: Princeton University Press, 2015; Jack L. Walker, *Mobilizing Interest Groups in America: Patrons, Professions, and Social Movements*, Ann Arbor, Mich.: University of Michigan Press, 1991.

[271] Office of the Director of National Intelligence, *Assessing Russian Activities and Intentions in Recent US Elections*, Washington, D.C., ICA 2017-01D, January 6, 2017, p. iii.

information to vulnerable demographics in order to sway their attitudes toward one of the two presidential candidates, with the aim of achieving an outcome preferable to Russian interests.[272] Russia aimed to do this by exploiting at least three of the trends that constitute Truth Decay: blurring the line between opinion and fact, increasing the relative volume of disinformation and opinion to essentially drown out fact, and undermining confidence in key institutions (namely the political establishment) as providers of information. However, Russia is not the only country whose use of information campaigns in the United States has contributed to Truth Decay. For instance, there is significant evidence that the Chinese government uses targeted disinformation and propaganda with the intention of fostering a positive view of China within the United States (especially among Chinese-speaking communities) both to solidify the control of the ruling party and to encourage investment in and business partnerships with Chinese firms. This propaganda includes efforts on social media as well as in traditional print media and advertising.[273] Furthermore, analysis suggests that these efforts have increased over the past decade.[274] Chinese propaganda has the same basic effects as Russian actors' in terms of contributing to the blurring of the line between opinion and fact and increasing the relative volume of disinformation and misinformation to that of fact.

### Summary and Way Ahead

It seems that a significant number of entities have played a role in contributing to the four trends that constitute Truth Decay. The role that these agents play in the challenges we observe today in U.S. political and civil discourse, policy debates, and governance is an area ripe for additional exploration and investigation. This might include externally driven research as well as inward-looking analysis by academic and research institutions, media corporations, and political actors to

---

[272] Office of the Director of National Intelligence, 2017.

[273] Sarah Cook, "Chinese Government Influence on the U.S. Media Landscape," testimony before the U.S.-China Economic and Security Review Commission, Hearing on China's Information Controls, Global Media Influence, and Cyber Warfare Strategy, May 4, 2017.

[274] Cook, 2017.

identify ways in which they could better promote transparency and the importance of objective facts. It is also an opportunity for concerned private citizens to consider the role in their own lives of facts, data, and analysis and to look for ways to fight biases, seek objective facts, and participate in civil discourse, all of which might make strides against Truth Decay. We return to possible research topics in this area in Chapter Six.

## Summary: Truth Decay as a System

This chapter has discussed four drivers of Truth Decay: characteristics of human cognitive processing and the power of cognitive bias; changes in the information system; constraints in the educational system; and polarization. We have presented each independently and discussed the ways each contributes to Truth Decay. In reality, however, these four drivers function together to cause Truth Decay, more like a system than a set of one-way causal relationships. Each driver influences and is influenced by the others. Changes in the information system exacerbate some of the challenges that cognitive biases create, presenting people with massive amounts of information and making it easier than ever for anyone to find information that matches preexisting beliefs. The rapid increase in the speed and volume of information creates new challenges for the U.S. educational system, and for the institutions that support adult civic development. Social media contributes to the formation of echo chambers, which are further reinforced by filters and search algorithms, and all this contributes to polarization. At the same time, polarization might create incentives for media organizations to present biased perspectives as a way to increase and retain viewership. Polarization and partisan identity also create new cognitive biases and new mental models, which can affect individual beliefs and openness to new information. This chapter also identified a number of agents that act to exploit the changes and conditions created by the drivers and, in so doing, worsen the problem and advance the agents' own political and economic interests.

Truth Decay, with its uncertainty about what is fact and what is opinion, its increasing disagreement about facts, its disregard for facts, and its low trust in institutions, is a complex problem, driven by these interactions simultaneously and together. This complexity is increased by feedback mechanisms through which Truth Decay also affects its drivers. Cognitive biases promote a privileging of opinion and experience over fact and create resistance to new facts among the electorate, but Truth Decay's blurred line between opinion and fact makes the challenge of identifying facts more difficult. The rise in polarization clearly contributes to Truth Decay's increasing disagreement about facts and analytical interpretations and a decline in trust in institutions, but Truth Decay's blurred lines between opinion and fact and its associated explosion of opinion also worsen polarization by creating competing narratives. Social media and its removal of information gatekeepers speeds the progress of Truth Decay and the irrelevance of facts, just as the increasing relative volume, and resulting influence, of opinion and personal experience over fact and the blurring of the line between opinion and fact affect the types and networks of information flow on social media platforms.

In the next chapter, we consider four consequences of Truth Decay: erosion of civil discourse; political paralysis at the federal level; an increase in alienation and disengagement within the electorate; and an increase in uncertainty in national policy that has diplomatic and domestic implications. There is, importantly, also feedback among Truth Decay's consequences, its four trends, and its causes. For example, increasing disagreement about basic facts and the blurring of the line between opinion and fact undermine the ability of people on two sides of an issue to have a meaningful debate. At the same time, without such discussions, agreement about objective facts and interpretations of those facts is likely to decline further as each group develops its own narrative. As another example, polarization drives Truth Decay, but it also undermines and weakens civil discourse, is a key cause of political paralysis, and contributes to policy uncertainty. At the same time, weak civil discourse and the inability of two groups to debate and discuss meaningful issues are likely to deepen the divide between them and worsen polarization. As a final example, polarization explains much of the political paralysis observed in the current government, but political paralysis and the cross-party stalemate that accompany it also worsens polarization. We explore some of these relationships in more detail in Chapter Five.

We point out these feedback mechanisms not to conflate causes and effects but to emphasize the multifaceted challenge that Truth Decay poses and to highlight the fluidity of Truth Decay, its causes, and its effects. We also note once again that the framework we propose is a first cut, and future research should consider whether the elements included in the framework need to be reorganized, combined, or expanded to include other factors. Figure 4.7 offers a graphical depiction of these relationships.

The challenge presented by Truth Decay, then, is a complex one, and will require a complex, multifaceted answer. The first step toward this answer is understanding these interrelationships and their specific consequences for society. Identifying and exploring these consequences are critical because a clear and empirical understanding of the costs of Truth Decay guide the search for policy responses. Chapter Five identifies four important consequences of Truth Decay, their implications for society, and what additional information is required to take the next step toward combating Truth Decay.

**Figure 4.7**
**Truth Decay as a System**

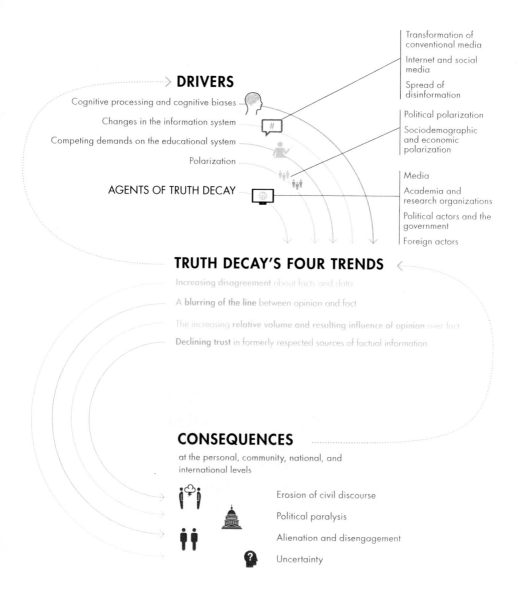

# CHAPTER FIVE

# The Consequences of Truth Decay

Truth Decay and its many manifestations pose a direct threat to democracy and have real costs and consequences—economic, political, and diplomatic. It is not enough, however, to identify these consequences. It is also necessary to explore and estimate the costs imposed on society at both the national and individual levels. This assessment of costs will not only clarify the necessity of addressing Truth Decay but might also help highlight possible solutions—or at least areas of emphasis for future research on possible solutions. In this chapter, we discuss the four consequences we have identified as potentially the most dangerous and damaging: erosion of civil discourse; political paralysis at the federal level; an increase in alienation and disengagement within the electorate; and an increase in uncertainty in national policy that has domestic and diplomatic implications. In this chapter, we present descriptive evidence that suggests that each of these consequences is currently present in American society at a higher level than in the past and is at least closely associated with Truth Decay and its drivers. We explore mechanisms that might explain these relationships, as well as the costs of each consequence. We also identify areas where research is needed to further understanding of the consequences and their relationship with Truth Decay. However, as in other areas explored in this report, there is a shortage of the rigorous empirical evidence needed to establish conclusively that the trends we define as part of Truth Decay have directly or indirectly caused the consequences discussed in this chapter. Establishing such causal relationships is one element of the research agenda provided in Chapter Six.

## Erosion of Civil Discourse

### How Truth Decay Erodes Civil Discourse

The first consequence of Truth Decay is the erosion of civil discourse throughout American society. By *civil discourse*, we mean "robust, honest, frank and constructive dialogue and deliberation that seeks to advance the public interest."[1] It is worth noting that civil discourse does not necessarily need to be polite or passive, but it should be informed and honest, with all participants approaching the conversation with an open mind, a willingness to hear alternative viewpoints, and a commitment to reaching a constructive outcome.[2] Within this general topic area, we are particularly interested in discourse related to policy issues and topics related to public well-being, broadly defined. Without a common set of facts, and with a blurring of the line between opinion and fact, it becomes nearly impossible to have a meaningful debate about important policies and topics. For example, consider the debate over immigration. The issue of immigration is one that deserves serious consideration. How to best secure U.S. borders, how to address the undocumented immigrant population, how to measure the need for immigrant labor, how to balance the needs and rights of U.S. citizens and legal residents with those of refugees who seek safety in the United States and of people seeking a better future for their families—all of these questions are important and deserve discussion. Having a constructive discussion about what policies toward immigrants should look like or what objectives and outcomes policy should aim to achieve is difficult without a common set of facts—such as the number of immigrants entering the United States, the economic role of immigrants, and the level of crime perpetrated by these immigrants. Instead of focusing on solutions, different stakeholders simply argue about the basic terms of the debate. This appears to occur, in part, because of the significant amount of information, some based on fact and some not, circulated about this

---

[1]   Brosseau, 2011.

[2]   Andrea Leskes, "A Plea for Civil Discourse: Needed, the Academy's Leadership," *Liberal Education*, Vol. 99, No. 4, 2013.

topic. Determining the terms of the debate might be a necessary part of the process, but in the current environment, no common ground on terminology ever seems to be found. In other words, the core of the debate—policy—is never reached. In the end, this dysfunction might lead to inefficient or ineffective government decisionmaking. Inability to reach a fact-based decision (or, indeed, any decision) on the topic also has meaningful implications outside of policymaking and governance—for example, individuals whose status in the United States might ultimately be affected by a policy decision in this area could face considerable uncertainty in the meantime.

Another example is the debate over how to address high violent crime rates in major cities, such as Chicago. Disagreements about the current violent crime rate, the trends in that violent crime rate, and the major causes of changes in the violent crime rate (many of which can be objectively determined) interfere with much-needed discussion about how to address what violent crime is occurring. An inability to establish a common set of facts does not just hinder meaningful debate about this and other important issues: It might also lead to policy choices that are not based on fact and do not address the causes of violent crime. The result could be deaths that might have been prevented or the misallocation of scarce public-sector resources. Thus, the decline in civil discourse does not simply undermine the quality of policymaking in an abstract way. It could also have real-world implications for citizens.

The case of the decline in civil discourse might also be an example of the way in which our framework for Truth Decay operates as a system, with feedback among Truth Decay, its causes, and its consequences. For example, it seems that the polarization and cognitive biases that drive Truth Decay might also drive the apparent decline in civil discourse by making it increasingly difficult for two people or two groups who are on opposite sides of any issue to have a meaningful debate about that issue. Not only will people on each side have their own version of the facts and their own narratives, but geographic polarization could mean that people on one side have very limited interaction with or exposure to people on the other, which, in turn, strengthens preconceptions and can weaken the skills people need to participate in civil discussion.[3] Furthermore, because of cognitive biases, individuals might even avoid debates with others who disagree and might not be at all open to hearing alternative perspectives.

Another example of such a feedback mechanism is found in changes in the information system—especially the rise of social media as a primary form of communication—that have likely contributed to the erosion of civil discourse. Research suggests that the anonymity provided by social media increases bullying, "trolling," and other types of negative commentary in ways that might not occur in face-to-face conversations.[4] Furthermore, the types of "discourse" that occur on social media platforms tend to involve limited amounts of deep or direct communication. Conversations tend to be more superficial and might not include meaningful discussion on substantive issues. Thus, even as social media platforms can stimulate some increase in political interest and activity—including online discussion boards and posts that go "viral"—these platforms cannot replace the public sphere[5] as a place for civic discourse.[6] To the extent that having a vibrant marketplace of ideas is important for a healthy democracy, the gradual growth of online communication and its slow replacement of direct or in-person communication could prove dangerous. Furthermore, some research suggests that relying solely on online forms of communication could slow the development of a person's ability to conduct meaningful, in-person discussions, especially if he or she uses online communication to avoid face-to-face discussions.[7]

---

[3]  Leskes, 2013.

[4]  Paul Best, Roger Manktelow, and Brian Taylor, "Online Communication, Social Media and Adolescent Wellbeing: A Systematic Narrative Review," *Children and Youth Services Review*, Vol. 41, 2014.

[5]  By *public sphere*, we mean a social space in which people can come together in person to share ideas and to identify and discuss societal problems, needs, and courses of action.

[6]  Christopher M. Mascaro and Sean P. Goggins, "Technologically Mediated Political Discourse During a Nationally Televised GOP Primary Debate," *Journal of Information Technology & Politics*, Vol. 12, No. 3, 2015.

[7]  Lisa M. Flaherty, Kevin J. Pearce, and Rebecca B. Rubin, "Internet and Face-to-Face Communication: Not Functional Alternatives" *Communication Quarterly*, Vol. 46, No. 3, 1998; Adam N. Joinson, "Self-Esteem, Interpersonal Risk, and Preference for E-Mail to Face-to-Face Communication," *CyberPsychology & Behavior*, Vol. 7, No. 4, 2004.

## Assessing the Decline of Civil Discourse

Although it is difficult to empirically assess the value of civic discourse to the quality of democracy, studies that assess the value of deliberative democracy note that, even when complicated or controversial, and even when no final decision is reached, public discourse and discussion can serve an important function in democracy, supporting the sharing of diverse perspectives and the formation of more-thoughtful and more-reasoned decisions and policy outcomes.[8] This can be true even in a representative democracy in which final decisions are made by elected delegates rather than the electorate itself. Civil discourse across identity-group lines can also have educational benefits for students who are encouraged to conduct this type of discussion, improving their ability to engage with information and raising their interest in participating in other civic activities.[9] Civil discourse is not just a necessary part of democracy: It is also an important part of societal advancement, and it might contribute to progress in areas, such as technology, social sciences, or the physical sciences, where discussion and sharing information can lead to innovations.[10]

### The Extent of the Empirical Evidence on Civil Discourse

There is little empirical data on the amount or the quality of civil discourse over time, but, by most accounts, both have been on the decline over at least the past decade. Examples of this decline are prevalent in contemporary society. For instance, discussions between political candidates and elected officials in 2016 and 2017 have led to physical altercations or threats. Name-calling is a common tactic in political campaigns. Colleges and universities have canceled speakers whose views students dislike or disagree with (and speakers who have proceeded despite this resistance have faced violent protests). Town halls with members of Congress have devolved into screaming matches.

[8] Mark Button and Kevin Mattson, "Deliberative Democracy in Practice: Challenges and Prospects for Civic Deliberation," *Polity*, Vol. 31, No. 4, Summer 1999.

[9] Patricia Gurin, Biren Ratnesh A. Nagda, and Gretchen E. Lopez, "The Benefits of Diversity in Education for Democratic Citizenship," *Journal of Social Issues*, Vol. 60, No. 1, 2004.

[10] Leskes, 2013.

These things seem to occur more often now, but it is worth noting that none of it is entirely new. Town halls were just as contentious in 2009 when the Tea Party emerged, and political campaigns have always produced confrontational and impolite language. However, the fact that almost anyone now has the ability to share and proliferate ideas through social media platforms raises the stakes and the prevalence of speech that runs counter to the premise of civil discourse—that is, speech filled with hostile accusations and disagreements that lacks the open-mindedness required to make meaningful debate possible.

In suggesting that civil discourse is eroding, we do not mean to imply that civil discourse in the United States has always been optimal and productive. In fact, limitations have always existed. Throughout U.S. history, political debates over high-stakes issues have degenerated into emotionally charged arguments, both among the electorate and within government institutions. Furthermore, in the past, civil discourse often excluded certain groups of people, such as women and African-Americans. Until given the right to vote, women were largely excluded from the practice of civil discourse, and their opinions were rarely valued or heard.[11] Today, women as a group do have a louder voice in civil discourse—even as individual women still work to achieve equal footing with male peers in areas such as politics and academia. African-Americans were not only excluded from civil discourse but also subject to hateful speech, threats, and humiliation—practices that run entirely counter to the very principle of civil discourse—during much of the 20th century and continuing to some degree even today.[12] Progress in addressing prejudice and discrimination and removing obstacles to the participation of some groups in civil discourse has been slow, but social media and other emerging communication channels have given minority populations a greater chance to voice to their perceptions, views, and preferences.

In the past, obstacles to civil discourse existed most often at the boundaries between different identity groups (i.e., race, gender, eco-

---

[11] Dorothy E. Smith, "A Peculiar Eclipsing: Women's Exclusion from Man's Culture," *Women's Studies International Quarterly*, Vol. 1, No. 4, 1978.

[12] Martin Reisigl and Ruth Wodak, *Discourse and Discrimination: Rhetorics of Racism and Antisemitism*, Abingdon, UK: Routledge, 2005.

nomic status); in contemporary society, however, challenges to civil discourse seem more pervasive and extend beyond identity group lines. Driven by cognitive biases and polarization, and enabled by changes in the communication landscape, people who prefer not to engage in meaningful discourse can avoid doing so by relying only on their insulated network and seeking confirmatory sources. This avoidance might undermine the value that has historically been placed on civil discourse, with potentially far-reaching consequences. Unfortunately, we do not yet have strong empirical evidence to document possible trends in the quality or amount of civil discourse, such as those discussed earlier, or to assess the quantitative and qualitative costs of the loss of civil discourse as a value. We address this point in more detail in the next section and in Chapter Six.

### Efforts to Increase Civic Discourse

A growing number of initiatives are attempting to promote civil discourse, and many are operating through colleges and universities. Research on civil discourse suggests that learning how to participate in a meaningful civil debate is a skill that must be taught: It is not something that can be learned through observation or experience.[13] Students must be given repeated opportunities to participate in civil discourse and to be evaluated. Thus, responding to the problem of civil discourse through the university system seems appropriate. Selected examples of these initiatives include

- Arizona State University's Arizona Humanities Council in Project Civil Discourse, which convenes diverse groups of people to discuss large and complex societal problems[14]
- a series of workshops and panel discussions held at Emory University that focused on encouraging civil discourse and the spread of intellectual diversity across disciplines[15]

---

[13] Leskes, 2013.

[14] Leskes, 2013.

[15] Leskes, 2013.

- making civil discourse a core value and including it in the key objectives of most course syllabi at Roger Williams University[16]
- a workshop held by Pardee RAND Graduate School in which students explored ways that technology, ranging from online videos to interactive tools and card games, can improve civil discourse.

However, such efforts to improve civil discourse are far from sufficient, especially considering the power of the opposing forces. A stronger response to the decline in civic discourse must include commitments at the local and national levels, among members of Congress, and among leading media organizations to have serious and civil discussions about important issues. This would involve a real effort by Democratic and Republican members of the House and the Senate to have serious debates about policy issues that include members of both parties and efforts by media organizations to host substantive discussions on topics of public interest and concern among experts with different backgrounds and viewpoints (rather than tailoring content to appeal to specific demographics). A return to civil discourse must also include changes in the way Americans consume information and the value that people place on facts. Restoring civil discourse will be challenging, but it is not impossible. In fact, working against Truth Decay could naturally move toward that restoration by rebuilding the emphasis on and respect for facts, which must be the foundation of any meaningful discourse.

Although civil discourse is a topic of increasing interest, it is also an area in which high-quality empirical research is limited and additional work is needed. Most important, there is limited empirical work that identifies precisely *how* civil discourse has changed over time and by *how much*. We have presented a number of episodic examples that suggest a decline in the amount and quality of civil discourse in recent years, but more-robust attempts to empirically evaluate trends in this year could lead to a greater understanding of how and why changes in civil discourse have occurred. Second, assessments that systematically

---

[16] Leskes, 2013.

and empirically demonstrate how civil discourse affects the quality and efficiency of American democracy will be valuable, as will assessments that reveal economic and other costs (to individuals and society) of a loss of civil discourse. These assessments could be qualitative but also quantitative, examining the costs of missed opportunities, decisions based on missed opportunities, and other areas where an increase in civil discourse and discussion might lead to better outcomes. Expected utility models that consider how an individual's own well-being might be affected by a decline in civil discourse might also be helpful and beneficial. These types of cost assessments would highlight more emphatically the reasons why civil discourse is important and worth protecting and advancing. Finally, although initiatives to advance civil discourse undertaken at the university level are important, research is also needed to identify the most-effective curricula for advancing civil discourse and to investigate ways in which to teach adults, outside of a formal school setting, how to participate in civil discourse and acquire the skills it requires.

## Political Paralysis

Aside from eroding civil discourse, Truth Decay also appears to contribute to political paralysis and stalemate in Washington. Although U.S. government has experienced periods of stalemate in the past, the data presented in this section highlight ways in which this paralysis appears to have worsened and to have become increasingly costly for the American public. We argue that Truth Decay is at least a contributing factor to this deepening stalemate.

There are some who would prefer a smaller, minimalist government that takes on fewer functions and interferes less in individual lives. Others may see political paralysis as a positive development that helps break the monopoly that "the establishment" holds over policy-making. However, most people would likely admit that there is a basic set of functions that should be the responsibility of the government, and political paralysis (and the Truth Decay driving it) can interfere with even these.

## How Truth Decay Causes Political Paralysis

Truth Decay can lead to political paralysis through a number of channels. First, uncertainty and disagreement about basic facts and the blurring of the line between opinion and fact both create divides between elected officials—often, but not always, along partisan lines that make it difficult for these representatives to agree to the terms of debate on key issues and, worse, that prevent compromise or agreement on key pieces of legislation. Low trust in government, another trend of Truth Decay, also contributes to political paralysis by weakening the authority of government institutions and strengthening the position of veto players, such as interest groups, that can interfere in government decision-making and have the power to sway public opinion.[17] Some of the factors driving Truth Decay might also play a role. For instance, the polarization that seems to drive Truth Decay creates significant obstacles and barriers between partisan camps, preventing communication, compromise, and agreement. Even Truth Decay's other consequences might play a role. The erosion of civil discourse, combined with the high volume of disinformation that raises uncertainty about what is fact, what is opinion, and what is simply false, also seems to worsen today's political stalemate because it is harder for policymakers to be sure that the opinions of their colleagues are grounded in fact and to begin a meaningful dialogue.

Although Truth Decay is clearly not the only factor driving political stalemate, increased uncertainty, low trust, and increasing disagreement over facts (all associated with Truth Decay) might be worsening this political paralysis in key ways. For example, low trust and increased disagreement over facts might interfere with Congress's responsibility to exercise key oversight functions or come to an agreement (sometimes even within a single party) on key legislative issues. These delays and periods of inaction have real financial and other consequences. RAND researchers who assessed the costs of paralysis caused by political polarization have found that drafting and passing laws, confirming presidential executive and judicial appointments (or at least bringing them to a vote), creating budgets and allocating funds, and ensuring

---

[17] Francis Fukuyama, "America in Decay: The Sources of Political Dysfunction," *Foreign Affairs*, Vol. 93, No. 5, 2014.

proper oversight are needed if the government is to function effectively and provide needed services efficiently, if the United States is to interact constructively with its partners and allies, and if the president and his advisers are to pursue policies that advance the well-being of U.S. citizens.[18] Thus, to the extent that Truth Decay interferes with any or all of these functions, it can pose a threat to the functioning of democracy.

**Assessing Political Paralysis and Its Costs**

A number of metrics underscore the sharp increase in political paralysis in recent years. Again, this increase cannot be attributed entirely to Truth Decay but, as already explained, Truth Decay is likely a contributing factor. Filibusters, a partisan tool used to delay a vote on a piece of legislation, could be one metric of friction within Congress and of its inability to pass laws and take other action. Figure 5.1 shows a gradual upward trend in the number of filibusters per year between 1947 and 2017 in the Senate and highlights the sharp increase around 2008, the end of George W. Bush's presidency and the start of Barack Obama's tenure. Data on congressional workload reveal similar signs of paralysis and stalemate. Figure 5.2 shows the percentage of total legislation proposed that was enacted by each Congress since 1973 (when the data were first collected). The rate of successful enactment has fallen markedly since its peak in the mid-1980s and declined fairly consistently since roughly 2003,[19] which suggests that a smaller fraction of proposed legislation makes it through to enactment. This trend exists despite the fact that the total number of pieces of legislation proposed has been roughly constant since the early 1980s, with the exception of a brief period between 1993 and 1996, when total proposed legislation per two-year period was somewhat lower.[20] It is reasonable to hypothesize that polarization and stalemate might be one cause of this decrease in the number of enacted laws in recent terms. However, it is also the case that this metric does not

---

[18] Unpublished research by Stephanie Young, Daniel Egel, Sarah Turner, and Michael Kennedy, RAND Corporation.

[19] GovTrack, "Statistics and Historical Comparison, Bills by Final Status," webpage, undated.

[20] GovTrack, undated.

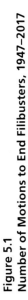

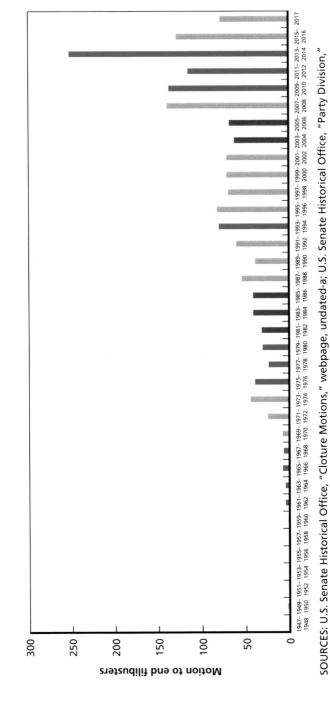

**Figure 5.1**
**Number of Motions to End Filibusters, 1947–2017**

SOURCES: U.S. Senate Historical Office, "Cloture Motions," webpage, undated-a; U.S. Senate Historical Office, "Party Division," webpage, undated-b.
NOTE: Gray bars indicate split control of the Senate and White House, red bars indicate Republican control of the Senate and White House, and blue bars indicate Democratic control of the Senate and White House.

RAND RR2314-5.1

**Figure 5.2**
**Percentage of Total Legislation Enacted, 1973–2015**

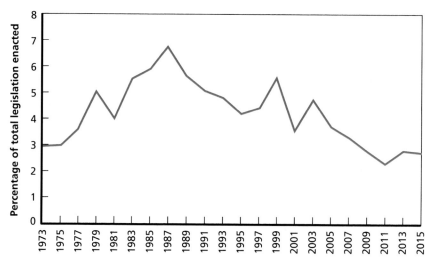

SOURCE: GovTrack, undated.
RAND RR2314-5.2

take into account the size or complexity of a given piece of legislation or whether bills passed by Congress in more-recent years are more likely than in prior decades to include many smaller pieces of legislation combined into one. Further analysis of the relative complexity and composition of proposed and passed legislation over the past four decades would be needed to fully explore possible reasons for the decline in the rate of law enactment in the past two decades.

Political paralysis has significant political and economic costs. Economically, the power and severity of these consequences were most clearly underscored during the government shutdown in 2013. Estimates varied, but most suggested that the shutdown led to a drop of 0.25 to 0.5 percentage points in real GDP growth, amounting to a loss of about $20 billion to the U.S. economy. Also affected were federal employees and government contractors who could not work during the shutdown.[21] A Congressional Research Service review that assessed cost estimates from the shutdown noted, "A review of third-party estimates of the effects of the shutdown on the economy finds a predicted reduction in GDP growth of at least 0.1 percentage points for each week of the shutdown."[22] The review also noted, however, that most forecasters did not attempt to include multiplier or indirect effects, so "the estimates reviewed can be thought of as a lower bound on the overall effects on economic activity."[23]

In addition to shutdowns, political paralysis has also contributed to a slower rate of judicial confirmation rates to lower courts, which leads to delays that have economic costs for the government and for people involved in legal proceedings.[24] Young et al. developed a framework for estimating some of the economic costs of political paralysis, including delays in executive and judicial confirmations and missed deadlines on must-pass legislative actions, such as spending bills. The results vary based on the specific type of delay considered, but here is an example: Using as a metric the opportunity cost of money held in risk-free accounts by litigants awaiting the adjudication of civil cases, Young et al. estimated that delays in judicial appointments could result in an annual reduction of $3.3 billion in GDP using the baseline conditions.[25] The authors also used the experience of the 2013 shutdown and the estimates discussed earlier to assess the cost of a future shutdown, this time including the indirect costs that other estimates omitted. According to Young et al., a future two-week government shutdown could reduce GDP by $9 billion.[26] The authors also note that, although it is more difficult to measure economically, the costs associated with a

---

[21] Marc Labonte, *The FY2014 Government Shutdown: Economic Effects*, Washington, D.C.: Congressional Research Service, September 11, 2015.

[22] Labonte, 2015.

[23] Labonte, 2015, p. 7.

[24] Sarah A. Binder and Forrest Maltzman, *Advice and Dissent: The Struggle to Shape the Federal Judiciary*, Washington, D.C.: Brookings Institution, 2009.

[25] Unpublished research by Young et al.

[26] Unpublished research by Young et al.

loss of global credibility or with an inability to avoid an international crisis due to clumsy decisionmaking could be just as large.

The quality and efficiency of government services are another victim of political stalemate. Legislative inaction interferes with government ability to modify programs to meet unexpected constituent needs and makes legislative and other government institutions rigid and inflexible.[27] Political paralysis can lead to delays in key policy decisions or to the adoption of minimally satisfactory policies that can be passed with support from only one party (or from one party and a few token members of the opposing party) and do not require true compromise. Although the passage of any policy may be preferable to paralysis in some cases, half-measures and policies that are written and passed without debate can create additional negative consequences for individual voters. Efforts to address such major issues as economic inequality and poverty, rising health care costs, and the effects of both trade and automation on certain jobs or workers are consistently hamstrung over disagreements across party lines regarding basic facts and analytical interpretations of those facts. These disagreements can lead to policy choices (or in the case of stalemate, the failure to craft policies) that have significant negative implications for people. For example, inefficiencies in the ACA that have caused higher premiums among some groups of Americans arose partly from political constraints, created by interparty competition, that affected the bill's final form.[28] Continuing uncertainty about the future of health care resulting from political paralysis has had further distorting effects on the market and led to further increases in premiums.[29] Delays in policy—or not implementing any policy—have not only economic costs but also possible direct fiscal and other effects on people's lives.

---

[27] Nolan McCarty, Keith T. Poole, and Howard Rosenthal, *Polarized America: The Dance of Ideology and Unequal Riches*, Cambridge, Mass.: MIT Press, 2008; unpublished research by Young et al.

[28] Sarah Kliff and Ezra Klein, "The Lessons of Obamacare," *Vox*, March 15, 2017.

[29] Chad Terhune and Julie Appleby, "Uncertainty over Obamacare Leaves Next Year's Rates in Limbo," National Public Radio, July 19, 2017.

Finally, the government's inability to reach quick decisions on key issues can create significant foreign policy risk. When external threats arise, the United States must be able to make immediate decisions to protect national security. When it cannot do this because of political paralysis, the safety of individuals and infrastructure are placed in serious jeopardy. Decisions about how and when to deploy U.S. ground forces must be based on clear data and information as well as a definitive understanding of relevant alliances and commitments. In cases when responses must be immediate, hesitation and indecision can have significant consequences. Furthermore, unintentional escalation and other consequences could also result from political paralysis caused by Truth Decay in such a situation.

Thus, the costs of political stalemate are substantial, whether measured in terms of economic losses, degradation of the quality of government, increased foreign policy risk, or simply the loss of credibility an ineffectual government suffers in the eyes of its electorate. Increasing disagreement about facts and analytical interpretations of facts and data and the blurring of the line between opinion and fact contribute to this political stalemate by preventing effective civil discourse and meaningful debate and by making compromise increasingly difficult. Because of the magnitude and seriousness of these costs, additional analysis would be valuable both for advancing researchers' understanding of areas where these costs are greatest and for designing responses to address them. Perhaps most important, although Young et al. make great strides in estimating the costs of government shutdowns, delays in judicial confirmation, and an inability to implement legislation, it is considerably more difficult to estimate the costs associated with foreign policy risk, erosion of diplomatic relationships, reduced government credibility, or a decrease in the overall quality of government legislation and services due to political stalemate. Efforts to estimate these costs would help policymakers and even voters understand the myriad ways in which a stalemate directly affects their livelihoods and national security. For example, efforts to assess the costs of inefficiencies in the ACA could underscore for individual voters how government stalemate directly affects their livelihoods and, in turn, could create electoral pressure for compromise.[30] Research on ways that polarization can be reduced (discussed in the previous chapter) will also be essential: The key to overcoming political paralysis is to reduce division and refusal to compromise across party lines. Potential solutions might include institutional or process changes at the state or national levels that incentivize compromise or at least ease its process. Still, it is important to remember that checks and balances in U.S. political institutions are intended to grind processes to a halt when the country is deeply divided and when agreement on key policies is limited. In this sense, government paralysis may be beneficial, serving as a check on the power of any one person or party. Research focused on identifying the benefits and opportunities of stalemate, if they exist, could be beneficial. The research agenda in Chapter Six proposes additional avenues for research into political paralysis.

## Alienation and Disengagement

### How Truth Decay Causes Alienation and Disengagement

Truth Decay appears to have contributed to an increase in the number of people who express feelings of alienation from major institutions, including government, media, and organized religion, and a decrease in expressions of political efficacy. By *alienation*, we mean detachment from, rejection of, and disaffection from major institutions, processes, and social norms.[31] Truth Decay appears to worsen political and social alienation in a few key ways. As people lose confidence in the government to do what is right, pass legislation, fulfill its basic responsibilities, and protect their interests, traditional institutions and the democratic processes on which they are founded also wind up at risk. Alienation is worsened by the blurring of the line between opinion and fact and resulting uncertainty about who and what to believe. This might lead

---

[30]  Kliff and Klein, 2017.

[31]  We use the term *social atomization* to refer to a process in which individuals become isolated, turning inward and doing things on their own, rather than engaging actively with others.

to disillusionment with government and, after a point, even a rejection of institutions and organizations of suspect credibility. The proliferation of disinformation and misinformation that might be a cause of Truth Decay is also relevant—another example of the ways in which the drivers and consequences of Truth Decay are interrelated.

### Assessing Alienation and Disengagement

Public opinion polls suggest dissatisfaction with both major political parties and a sense that Congress does a poor job of representing voter interests. For example, a 2015 Pew Research Center survey found that 47 percent of voters report that ordinary citizens have few avenues through which to influence government, and that 39 percent report that voting does not affect how the government runs things—sentiments that have increased in prevalence compared with previous decades.[32] Since the 1950s, the American National Election Studies has tracked trends in perceived political efficacy.[33] As Figure 5.3 shows, perceived political efficacy declined consistently between 1952 and 1980 and, since then, has swung through a series of cycles, rising and falling over the decades. However, after a period of increasing perceived efficacy between 1994 and 2002 (during which the average political efficacy score passed 60 on the 0 to 100 index), reported efficacy once again plunged sharply to just 36 in 2012. This level is near the historic low, as measured by the American National Election Studies, and has been lower only twice: in 1990 (35) and 1994 (33). This sense of political inefficacy, which is highest among young voters and those with lower levels of education, can weaken motivation and willingness to participate in civic and electoral activities, including attending community meetings and voting.

As we have noted, trust in all government institutions and their ability to "do the right thing" is abysmally low, and this is yet another

---

[32] Pew Research Center, "Beyond Distrust: How Americans View Their Government—9. Views of the Nation, How It's Changing and Confidence in the Future," webpage, November 23, 2015b.

[33] The American National Election Studies tracks the attitudes, opinions, and political participation of the American electorate using a nationally representative survey. For more information, see American National Election Studies, homepage, undated.

**Figure 5.3**
**Trends in Political Efficacy, 1952–2012**

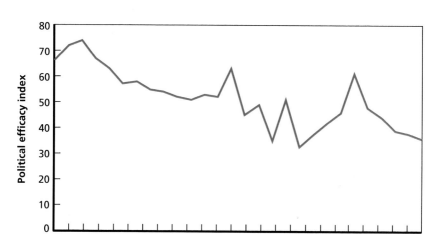

SOURCE: American National Election Studies, "Average Score on Index 1952–2012: External Political Efficacy," webpage, undated.
NOTES: The political efficacy index asks respondents to rate on a scale from 0 to 100 how strongly they agree or disagree with one of the following statements (depending on the version of the survey used): (1) "People like me don't have any say about what the government does," or (2) "I don't think public officials care much what people like me think." A score of "0" indicates full agreement and "100" indicates full disagreement, or high feelings of efficacy. Data on this metric have been collected every two or four years since 1952. The years shown in the figure reflect all the years in this range when some form of this question was asked in the survey.
RAND RR2314-5.3

manifestation of disengagement.[34] But perhaps the most-powerful evidence of the consequences of alienation and disillusionment with the establishment was the success of outsider candidates in 2016 in both the Democratic and Republican parties—candidates supported by groups of voters who felt ignored and forgotten. These candidates include not only Bernie Sanders and Donald Trump, but also third-party candidates, who won 5.7 percent of the popular vote,[35] compared

---

[34] Pew Research Center, 2015a.

[35] The 2016 election has a number of unique dynamics which might have led to higher vote totals for third-party candidates in 2016 compared with previous elections. However, at least

with just 1 percent, 1.5 percent, and 1.8 percent in the three previous presidential elections.[36] Trends in civic participation also reveal consistently low levels of engagement, particularly among certain ethnic and age groups. In 2016, overall turnout (defined as the percentage of the voting eligible population that voted) reached just 59.3 percent, which represented a small decrease from 2004 and 2008 but a slight increase compared with 2012.[37] However, the trend in turnout was substantially more negative among specific segments of voters: Turnout among African-American and Hispanic voters also declined between 2012 and 2016, with the largest decline among African-American voters.[38] Part of this could be because of the specific candidates on the ballot, but evidence suggests that disengagement and alienation were at play as well. An apparent trend in disengagement is not unique to minority voters, however. When asked why they do not vote, many eligible voters reply that they do not have time or they do not feel bound by the participatory norms of a representative democracy. A smaller share of the voting-age population was registered to vote in 2012 (65 percent) than in 1972 (72 percent). Participation in other types of civic activity in the United States is also low compared with the past. For example, between 1974 and 2016, the percentage of Americans who reported spending significant time with a neighbor declined from 30 percent to 19 percent.[39] Civic participation in the United States is also low compared with rates in other democratic countries. In the United States, 29 percent of respondents to a survey reported attending a campaign event or speech in 2016, compared with 42 percent in Greece and 38 percent in India. Sixteen percent of Americans reported participat-

---

some portion of these voters likely chose a third-party candidate because they felt alienated by establishment political figures and parties.

[36] "Popular Votes 1940–2012," Roper Center, webpage, undated; David Wasserman, "2016 National Popular Vote Tracker," Cook Political Report, January 2, 2017a.

[37] "Voter Turnout," United States Election Project, webpage, undated.

[38] Jens Manuel Krogstad and Mark Hugo Lopez, "Black Voter Turnout Fell in 2016, Even as a Record Number of Americans Cast Ballots," Pew Research Center, May 12, 2017.

[39] Vice Chairman's Staff of the Joint Economic Committee, *What We Do Together: The State of Associational Life in America*, SCP Report No. 1-17, May 2017.

ing in an organized protest, compared with 25 percent in both Italy and India and 27 percent in South Africa.[40]

Evidence also suggests that Americans have been replacing active, in-person civic participation with online civic participation.[41] Research reveals that levels of political activity via social media platforms are higher than those done in person. By 2013, about two-thirds of Americans with social media accounts used those platforms to obtain or share political information.[42] Political figures, from the president and members of Congress to city mayors and police and fire chiefs, are also taking to social media, using those platforms to share ideas and connect with voters—and a growing number of voters are using social media to follow their representatives.[43] Although political participation and engagement via the internet and social media are valuable and important because they open new channels of access and involvement, they do not replace direct, in-person participation. Engagement through the internet and social media is less direct and often represents a more superficial and fleeting commitment to engagement. In fact, some researchers argue that being involved in nonpolitical civic organizations or replacing face-to-face interaction with membership in an online community can actually reduce and degrade a person's quality and amount of political participation.[44]

Disengagement is highest among the youngest cohort, ages 18–29. This group is the least likely to participate in elections, the least likely to feel a sense of civic identity, and the least knowledgeable about public affairs. In fact, only one in ten can name both of his or her state's U.S.

---

[40] Pew Research Center, "Even in an Era of Disillusionment, Many Around the World Say Regular Citizens Can Influence Government," webpage, October 24, 2016c.

[41] Pew Research Center, "Civic Engagement," webpage, April 25, 2013.

[42] Aaron Smith, "Part 2: Political Engagement on Social Networking Sites," Pew Research Center, April 25, 2013.

[43] Monica Anderson, "More Americans Are Using Social Media to Connect with Politicians," Pew Research Center, May 19, 2015a.

[44] Jeffrey M. Berry, "Nonprofits and Civic Engagement," *Public Administration Review*, Vol. 65, No. 5, 2005; Mark E. Kann, Jeffrey M. Berry, Connor Gant, and Phil Zager, "The Internet and Youth Political Participation," *First Monday*, Vol. 12, No. 8, 2007.

senators. Compared with older cohorts, members of this group are also less likely to participate in other political activities, and only slightly more than one-third report that they follow the news every day. Much of this disengagement resembles the youthful behavior of older generations and is not new, but the advent and prevalence of the internet and the role the internet increasingly plays in activism and civic participation may exacerbate existing disengagement even as it provides new opportunities for participation.[45]

The decline in public engagement that seems to be driven, at least in part, by Truth Decay is important for a number of reasons. Public engagement serves a number of functions in a democracy. First, as Verba and Nie argue, civic engagement allows voters to put pressure on the political elite to recognize and respond to constituent preferences.[46] Second, public engagement can foster learning, relationship-building, transparency, and understanding among people with diverse perspectives because it allows for the expression and modification of beliefs and opinions and can foster cooperation and compromise.[47] Third, civic engagement can also improve the quality of democracy by fostering other types of community participation and engagement.[48] Proponents of civic engagement argue that this widespread participation in society can foster trust and tolerance and decrease polarization—all badly needed traits that are seemingly on the decline in many aspects of today's society.[49] Restoring civic engagement, if it can also promote increased trust in institutions and reduced polarization, could be a way to combat Truth Decay and its negative consequences.

There are, however, important limits to the benefits that broader civic engagement provides. Putnam argues that only "bridging social

---

[45] Ellen Quintelier, "Differences in Political Participation Between Young and Old People," *Contemporary Politics*, Vol. 13, No. 2, 2007.

[46] Sidney Verba and Norman H. Nie, *Participation in America*, New York: Harper & Row, 1972.

[47] National Academies of Science, Committee on Science Communication, 2017.

[48] Verba and Nie, 1972.

[49] Elizabeth Theiss-Morse and John R. Hibbing, "Citizenship and Civic Engagement," *Annual Review of Political Science*, Vol. 8, 2005.

capital" (i.e., those ties that bridge social, political, and ethnic lines) is beneficial, while "bonding social capital" (i.e., ties that strengthen connections within groups) can be detrimental.[50] Given concerns about demographic and ideological segregation, a warning about the dangers of bonding social capital is particularly striking and important. It is possible that Truth Decay has actually had different effects on different forms of social capital. It might have strengthened the bonds and ties within partisan, ethnic, or demographic groups (generally seen as the negative and harmful form of social capital), which are often made up of people who share a single narrative and interpretation of events, while degrading social bonds and consensus that cut across ethnic, political, or economic lines (the more-beneficial form of social capital).[51] Cross-group interaction seems to have become increasingly contentious and polarized. This may be attributed—at least, in part—to the increasing disagreement about facts that is part of Truth Decay—and these divides could further weaken levels of productive civic engagement. As each group develops its own set of facts and its own narrative, there is less and less common ground for productive cross-group interaction in political and other civic activities. Furthermore, the erosion of civil discourse, discussed earlier, could hasten the decline in civic engagement. Specifically, civil discourse could be one way in which people become and stay engaged and interested in the political sphere: Without it, political debate might seem inaccessible, and people could turn away from the political sphere altogether.

Empirical support for the relationship between engagement and the quality of democracy and representation is somewhat mixed, largely due to challenges in identifying the appropriate measures of participation and precisely assessing the effects of engagement on government output. Some evidence suggests a relationship between higher levels of civic participation and the quality of representation, especially in communities with high levels of participation.[52] In addition, research

---

[50] Robert D. Putnam, *Bowling Alone*, New York: Simon & Schuster, 2000.

[51] Theiss-Morse and Hibbing, 2005.

[52] Jeffrey M. Berry, Kent E. Portney, and Ken Thomson, *The Rebirth of Urban Democracy*, Washington, D.C.: Brookings Institution, 1993.

that distinguishes between bonding and bridging social capital offers some support for Putnam's argument. That same analysis finds no statistically significant relationship between bridging forms of civic engagement and quality of representation but reveals a clear negative relationship between bonding social capital and quality of representation.[53] Assessments of other types of outcomes, such as the quality of policy outputs and the number of policy innovations, suggest that civic engagement does have a positive effect, possibly because it spurs richer and more-diverse conversations, even if it does not directly improve the quality of representation.[54] Thus, it is reasonable to be concerned about alienation and disengagement and their effect on the health of American democracy, especially among young people, who will become the next generation of leaders. However, it is worth noting that wider civic engagement is not without dangers, including more-negative views of the government that result from wider exposure.[55]

There are ongoing efforts to identify ways to increase civic participation, especially among younger voters. At the local government level, these tend to focus on increasing community participation in local political activities. Other interventions have focused on exploiting the internet and social media as a way of fostering wider and more-robust political interest, knowledge, and even communication (through blogs or discussion forums).[56] Another approach, described in Chapter Four, aims to increase civics-oriented education in schools to build more-robust political awareness and enthusiasm, which educators hope will translate into

---

[53] Kim Quaile Hill and Tetsuya Matsubayashi, "Civic Engagement and Mass-Elite Policy Agenda Agreement in American Communities," *American Political Science Review*, Vol. 99, No. 2, 2005.

[54] Stephen Knack, "Social Capital and the Quality of Government: Evidence from the States," *American Journal of Political Science*, Vol. 46, No. 4, October 2002.

[55] Theiss-Morse and Hibbing, 2005.

[56] Michael X. Delli Carpini, "Gen. Com: Youth, Civic Engagement, and the New Information Environment," *Political Communication*, Vol. 17, No. 4, 2000; Howard Rheingold, "Using Participatory Media and Public Voice to Encourage Civic Engagement," *Civic Life Online: Learning How Digital Media Can Engage Youth*, Cambridge, Mass.: MIT Press, John D. and Catherine T. MacArthur Foundation Series on Digital Media and Learning, 2008.

greater participation.[57] Still other approaches seek to build wider civic participation in such forums as churches and synagogues.[58] Additional research is needed to evaluate the success of these efforts to build civic engagement through new channels and using innovative means.

Attempts to build civic engagement face significant challenges, however. First, some members of the electorate simply have little or no interest in participating in political activities, regardless of the stakes and the rewards.[59] Second, the forms of social capital and civic engagement that are most likely to improve the quality of democracy are still unclear, as are the areas of government functioning in which civic engagement plays the greatest role. Research in this area is growing, but significant gaps remain. One of the most fundamental gaps is the lack of clear metrics and a methodology for measuring changes in civic engagement over time. The metrics currently in use—voter participation, feelings of political efficacy, and the representativeness of congressional votes—are not perfect, and data on participation in activism are inconsistent and do not provide the historical coverage needed for a rigorous assessment. Because political disaffection can manifest as general indifference, one possible approach is to consider how the number of "no opinion" or nonresponse answers on politically focused surveys changes over time. Another is to track voting for third-party candidates or the percentage of write-in votes, either of which might suggest general rejection of the existing political system. Identifying periods in the past when civic engagement has been low might offer insights into both root causes and possible solutions.

Additional work is also necessary to understand how civic engagement affects the functioning of a democracy, the quality of electoral and policy outcomes, and the political efficacy and satisfaction of citizens. There appears to be a relationship, but empirical work has not yet firmly established a connection. Research that builds an understanding

---

[57] iCivics, undated.

[58] Kraig Beyerlein and John R. Hipp, "From Pews to Participation: The Effect of Congregation Activity and Context on Bridging Civic Engagement," *Social Problems*, Vol. 53, No. 1, 2006.

[59] Theiss-Morse and Hibbing, 2005.

of the effects civic engagement has on democracy—and which types of civic engagement have the strongest and most-significant effects—is a high priority for future work.

Finally, research is needed to identify how to increase civic engagement most effectively. This requires a better understanding of the ways in which changes in the information system, polarization, and declining trust in institutions contribute to disaffection. Possible approaches to overcoming the loss of civic engagement associated with Truth Decay include tailored civics-focused education, changes to existing institutions to ensure that voters feel represented and empowered in their democracy, and (possibly) improvements in the way information is disseminated that would promote transparency and openness. The research agenda in Chapter Six proposes additional avenues for research into civic engagement.

## Uncertainty

### How Truth Decay Causes Policy Uncertainty

The final consequence of Truth Decay is uncertainty. There are many different types of uncertainty, but we focus in this section on policy uncertainty at the national and international levels. The Truth Decay trends that seem to increase policy uncertainty are the blurring of the line between opinion and fact and the decline in trust of formerly respected sources of information. When individuals, businesses, and even foreign actors do not trust information provided by the U.S. government, the news media, or other interest groups, and when information provided by these same sources consistently blur opinions, falsehoods, and facts, the resulting uncertainty can have significant implications for decisionmaking and for both state and individual behavior. At the international level, uncertainty about U.S. policies or commitment might lead adversarial states to aggressive moves that escalate to conflict, or it might cause allies to question U.S. commitments and act in ways that run counter to U.S. interests. At the national level, businesses may defer investments and forgo growth opportunities. In addition, Truth Decay works alongside one of its drivers, polarization, to further exacerbate policy uncertainty. When there is a lack of agreed-upon facts or analytical interpretations of data to drive policy decisions, policy decisions in areas as varied as health, finance, and foreign relations may be subject to reversals every time there is a change in administration or congressional leadership. These changes, the threat that they might occur, and an inability to predict when they might occur all contribute to policy uncertainty both domestically and for allies and partners.

### Assessing the Costs of Uncertainty at the National and International Levels

As we have noted, policy uncertainty can have serious consequences at the national and international levels. In this section, we discuss some of these consequences, which range from economic implications to the risk of international conflict. For example, policy uncertainty has been shown to have significant economic costs in the form of declines in business investment and production.[60] One study estimates that firms reduce their investment by about 4.8 percent in election years due to concerns about postelection economic policy changes.[61] In theory, this should not affect every year's investment decisions, but in an environment distorted by Truth Decay, in which policy uncertainty is increased by the blurring of the line between opinion and fact and by increasing amounts of disinformation, it is possible that these effects would extend over longer periods. There are also other economic effects. At the corporate level, these include increased stock price volatility and reduced employment in sectors related to areas of policy uncertainty (e.g., defense, health care, infrastructure); at the macro level, public investment, employment, and output can be affected.[62]

[60] Baker et al., 2014; Scott R. Baker, Nicholas Bloom, and Steven J. Davis, "Measuring Economic Policy Uncertainty," Cambridge, Mass.: National Bureau of Economic Research, NBER Working Paper 21633, October 2015.

[61] Brandon Julio and Youngsuk Yook, "Political Uncertainty and Corporate Investment Cycles," *Journal of Finance*, Vol. 67, No. 1, 2012.

[62] Baker, Bloom, and Davis, 2015.

Policy uncertainty can also affect the functioning and efficiency of government. For example, some researchers have found that policy uncertainty can increase bureaucracy: Different groups within the government protect their own interests by "stovepiping," or isolating their activities, acting on the fear that future policy changes could diminish the group's role or importance.[63] This, in turn, can slow political decisionmaking. Uncertainty can also hinder the political decisionmaking process more directly in highly complex areas where ambiguity about basic facts makes it difficult to choose among policy options. Slow and bureaucratic processes can have serious implications if they delay important social, economic, or foreign policy decisions. For instance, when confronted with a credible threat of an attack on the U.S. homeland, policymakers must be able to select a response nearly immediately. Uncertainty about information could impede this decisionmaking and thus compromise national security and readiness. The same could be said of a response to economic trends or events that is not based on data.

Uncertainty can negatively influence policy decisions in the domestic sphere as well. Decisions based on opinions, perceptions, or ideology rather than on facts—a situation that appears increasingly common in an environment of Truth Decay, even among policymakers—can lead to policies that have deleterious and unintended consequences. For example, an approach to climate change based on disinformation rather than scientific fact might risk either overreacting to a minor threat in a counterproductive way or ignoring a serious concern until it is too late.

Policy uncertainty that seems to derive, at least in part, from Truth Decay could also have diplomatic implications. Allies and adversaries that are uncertain about whether to trust prior policy positions taken by U.S. leaders, or that are unable to determine whether a commitment (or, in the case of an adversary, a threat) is authentic, could act in ways that run counter to U.S. interests. For example, an ally that lacks confidence in the strength of a U.S. commitment might turn to another partner for additional support, depriving the United States of a potentially important political or economic relationship. An adversary that

---

[63] Rui J. P. de Figueiredo, Jr., "Electoral Competition, Political Uncertainty, and Policy Insulation," *American Political Science Review*, Vol. 96, No. 2, 2002.

believes a prior U.S. position is not an accurate reflection of U.S. intent might challenge the United States and contribute to an escalation of hostilities. Such institutions as the North Atlantic Treaty Organization and the post–World War II alliance structure have reduced some of the uncertainty surrounding diplomatic commitments, but, in the first half of 20th century, there were no such guarantees, and uncertainty was considerably higher. Should Truth Decay contribute to an increase in this uncertainty, it is possible that the risk of unintentional escalation and even conflict would increase.

Finally, as alluded to previously, Truth Decay alongside polarization (one of its drivers) can further exacerbate policy uncertainty with additional domestic and international implications. Policies that are based not on shared and commonly accepted facts but on selective adoption and rejection of facts may be subject to rapid change and reversal when congressional leadership or the presidency changes hands or parties. Polarization exacerbates this tendency, as it increases the ideological distance between policymakers on each side of the spectrum and increases the chances of "policy whiplash" when legislative or executive power shifts from one party to the other. At the domestic level, rapid policy reversals may lead to any number of negative consequences, including financial loss for individuals or corporations, wasted resources at the government and individual level, and instability in economic, health care, or insurance markets that have direct implications for individual constituents. In addition, policy reversals may further undermine trust in key institutions. At the international level, policy reversals compromise U.S. credibility, can harm alliances and partnerships, and risk triggering escalation that may lead ultimately to full blown conflict.

## Managing Uncertainty at the National Level

A large body of research in business and psychology literature explores how to contend with, manage, plan for, and profit from existing uncertainty. However, none of this work truly addresses the challenges at the national or international level presented by uncertainty associated with Truth Decay. Overcoming the uncertainty associated with low trust and a proliferation of disinformation will be challenging. Research on ways to provide individuals and government decisionmakers with un-biased and objective information would be valuable. Some efforts along these lines are under way. For example, some social media companies are attempting to reduce the amount of false information disseminated on their platforms, and fact-checking organizations help identify false and misleading statements and assertions. As noted elsewhere, however, in many cases, objective facts are not sufficient to project a sense of certainty about a given piece of information. Furthermore, there is little ongoing research into ways to decrease uncertainty in diplomatic and international relations—and it is in this area where Truth Decay–related uncertainty may be most dangerous. Therefore, research on overcoming the effects of Truth Decay–related uncertainty must also consider the types of messages, platforms, and messengers that are needed to provide both domestic and international actors with objective facts in a way that makes them willing to accept and engage with these facts.

There are several other areas where additional research on the topic of uncertainty could be relevant. First, identifying and tracking additional measures of uncertainty could provide more-complete insight into how uncertainty has changed over time, in what ways and areas it has increased, and in what ways and areas it has not changed. For example, although public opinion data reveal perceptions of uncertainty, additional metrics could be useful, including more-systematic analysis of instances when leading political figures have drastically changed their positions, of instances when national policy has changed substantively, and of the extent of policy reversal or change following the handover of administration. Also valuable would be more-rigorous assessment of the different costs of uncertainty, whether economic, policy, or diplomatic. Although there are fairly good estimates of economic costs of uncertainty, assessments of the costs of uncertainty in terms of national security risks or damage to diplomatic partnerships are less robust. It would also be valuable to know which types of uncertainty are most damaging and to assess this damage in quantitative or other terms in a variety of realms, such as foreign policy, economics, and individual mental health. Finally, although the simple solution to uncertainty would be policy consistency, other policy or institutional interventions might be able to ameliorate and reduce uncertainty. Research to identify possible interventions and how they would work would be valuable. The research agenda in Chapter Six proposes additional avenues for study of uncertainty.

## Summary

The costs highlighted in this chapter underline the severity of the challenges posed by Truth Decay. It is likely that the trends we have identified will result in consequences beyond the ones examined in this report—consequences that will emerge as research in this area continues and the collective understanding of Truth Decay evolves. An in-depth focus on the four consequences mentioned here is important not only for the insight it provides into the ways Truth Decay might erode the institutions and foundations of American society but also because it can identify areas where policy responses could form a cornerstone to fighting Truth Decay. Additional research on these four areas would be valuable in identifying these responses. The discussion in this chapter provides some possible directions for this research. First, as noted elsewhere, targeted changes to government institutions and media organizations could incentivize compromise and transparency, either of which could restore trust and confidence in these institutions and even help clarify the distinction between opinion and fact. Second, there are areas where legislative responses, either to mandate forums for meaningful social discourse or to reduce policy uncertainty, could serve a valuable function in the fight against polarization and Truth Decay. Finally, the use of behavioral economics to identify ways to structure situations to encourage desired behaviors—such as civic engagement, participation in civil discourse, more easily updating prior beliefs, and giving more weight to objective facts—could also help ameliorate some of Truth Decay's most troubling characteristics and consequences. In each of these areas, however, additional research is needed. Chapter Six lays out a research agenda that can serve as a map to guide further exploration.

# CHAPTER SIX

# The Road to Solutions: A Research Agenda

This report has presented a definition of Truth Decay and offered examples—and, where possible, evidence—of ways in which Truth Decay appears to be affecting today's political arena and political discourse. It has discussed four apparent drivers of Truth Decay, explored possible causal mechanisms linking these drivers and Truth Decay, and described the research and evidence that suggest a connection between each driver and the four trends associated with Truth Decay. It has also identified four consequences that appear to be, at least in part, attributable to Truth Decay, investigated the costs associated with each, and suggested ways in which Truth Decay leads to these consequences.

Throughout, we have emphasized ways in which Truth Decay, its drivers, and consequences appear to be different from similar trends observed in recent decades, although we acknowledge that some components of Truth Decay are not entirely new. The historical analogues presented in Chapter Three highlight periods in U.S. history that have exhibited trends that bear some of the hallmarks of what we have defined as Truth Decay, as well as sharing some of its drivers. However, we have also aimed to show how these past periods differ from today.

As we have noted throughout this report, substantial further research is required in a number of important areas, both to better understand Truth Decay and to understand more fully how conditions are different from and similar to the past. We have suggested a need to mine historical and international analogues for lessons and comparisons; to gather more and more-rigorous empirical evidence about the extent to which Truth Decay is pervading today's society;

to explore (and, where possible, establish) causal mechanisms linking Truth Decay to its drivers and consequences; and to identify, test, and implement responses that can help address areas where Truth Decay's effects are most severe. The research and evidence presented in this report, although imperfect and incomplete, create a foundation on which to build.

We believe that taking action on this research agenda should be an immediate and high priority. As we note throughout this report, a healthy democracy requires a vibrant marketplace of ideas, with rigorous debate and discussion of key policy issues serving as a way to reach more-informed policy outcomes that protect individual rights while advancing security, prosperity, and the national interest. Without a common set of facts and general agreement about how to treat—and when to trust—analytical interpretations of those facts and data, it becomes increasingly difficult to have this type of meaningful debate. Under Truth Decay, competing narratives emerge, tribalism within the U.S. electorate increases, and political paralysis and dysfunction grow where there would ideally be a vibrant discourse on civic and political issues. In Chapter Four, we discussed the complexity of Truth Decay's drivers. In Chapter Five, we discussed some of the effects of Truth Decay on civil discourse, policymaking, civic engagement, and the international reputation and security of the United States. Truth Decay and the declining use of and respect for facts, data, and analysis in civic and political discourse have far-reaching implications in all areas of American public and political life and create many levels of risk: that democracy will be fundamentally weakened, that the electorate will be permanently divided, that U.S. political and civic institutions (including those responsible for governing) will become increasingly or completely irrelevant, and that the United States' position in the world order and even national security will be irreparably damaged. For all of these reasons, we believe that the challenges presented by Truth Decay are urgent and must be taken seriously and addressed immediately and comprehensively. The research agenda proposed in this chapter is a first step toward action, outlining a set of research priorities that aim to develop a better understanding of Truth Decay and to help individuals and organizations find actionable solutions that can address Truth Decay in the near and medium terms.

This chapter presents a research agenda that identifies research priorities. It aims to guide further study of Truth Decay, address some of the gaps in data, understanding, and knowledge highlighted in this report, and support the pursuit of solutions and responses. We describe four research streams and present research priorities and specific research questions in each:

1. historical and international analogues
2. data and trends
3. mechanisms and processes
4. solutions and responses.

We discuss how each stream would contribute to a deeper understanding of Truth Decay and aid the search for highly effective responses. It is worth noting that there can be overlap across research streams: Some questions might fit into more than one stream, and a single project might combine research questions from several streams, depending on its size and objectives. For example, a project focused on disinformation could look at trends in the amount of disinformation over time, reasons for increases and decreases in this volume, and ways to decrease or control the amount of disinformation proliferated by various sources. We conclude the chapter with a way ahead for pursuing this agenda. Importantly, this research agenda is meant to be flexible and responsive. As research progresses, new questions and focus areas might emerge. Thus, the agenda should be updated as needed to ensure currency and relevance.

## Research Stream 1: Historical and International Analogues

Through research stream 1, we propose a continuation of the work presented in Chapter Three, exploring in greater depth past manifestations of Truth Decay in the United States as well as current and past analogues in other countries. Research stream 1 aims to (1) identify similarities and differences, as well as lessons and insights, that can be gained from past experience and (2) to shed light on how Truth Decay as we have defined it might be new and different from the past. On this topic, additional insight into whether there has been declining agreement about facts and data—and analytical interpretations based on these data—in past periods, would be especially valuable because this seems to be a defining characteristic of the present era. Most importantly, research into how past Truth Decay–like episodes have ended could aid in identifying responses or policy levers that can be used to fight Truth Decay today. Chapter Three suggested initial areas for focus, including the roles played by economic prosperity and national unity (the opposite of cohesion), the function served by investigative journalism, and the extent to which society's concerns about objectivity and fact-based analysis swing like a pendulum, prompting a natural correction to Truth Decay–like events. Table 6.1 presents research priorities for this stream and samples of associated research questions. Here and elsewhere in this chapter, the questions we propose are not exhaustive; rather, we provide a sampling of the types of questions that need to be addressed within the research stream.

There are two research priorities within research stream 1. First, we propose continued exploration of analogues in U.S. history (research priority 1.A), including the three prior periods identified in this report but also others that could provide additional parallels and insights. Table 6.1 outlines possible research questions. Historical research would likely need to rely most heavily on archival research to deeply investigate evidence of the four trends that constitute Truth Decay. Second, we propose extending this analysis to international analogues (research priority 1.B). In both cases, the research questions are similar:

- Each potential analogue should be mined for similarities and differences in areas relevant to Truth Decay. This will help advance researchers' understanding of which aspects are new and which have clear historical precedents. The questions we propose will need to be made more specific. For instance, rather than focusing broadly on all similarities and differences, a researcher might

**Table 6.1**
**Research Priorities for Historical and International Analogues**

| Research Priority | Sample Research Questions |
| --- | --- |
| 1.A: Analogues in U.S. history | • What are the similarities and differences between past periods and today in areas relevant to Truth Decay? Are the trends observed today unique, or are they continuations of the past?<br>• If there are similarities with the past, what can we learn from them? If there are differences, what are their implications?<br>• How do today's levels of polarization, challenges in the information system, and the state of civics education compare with the past?<br>• How do today's levels of political paralysis, civil discourse, alienation, and uncertainty compare with the past?<br>• How did these prior periods end? What were the most important factors? What insights can inform a response today? |
| 1.B: International analogues | • What are the similarities and differences between international analogues and those of the United States in areas relevant to Truth Decay?<br>• Are the key drivers in international analogues similar to or different from the drivers of Truth Decay in the United States? The consequences?<br>• What lessons can be learned from these international analogues? |

focus specifically on declining trust in institutions, or on the increasing disagreement about facts and analytical interpretations of those facts, data, or analysis, and researchers could explore how the current manifestation of this trend differs from the past (and why).

• Each potential analogue should be evaluated to determine whether the key drivers and consequences are similar to or different from those of today's Truth Decay in the United States. Differences could point to additional factors that should be explored. Answers to these questions could help researchers understand the ways in which Truth Decay is new and ways in which it may be a continuation of the past. In the case of historical examples, this might include a focused analysis of changes in polarization over time that addresses remaining questions in existing work and explores how this factor contributes to Truth Decay.

• Each potential analogue should be mined for key insights and lessons than could be extended to today. Areas for exploration include assessing why past manifestations of Truth Decay–like phenomena ended and understanding ways that the unique characteristics or dynamics of today's Truth Decay can be used to motivate solutions. This final question is essential if researchers are to learn from previous experience and use these experiences to hasten the end of today's Truth Decay.

## Research Stream 2: Data and Trends

Through research stream 2, we propose a focus on identifying, collecting, and assessing metrics on each aspect of Truth Decay. This will allow researchers to better identify and document areas where Truth Decay is most severe, to chart phases in the emergence of today's Truth Decay, and to demonstrate more clearly and rigorously the ways in which Truth Decay is a unique phenomenon that is different from the past. We have noted elsewhere that it will be difficult to define and quantify certain measures of Truth Decay's trends, drivers, and consequences. However, we have tried to identify possible directions and specific types of data that might make this task more achievable.

First, better evidence on the four trends that define Truth Decay itself will facilitate a better determination of the extent to which Truth Decay has affected the U.S. political arena and discourse. A number of specific metrics of interest are identified in Chapter Two. These metrics could also help researchers understand which elements of Truth Decay are new and which are not. Second, better information on such phenomena as the speed of information flow, the amount of information available, and the extent to which polarization has changed over time will help researchers identify the key drivers and consequences of Truth Decay and develop a more complete assessment of its extent and the ways in which it is (or is not) an unfolding process. Research produced as part research stream 2 could help focus attention on those drivers and consequences that seem the most dynamic and influential and that have resulted in the most-meaningful or most-important changes over

time. Finally, better data in such areas as the costs of political stalemate, combined with more-precise ways to measure the costs of declining civil discourse, will provide insight into the effects of Truth Decay
and the damage it inflicts on American democracy, political efficacy,
and national security.

As this report has noted, there are areas, such as political polarization and trust in institutions, where there is already a great deal of
information on trends over time, while other areas are less documented.
Table 6.2 outlines key priorities in research stream 2, focusing on those
areas where good data are lacking. The challenge in many of these
cases is that good metrics could be difficult to identify and data could
be hard to collect. Nonetheless, Table 6.2 supplies associated sample
research questions in these areas to stimulate thinking and innovation
about how these challenges might be overcome. Once again, some of
these questions are too broad to become research questions without
additional refinement. We provide more-specific thoughts in the next
several paragraphs.

**Table 6.2**
**Research Priorities for Data and Trends**

| Research Priority | Sample Research Questions |
|---|---|
| 2.A: Truth Decay and its trends | • In which areas has agreement about facts and analytical interpretations of those facts decreased? Where does agreement remain? What drives this decrease when it occurs?<br>• What are the costs associated with the increase in disagreement about facts?<br>• In what ways and in which substantive areas have opinion and fact become blurred?<br>• How has people's ability to distinguish opinion and fact changed over time? How have changes in the information system contributed to that?<br>• How has the use of facts and fact-based analysis evolved in various forms of media and communication?<br>• In which areas is Truth Decay most severe?<br>• Which aspects of Truth Decay are new? Which are not? |
| 2.B: The spread of information | • What would a "map" of the information system look like? What are the different types of information, audiences, senders, and intents (e.g., disinformation, misinformation)?<br>• How has the volume of information generally and disinformation in particular changed over time?<br>• How has the speed of information flow changed over time? |

**Table 6.2—Continued**

| Research Priority | Sample Research Questions |
|---|---|
| 2.C: Changes in the media industry | • How has the number of sources changed over time? Are there more now than in the past?<br>• How has the proportion of opinion and fact in various forms of media coverage changed over time? The content of coverage?<br>• How has the accuracy of news coverage changed over time?<br>• How have the economics of media changed? How have these changes affected Truth Decay? |
| 2.D: Polarization and political stalemate | • Beyond metrics that already exist, how can changes in demographic and social polarization over time be assessed? What do these trends reveal?<br>• What are the diplomatic and foreign policy costs of political stalemate?<br>• What are the costs associated with lost credibility domestically and internationally due to political stalemate? |
| 2.E: Civil discourse and civic engagement | • How have the quality and quantity of civil discourse and civic engagement changed over time?<br>• How have attitudes toward civil discourse and civic engagement changed over time?<br>• How can the costs of a decline in civil discourse and civic engagement be measured? What do these trends reveal?<br>• What are the costs of declining civil discourse and civic engagement for the quality of government? In other areas? |
| 2.F: Educational opportunities | • How have the quality and quantity of civics education in schools, colleges, and universities changed over time?<br>• How have the quality and quantity of civics education outreach for adults changed over time?<br>• How have the quality and quantity of training in critical thinking changed over time?<br>• How do the quality and quantity of civics education and of training in critical thinking vary across states? Across different demographic groups? Across types of schools (e.g., public, private)?<br>• How have the critical-thinking skills of students changed over time?<br>• How have youth and adult political awareness and media literacy changed over time? |
| 2.G: Uncertainty | • How has policy uncertainty changed over time?<br>• What are the diplomatic and foreign policy costs of policy uncertainty?<br>• What are the costs associated with lost credibility domestically and internationally due to policy uncertainty?<br>• Which types of uncertainty cause the most-significant damage? |

We identified seven research priorities in research stream 2 and supply a number of sample research questions in each. The questions fall into two key areas:

- Some questions focus on trends over time. These questions are intended to identify ways in which key drivers and consequences have evolved so as to better understand the emergence and spread of Truth Decay and identify which aspects of Truth Decay are truly new and which are more consistent with past levels or trends.
- Other questions focus on the costs imposed by specific elements of Truth Decay. As discussed at length in Chapter Five, the reason for digging into the costs of Truth Decay is to better describe its negative effects on society and to develop a better understanding of consequences and costs that could point to possible responses.

The seven research priorities emerge from aspects of our Truth Decay framework where good data and a clear understanding of historical trends are missing. Those that would benefit most from research on data and trends are research priorities 2.A (Truth Decay and its trends), 2.B (the spread of information), 2.C (changes in the media industry), 2.D (polarization and political stalemate), and 2.E (civil discourse and civic engagement). As we have noted elsewhere, the first step in any research agenda on Truth Decay is to gather and assess more-rigorous data on the phenomenon we have defined as Truth Decay (research priority 2.A: Truth Decay and its trends). This includes identifying areas where agreement about facts has decreased and measuring the extent of any change; identifying obvious examples of areas where the line between opinion and fact has been blurred; assessing how the relative volume of opinion and anecdote has changed in relation to the volume of facts disseminated through various forms of media and communication; and more extensively analyzing data on declining trust in institutions. Some of these metrics will be difficult to collect and assess, but content coding using language-processing tools might prove useful for approaching several of these areas. For instance, coding and analysis of the tone or of types of words used in newspapers or broadcast news might facilitate an assessment of how news content has changed over time and how the mix of opinion and fact have changed. Such analysis could also be used on social media platforms to study the formation and perpetuation of echo chambers and to evaluate how the quality and quantity of civil discourse and civic engagement conducted on social media platforms have changed and evolved.[1] In each of these areas, it could prove necessary to focus on specific topics as a starting point. We suggest an initial focus on areas that have the most-direct effects on people's lives, such as health care, crime, and personal finance.

Research priority 2.B (the spread of information) is important because of the scope of changes in the information system. Although further research is needed to confirm this hypothesis, the extent of changes in the information system could be one aspect of the current manifestation of Truth Decay that is distinct from prior periods. It could also be an area in which solutions and responses to Truth Decay prove relevant. With additional data concerning how the information system has changed (including the volume and speed of information flow; the amount of disinformation; and the quality, content, and quantity of different types of media coverage), researchers could better diagnose which aspects of the media environment contribute the most to Truth Decay, which are most in need of additional resources or analysis, and which are being unfairly blamed for contributing to the problem. A 2001 study that assessed the quality of health information online might offer a reasonable framework for conducting a more holistic review of the quality of online information.[2] Evaluating the volume of information transmitted by the current information system and the amount of disinformation that flows through it would be more complicated. However, it might be possible to build on usage and traffic data already collected by media organizations, social media platforms, and

---

[1]   For a similar study, see Elizabeth Bodine-Baron, Todd Helmus, Madeline Magnuson, and Zev Winkelman, *Examining ISIS Support and Opposition Networks on Twitter*, Santa Monica, Calif.: RAND Corporation, RR-1328-RC, 2016.

[2]   Gretchen K. Berland, Marc N. Elliott, Leo S. Morales, Jeffrey I. Algazy, Richard L. Kravitz, Michael S. Broder, David E. Kanouse, Jorge A. Munoz, Juan-Antonio Puyol, Marielena Lara, Katherine E. Watkins, Hannah Yang, and Elizabeth A. McGlynn, "Health Information on the Internet: Accessibility, Quality, and Readability in English and Spanish," *Journal of the American Medical Association*, Vol. 285, No. 20, 2001.

search engines to establish a reasonable estimate of how much information each organization believes passes through its portal, site, or platform on any given day. The search for measures of disinformation might
need to rely on automated tools or some analogue, akin to some of the
fact-checking and verification tools discussed earlier in this report. This
research priority would also collect and analyze what evidence exists to
support the perception that disinformation has increased in volume or
that the amount of opinion disseminated through media sources has
increased so significantly that facts are being overwhelmed.

Research priority 2.C (changes in the media industry) focuses on
measuring and analyzing the ways in which the form and content of
media have changed over time. While it seems that the amount of disinformation and misinformation available has increased, empirical evidence to support such an assessment is limited. Research in support of
this priority would focus on identifying appropriate metrics that can be
used to study trends such as the blurring of the line between fact and
opinion, the ways in which media content and tone have changed over
time, and the accuracy of news coverage across media formats in the past
and today. A more precise and data-backed assessment of these trends
will allow researchers and journalists to better understand the ways in
which Truth Decay has affected the media industry and develop solutions to address related challenges. Textual analysis software will provide
a powerful tool in this research, able to inductively capture changes in
tone and content and to deductively explore specific hypotheses or types
of media in more depth.[3] Work is already under way in this particular
area, with researchers working on improving the application of textual
analysis to both conventional media and social media to provide a richer
picture of how the form and content of media have evolved over time
and to study how changes in media content are linked with political and
social change.[4] Natural language processing and textual analysis are also

---

[3]  See, for example, Doug Irving, "Big Data, Big Questions," RAND Blog, October 16,
2017.

[4]  Philip N. Howard and Malcolm R. Parks, "Social Media and Political Change: Capacity,
Constraint, and Consequence," *Journal of Communication*, Vol. 6, No. 2, 2012.

being used to separate fact from fiction in digital news.[5] Research on this priority might also consider collecting data on how the media market has changed from a business perspective, in terms of consolidation and competition. Better data in this area would facilitate analysis of how the economics of the media industry play a role in Truth Decay, an important but sometimes underestimated relationship.[6] The challenge in this particular research priority will be the development of metrics that can serve as good approximations but can also realistically be collected.

Additional work in research priority 2.D (polarization and political stalemate) will be valuable. Data on polarization and some of the costs of political stalemate are already fairly robust. However, additional analysis of existing data and the collection of additional metrics might be valuable in several areas. First, most measures of polarization focus on political polarization. However, as we have noted, demographic and social polarization are equally important. The development, collection, and analysis of new measures of these other types of polarization would be valuable. Second, further assessment of the costs of political stalemate, particularly those that do not have easy economic proxies, is needed. Young et al. provided both a first step and a clear outline for additional work in this vein.[7] This includes an assessment of the diplomatic and foreign policy costs of political paralysis and of the costs that result from a loss of domestic or international credibility when the government is unable to make decisions and pass legislation. Similar approaches could be used to quantify the cost of political paralysis in the foreign policy realm by looking at how trade has been affected by delays in foreign policy decisionmaking or how diplomatic tension has emerged as the result of domestic political paralysis. Like the changes in the information system, polarization is at the heart of Truth Decay,

---

[5]   William Yang Wang, "'Liar, Liar Pants on Fire': A New Benchmark Dataset for Fake News Detection," *Proceedings of the 55th Annual Meeting of the Association for Computational Linguistics*, Vancouver, July 30–August 4, 2017.

[6]   See, for example, Eli Noam, *Media Ownership and Concentration in America*, New York: Oxford University Press, 2009; Ryland Sherman and David Waterman, "Technology and Competition in U.S. Television: Online vs. Offline," working chapter, September 21, 2013.

[7]   Unpublished research by Young et al., 2016.

and understanding its extent, manifestations, and costs will be important in the search for solutions.

Research priority 2.E (civil discourse and civic engagement) appears on this list for two reasons: There is a shortage of data on discourse and engagement, and this area holds potential for responses to Truth Decay. Better data on the levels and quality of civic engagement and civil discourse could point to opportunities for improvement while also identifying what is already working and where discourse and engagement are already thriving. Examples include defining metrics and collecting data on different types of online engagement (e.g., blogs, online petitions or discussions, and even politically oriented social media posts) as well as potentially using the same text-analysis tools already discussed to evaluate the quality and tone of discourse on various social media platforms and between different communities on those platforms. Similar tools could be used to evaluate discourse and engagement in the nonvirtual world as well. This might include assessing the quality and tone of discourse at town hall meetings across various states (possibly for a comparison across states) or during congressional debates. Although it would likely be impossible to get historical transcripts of town hall meetings, transcripts of congressional debates are public and thus could provide a historical record of the ways in which civil discourse and the willingness to debate and discuss have evolved—or stayed the same—over time. This information could guide and direct future efforts to increase civic engagement and to encourage or promote civil discourse and the skills it requires.

Research into research priority 2.F (educational opportunities) should also yield data valuable to informing an investigation of Truth Decay. In the area of educational opportunities, more-accurate and more-recent data on the prevalence and content of civics education courses nationwide could provide insight into how access to civics courses varies across states, demographic groups, types of schools, and levels of education. Information on how the training offered today differs from that supplied in the past will enable a better understanding of the extent to which civics training has declined in either quality or quantity. Better information on how schools currently teach higher-level critical-thinking skills and assessments of student performance on this dimension will be similarly important to the study of how both characteristics of the educational system and changes in the information system might contribute to Truth Decay. Areas of particular interest include data on instruction in science and statistics, two courses that provide a good vehicle for the delivery of training in critical thinking and that might also address other aspects of Truth Decay. Finally, although it will be difficult to collect the necessary data retrospectively, data on media literacy and political awareness among today's students and young adults could help researchers identify areas where students seem particularly unprepared or uninformed. Once identified, these areas might suggest points of focus for responses. Work in this particular area can build on existing education research and evaluations, of which there are many. In 2017, for example, RAND researchers evaluated the benefits of personalized learning programs, collecting data on teaching strategies, practices, challenges, and outcomes to offer a holistic assessment of how these programs affect student achievement, time use, and teacher efficacy. The researchers were able to use these data and analyses to offer suggestions about increasing the use and improving the efficacy of personalized learning curricula.[8] A similar model, tailored to this specific topic area and with outcome measures more directly relevant to the topic of media literacy (e.g., ability to evaluate sources, the ability to identify false information) could be promising.

Finally, research priority 2.G (uncertainty) focuses on gathering data that will allow researchers, policymakers, and other parties to better understand not only how uncertainty at the national level has changed over time, but to estimate the costs of uncertainty in national policy more precisely. This should include not only economic costs to businesses but also the costs in terms of compromised national security and damage to alliances and international reputation. A more precise accounting of these costs and their far-reaching impacts may better inform the development of targeted responses that address uncertainty in specific areas of national policy where the damage of continued

---

[8] John F. Pane, Elizabeth D. Steiner, Matthew D. Baird, Laura S. Hamilton, and Joseph D. Pane, *Informing Progress: Insights on Personalized Learning Implementation and Effects*, Santa Monica, Calif.: RAND Corporation, RR-2042-BMGF, 2017.

uncertainty is likely to be highest. These costs will be difficult to measure. Research in this area can start by building off an already strong body of political science literature into the effects of uncertainty on international conflict[9] and research focused on quantifying the reputational effects that leaders and countries face when reneging on a commitment, starting a war, or violating a norm.[10] While the substantive findings of this work will be of interest, the approaches researchers in this area take to measuring the costs of uncertainty and the value of reputation and credibility may be most relevant to an assessment of uncertainty and Truth Decay.

## Research Stream 3: Mechanisms and Processes

Research stream 3 lies at the core of understanding Truth Decay and focuses on the dynamics of each element of Truth Decay as well as Truth Decay as a system. These questions are essential because they will help researchers unpack the elements of Truth Decay, its drivers, and its consequences. By understanding how each process works, the research community can begin to devise solutions and responses to address the ills and distortions of Truth Decay.

In addition to helping researchers understand the mechanisms within each driver or consequence, work in research stream 3 will investigate relationships among the drivers (e.g., how cognitive bias affects polarization) and among the consequences (e.g., how political paralysis contributes to uncertainty). It will also consider relationships between

---

[9]  See, for example, Adam Meirowitz and Anne E. Sartori, "Strategic Uncertainty as a Cause of War," *Quarterly Journal of Political Science*, Vol. 3, No. 4, 2008; and James D. Morrow, "Capabilities, Uncertainty, and Resolve: A Limited Information Model of Crisis Bargaining," *American Journal of Political Science*, Vol. 33, No. 4, November 1989.

[10]  See, for example, Allan Dafoe and Devin Caughey, "Honor and War: Southern US Presidents and the Effects of Concern for Reputation," *World Politics*, Vol. 68, No. 2, 2016; Joshua D. Kertzer and Ryan Brutger, "Decomposing Audience Costs: Bringing the Audience Back into Audience Cost Theory," *American Journal of Political Science*, Vol. 60, No. 1, 2016; James D. Morrow, "Alliances, Credibility, and Peacetime Costs," *Journal of Conflict Resolution*, Vol. 38, No. 2, 1994; and Jack Snyder and Erica D. Borghard, "The Cost of Empty Threats: A Penny, Not a Pound," *American Political Science Review*, Vol. 105, No. 3, 2011.

drivers and consequences, such as how polarization and changes in the information system affect civil discourse and political alienation. Assessing the direction of causality between Truth Decay and each of the drivers will also be important because that will help build an understanding of how Truth Decay feeds each driver even as each driver contributes to Truth Decay. Finally, this research stream includes an examination of the question of agency. Table 6.3 presents research priorities for this stream and supplies sample associated research questions, once again focusing on areas where significant gaps exist and where additional research would provide the most impact.

Research priority 3.A (information dissemination, processing, and consumption) concerns questions related to reducing cognitive bias and some aspects of changes in the information system, such as the dissemination and consumption of disinformation and the relationship between media and its audience. Much of Truth Decay concerns information—how it is shared, how opinion and fact are increasingly comingled, and how media framing and disinformation affect attitudes and decisions. This research priority is intended to cover these aspects of Truth Decay. Network analysis might be useful here to study how information travels through a network and changes over time. This might allow for the identification of key nodes or individuals who play a role in the spread of this information. Content analysis that assesses both tone and specific themes might be valuable, as might work that identifies ways in which cognitive biases can be reduced outside of the laboratory setting. Also included in this research area is the issue of cognitive biases, how they work, and how they can be reduced, especially in areas involving the analysis and interpretation of facts and data. Work currently under way through the Annenberg Policy Center could be a starting point for additional research in this area. Specifically, the Annenberg Policy Center's project on the "Science of Science Communication" is exploring how scientific findings can be conveyed to the general public in a way that is both more understandable and more persuasive, with the aim of closing the gap between scientific knowledge and research findings and public beliefs on such issues as the safety of vaccines and GMOs.[11]

---

[11] Annenberg Public Policy Center, "Science of Science Communication," webpage, undated.

**Table 6.3**
**Research Priorities for Mechanisms and Processes**

| Research Priority | Sample Research Questions |
|---|---|
| 3.A: Information dissemination, processing, and consumption | • Under what conditions and in which areas can cognitive biases be reduced? Which messengers or media types are most effective?<br>• Under what conditions are people most susceptible to disinformation? Can they be "inoculated" against it with prior warning or training?<br>• How is information most effectively weaponized? Which actors are most likely to accomplish this? Which types of media are most likely to be affected?<br>• How does partisanship in media organizations affect viewer beliefs and decisions? Do viewer beliefs drive media partisanship?<br>• How does the current information system heighten the impact of cognitive biases?<br>• Can the costs a person incurs when he or she updates prior beliefs (e.g., damage to personal beliefs, loss of social network) be measured? If so, can the incentive structure be changed so that people are more willing to consider changing their minds?<br>• How do characteristics of the internet or social media exacerbate cognitive bias and Truth Decay? |
| 3.B: Institutions, authorities, and intermediaries | • Why has trust in institutions declined so severely? Why have some institutions been able to retain public confidence?<br>• What are the challenges and benefits associated with the loss of information mediators or gatekeepers?<br>• What is the role of political, social, and other institutions in the problem of Truth Decay? In its solutions?<br>• If Truth Decay continues unchecked, what are the implications for the educational system? For political institutions? For the media industry? |
| 3.C: Polarization, engagement, and discourse | • How are political, social, economic, and demographic polarization interrelated? Can they be solved independently, or must they be solved together?<br>• How do polarization and political stalemate contribute to declining trust in institutions? To declining civic engagement and civil discourse?<br>• What are the most-important drivers of polarization? Are they institutional? Ideological? Legislative?<br>• Is the United States more polarized now than ever before? What evidence supports either answer?<br>• How has uncertainty fed polarization? How has polarization fed uncertainty?<br>• How have changes in the information system affected polarization?<br>• In what ways has increasing uncertainty contributed to the decline in civil discourse and civic engagement?<br>• How are competing demands on the educational system contributing to the decline in civil discourse and civic engagement?<br>• How might a decline in civil discourse and civic engagement or an increase in polarization (or all three) affect the quality of American democracy?<br>• What factors drive feelings of political alienation? |

**Table 6.3—Continued**

| Research Priority | Sample Research Questions |
|---|---|
| 3.D: The benefits and challenges of technological advancement | • In what ways have social media platforms contributed to a decline in trust in institutions? The increasing disagreement about facts?<br>• In what ways can increased speed and access to information serve as a check on false information?<br>• How does online activity change the nature of civil discourse and civic engagement? What are the benefits and costs to democracy?<br>• How does technological change affect the nature of the media industry? What does this mean for Truth Decay?<br>• How does technological change affect democracy? What does this mean for Truth Decay?<br>• How have technological advances enabled the spread and power of disinformation? |
| 3.E: Agency | • How do media corporations intentionally and unintentionally accelerate Truth Decay? How do they exploit other drivers? With what consequences?<br>• How do governments and political actors intentionally and unintentionally accelerate Truth Decay? What are the consequences for policymaking?<br>• How do academia and research organizations intentionally and unintentionally contribute to Truth Decay? How do norms and standards in these areas prevent or allow this?<br>• How do foreign actors intentionally and unintentionally accelerate Truth Decay? How do they exploit other drivers? Which foreign actors pose the greatest threat?<br>• Which agents appear to play the largest or the smallest roles? Which have short-term effects? Which have longer-term effects?<br>• What is the balance between intentional and unintentional agents of Truth Decay? What does this mean for the search for responses? |
| 3.F: Truth Decay as a system | • In what ways are the different drivers of Truth Decay interrelated? How do they feed into each other and into Truth Decay?<br>• In what ways are the different consequences of Truth Decay interrelated? How do they feed into each other and into Truth Decay?<br>• What symbiotic relationships exist between Truth Decay and its drivers and consequences? In what ways does Truth Decay worsen or affect its drivers? |

Research priority 3.B (institutions, authorities, and intermediaries) considers such aspects of Truth Decay as the decline in trust in institutions; the loss of trusted sources of information in the area of information; the role of institutions and intermediaries in Truth Decay more generally; and the ways in which Truth Decay can distort or harm U.S. political institutions, educational systems, or media infrastructure. As noted throughout this report, the decline in trust in institutions is a defining aspect of Truth Decay, and so is the fact that access to information and the ability to be a source of information have become so completely democratized. Research in this area might explore ways in which the institutional structures that constitute the U.S. government or media market create the conditions that allow Truth Decay to prosper. It might also identify characteristics of political or media institutions that could serve as checks on Truth Decay, or focus on how Truth Decay undermines each set of institutions.

Research priority 3.C (polarization, engagement, and discourse) explores not only the dynamics within each of these three elements but also the relationships among polarization, political stalemate, civil discourse, and civic engagement. This research area continues the emphasis this report has placed on both the key role that polarization in its many forms plays in driving Truth Decay and the central place of engagement and discourse in its solution. Understanding the causes of disengagement, how disengagement manifests itself in political or other behaviors—or in more-fundamental areas, such as physical or mental health—and the role played by the erosion of civil discourse might help identify possible policy actions that could reverse these trends. Similarly, an intimate understanding of polarization and its many forms and drivers can support the development of responses, whether institutional, legal, or social, to help overcome it. Work focused on teasing out the causes of social and demographic polarization—possibly using new mapping software or other technologies to track migration patterns within the United States or social surveys to understand individual decisions to relocate—would be particularly valuable. Also needed are studies of the true extent of changes in polarization at the level of the electorate, an area where there is still extensive disagreement about how to interpret recent trends.

Research priority 3.D (the benefits and challenges of technological advancement) concerns changes in the information system, such as the rise of social media, the dominance of the internet, and the development of sophisticated filters and algorithms that have changed the nature of communication, the prevalence of and access to information, the ways in which people participate in democracy, and the methods and forums used for education. All of these changes play a role in Truth Decay and all are also affected positively and negatively by Truth Decay. For this reason, it is important to develop a more detailed understanding of these changes, focusing not only on the challenges that such changes create but also on the opportunities presented for responses to Truth Decay. There is already much work focused on questions related to the development of filters and algorithms and the role played by artificial intelligence, but much of it has focused on practical applications, such as self-driving cars. Additional attention to the ways in which these emerging technologies can both contribute to and check Truth Decay would be valuable. Rigorous research on how a shift toward online political activism and engagement affects the quality and durability of democracy is also lacking, even as changes in the information system and the political sphere seem to be moving activism and engagement in this direction. Understanding this relationship and its implications for such factors as trust in institutions, the erosion of civil discourse, and even the blurring of the line between opinion and fact will be important both for developing a fuller understanding of Truth Decay and for assessing how changes in the information system might change civic participation and even the definition of citizenship.

Research priority 3.E (agency) focuses explicitly on questions related to agency and the entities, organizations, and institutions that intentionally and unintentionally accelerate Truth Decay. A primary focus of this research area is to identify and understand actors that are explicitly exacerbating Truth Decay to advance political, economic, or other goals. The aim of this research is to subsequently identify ways that these actors can be dissuaded or prevented from contributing to associated challenges. A secondary focus should be to explore the extent to which Truth Decay is caused by changes and conditions (*drivers*, in our terminology) or by intentional agents who exploit those changes and conditions. The answer to this question might have implications for the search for responses—particularly in terms of where to look. Some of the research in this area may overlap with that of research priority 3.B, which focuses on institutions. Although institutions might prove relevant, they need not be the focus here. Studies that consider which types of media contribute most directly to Truth Decay by looking at the volume of disinformation or misinformation, and studies that explore the primary factors that drive skepticism about science and research findings (through a survey or interactive web application, for example), would also fit in this research area. Other research might focus explicitly on identifying the pathways that foreign actors can use to exploit Truth Decay, assessing different actors' abilities to do so, and designing defenses to counter such attempts.

Research priority 3.F (Truth Decay as a system) focuses primarily on the feedback mechanisms between drivers, consequences, and Truth Decay as a phenomenon. As noted throughout this report, Truth Decay is conceptualized as a multifaceted problem with many interconnected pieces. Truth Decay is shaped by its drivers, but it might also affect those same drivers in a symbiotic feedback relationship. This research area seeks to explore and assess these bidirectional relationships to understand the relative importance of different factors and how each can affect the others. Any solution or response that targets one piece of the system could have a ripple effect on other pieces of the system. This research area is intended to ensure that those ripple effects are identified and fully understood, both to prevent unintended consequences and to make use of synergies where possible. Work in this area will necessarily combine qualitative with quantitative analyses, including possibly statistics, network analysis, content analysis, and process tracing. Research that is able to blend these methods will likely be most successful at further exploring the Truth Decay system and for understanding how various feedback mechanisms contribute to Truth Decay and might be harnessed to identify solutions. Relationships of greatest interests might be those between Truth Decay and its drivers (which might operate in both directions) as well as those between agents of Truth Decay, its drivers, and its constituent trends.

## Research Stream 4: Solutions and Responses

Projects investigating questions in research streams 1–3 will likely consider or suggest possible responses, but work in research stream 4 focuses explicitly on identifying solutions and responses to Truth Decay. In many ways, it is difficult to define an agenda for studying solutions and responses without completing at least some of the projects identified in the first three research streams. It will be important to gather evidence on Truth Decay, its drivers, and its consequences; understand causal mechanisms; and better understand historical analogues when identifying research questions that can lead to responses. Insights derived from the first three research streams will allow researchers to focus their search for solutions in areas where Truth Decay is most severe, that seem the newest or most dynamic, and where solutions and responses seem most likely to have a significant impact.

However, research and evidence discussed and presented in this report already suggest some possible paths and directions where additional research might be valuable. For example, there is hope in the finding, previously cited, that polarization among those who use social media seems to increase the least among those who use it most.[12] This suggests that simply being exposed to diverse ideas through social media, even if one chooses not to engage with those ideas, can reduce polarization. Social media is decried for its negative consequences and the ways in which it appears to feed Truth Decay. But there could be ways to control its harmful aspects and harness its productive ones, including its apparent ability to increase and support political engagement. In theory, democratized access to information should be beneficial for democracy and should foster a wider and more efficient marketplace of ideas, but it will be valuable to consider ways to ensure access while also constraining the flow of disinformation. Research into the tools that allow people to choose what news and information they see could reveal ways to encourage greater exposure to different media sources. Here, education may be a powerful tool, used to teach youths *and adults* what it means to engage with and analyze information rather than just accept it. The ways in

---

[12] Boxell, Gentzkow, and Shapiro, 2017.

which social media or education can be used as responses to Truth Decay should be areas for further exploration.

The significant roles that polarization and loss of trust in institutions appear to play in Truth Decay could also be important. Further research into both ideas would be valuable and seems necessary. Reducing polarization will be difficult, but it is not impossible. As noted earlier, research that has convened diverse groups with opposing views can help overcome intergroup divides.[13] Programs that encourage the development of crosscutting social organizations at the local level could be one way to reduce polarization. Policies that target economic inequality might be another. The solution to polarization at the political level seems more difficult. One avenue where additional research might be valuable is the role of institutional changes. Changes in the way primaries are organized, for example, might allow political parties and elected officials to better represent the preferences of the electorate and could help address some of the distortions of the political system we have described, such as the significant roles played by certain donors.

Another area worth additional research as a response to Truth Decay is how a reconfiguration of major media organizations and a change in the way they provide information might address some of Truth Decay's drivers. One alternative that deserves serious consideration is a system in which philanthropic organizations fund media outlets, thus removing some of the profit motive and competition that feed bias, partisanship, and a shift from objective fact to commentary. This is largely the function that the Public Broadcasting Service and National Public Radio are intended to serve, but even these sources have not been able to avoid charges of bias. It is possible that public funding and private donations could increase the value placed on facts in the current media environment in other ways. For example, this funding could go toward editors and ombudsmen charged with supporting and promoting the use of facts and sounding the alarm when standards appear to have been violated. Another option is to use donations or public money to support long-form and investigative journalism, which often relies more heavily on facts than does daily news

---

[13] See, for example, Pettigrew, 1997; Pettigrew and Tropp, 2006.

coverage (in print or on television). Additional research into whether such a system would have the intended outcome, how it would work, and how it would be implemented is needed before firm recommendations can be made. It does seem, however, that implementing changes that can address some of the challenges present in the existing media landscape will take a truly bipartisan effort of individuals willing to work not for either party or for any political agenda but for the cause of objectivity, facts, and evidence and their fundamental importance. As it stands, this seems like a fanciful goal. But pieces of this vision could lead to smaller changes that move incrementally toward a better media environment.

Table 6.4 outlines research priorities and research questions focused in six main areas. Again, this is a starting point that should be updated and revised based on insights gained from the first three streams as well as initial work in this one.

As noted earlier, each of these research priorities emerges from observations and insights that flow from research and evidence presented in this report. Projects in this research stream will not simply explore possible interventions but also pilot-test them and evaluate outcomes, where possible. For example, research priority 4.A (educational interventions) will consider the many ways in which educational programs in schools (K–12 schools, colleges, and universities) and outreach programs at the local level might be able to address certain drivers and consequences of Truth Decay: The decline in civic education and civil discourse, low political awareness and engagement, and even polarization, for example, could be areas where targeted education programs could be effective. Importantly, research on educational interventions should consider not only those targeted at young people in traditional educational settings but also those aimed at adults, such as through civic centers or programs offered at local YMCAs—as well as the possible use of community engagement activities. As we noted earlier, there are already a number of efforts in this area, focused mainly on media and civic literacy. Future work should concentrate on evaluating these efforts and considering ways to scale them so that they can reach more students. Another approach is to explore ways in which computer-based adaptive learning programs might be used to advance the current state of civics education, media literacy, and

**Table 6.4**
**Research Priorities for Solutions and Responses**

| Research Priority | Sample Research Questions |
|---|---|
| 4.A: Educational interventions | • What sorts of community outreach programs might increase political engagement and awareness in local communities?<br>• What channels exist for providing media literacy or civics education to adults?<br>• How can civics education and training in critical thinking be provided more effectively in schools, colleges, and universities? How can these programs be scaled to reach a wider audience?<br>• How can media literacy and civic principles be integrated into existing courses in high school and college?<br>• How can we train engaged citizens for the 21st century?<br>• What types of community engagement activities could be used to teach the importance of objective facts, the value of civic participation, and the skills needed to critically evaluate information? |
| 4.B: Improving the information market | • How can the standards of journalistic quality be restored and institutionalized across media platforms?<br>• What policy or legal interventions might slow the flow of disinformation? What technological innovations might help in this goal?<br>• What alternative funding models for the media industry might reduce bias? What other structural or legislative changes might accomplish this goal?<br>• How can the high level of access to information Americans have now be maintained while also restoring some of the benefits that come from having only credible sources proliferating information?<br>• How can the United States prevent and dissuade adversaries from using disinformation or other influence campaigns to interfere in U.S. policymaking, elections, or other affairs?<br>• How might changes in the information market reduce uncertainty?<br>• What mechanisms can be used to increase the demand for unbiased, objective information among consumers? |
| 4.C: Institutional development and rebuilding | • What changes to institutions might help reduce polarization? What legislative changes might be needed?<br>• How can trust in institutions be rebuilt? Is rebuilding trust possible, or are fundamental institutional changes required?<br>• What changes to the media industry would be needed to restore credibility? To restore transparency?<br>• Could changes to political, educational, media, or other institutions be used to promote facts and analysis over opinion and experience?<br>• How can the research profession (e.g., academia, think tanks) be altered to better promote transparency and accuracy? To guard against conflicts of interest? Is a new, more-rigorous set of standards required?<br>• How can agents of Truth Decay be prevented or dissuaded from contributing to the problem? What institutional changes would be required? |

**Table 6.4—Continued**

| Research Priority | Sample Research Questions |
|---|---|
| 4.D: Bridging social divides | • How can social and demographic polarization be reduced?<br>• What types of forums are needed to increase civic engagement and restore civil discourse?<br>• What institutional changes might be needed to encourage or facilitate wider civic engagement?<br>• What legal or legislative changes could promote and restore civil discourse?<br>• Can polarization be overcome by constituent pressure? Or are institutional and legal changes required? |
| 4.E: Harnessing new technologies | • How can social media be used to reduce polarization?<br>• How can civil discourse and civic engagement be promoted through social media and other online spaces? What policy or legal changes would be needed to facilitate this?<br>• How can new technologies be used to improve U.S. democratic processes, including access to participation, representation, and ease of communication?<br>• How can new technologies be used to champion facts and analysis over opinions and experience?<br>• How might new technologies be applied to dissuade agents of Truth Decay from exacerbating associated trends? |
| 4.F: Behavioral economics, psychology, and cognitive science | • Can situations in which people process information, make decisions, or exchange views be structured to facilitate effective use of facts and data? What structural changes to the media industry might increase commitment to facts and data?<br>• What structural changes to academia or the broader research community might increase commitment to objective and transparency?<br>• What structural changes to the political infrastructure might increase commitment to objective facts and accountability among political actors?<br>• How can expectations and beliefs around civic engagement be updated?<br>• What types of cues, frames, or tools would be required to encourage private citizens and political actors to consider compromise and welcome debate? |
| 4.G: Organizational self-assessment | • How can an organization's institutional quality standards be improved to better promote transparency, accuracy, and objectivity?<br>• How can an organization advance intellectual diversity? Other types of diversity?<br>• How can the policies and procedures used by an institution ensure quality, transparency, and objectivity?<br>• What can an organization do to spread the values of transparency and objectivity?<br>• What can an institution do to promote the value and necessity of objective data and facts? |

training in critical thinking. Finally, efforts to establish clear standards for civic and media literacy and critical thinking would be valuable. The methodology and approach used for the development of the Next Generation Science Standards might be one model to build on.[14]

Work in research priority 4.B (improving the information market) might consider legal, financial, or other changes that could help reduce bias and misleading media framing, control the spread of disinformation, improve the quality of journalism offered through traditional formats and online, and eliminate filters that skew search results and information, among other goals. We have mentioned potential areas for investigation, including media organization funding changes that would reduce the power of the profit motive and powerful media moguls, the establishment of standards of conduct for both research organizations and media corporations, legislation that imposes consequences on media organizations or platforms that spread disinformation, and technological innovations that might help stem the proliferation of disinformation and "fake news" and, in turn, reduce uncertainty. Work focused on ways to harness the benefits of the changing information system while reducing negative and unintended consequences is needed and essential. Research in this area might examine how social media can be used to connect diverse groups and protect minorities without creating echo chambers or promoting discrimination.[15] Another option is to focus on the demand side, exploring ways to increase public demand for fact-based and objective information. The use of incentives could be one approach. Education could be another. This is one area where individual questions might span research streams.

Research priority 4.C (institutional development and rebuilding) has two main focal points: reducing political and economic polarization and restoring or rebuilding trust in institutions. Such institutional changes could reduce many of the consequences of Truth Decay, as well as some of its root causes. Examples include exploring how legislative changes, changes to campaign finance, or changes to the primary system might affect polarization, reduce the sway of rich organizations

---

[14] Next Generation Science Standards, 2013; National Science Teachers Association, 2014.

[15] For additional ideas in this area, see West, 2017.

and wealthy donors on political campaigns and party platforms, and identify actionable ways to reduce political friction and policy uncertainty. The use of computer-based simulations and agent-based modeling might be valuable by allowing researchers to consider multiple potential scenarios under different policy changes. Research into the characteristics of trusted institutions and ways in which those characteristics can be built or integrated into existing institutions facing a crisis of credibility could create a strategy for restoring trust in institutions that serve as information providers. This might include considering why science is trusted as an institution but questioned at the level of individual findings or exploring models of delegation and representation that differ from those currently used, especially those that increase the quality of political discussion and the prevalence of facts, analysis, and transparency in the political arena. Research into how to rebuild trust in institutions should focus not just on political institutions but also on institutions in media, academia and research, and science and medicine.

Research priority 4.D (bridging the social divide) seeks to identify ways to address social and demographic polarization and promote and advance civil discourse and civic engagement. Research in this area might explore the benefits of education, communication, and grassroots local activism. By necessity, it will also overlap with work on institutional and legal responses (e.g., in the area of redistricting). It might also overlap with research focused on improving the information market, as the issues of echo chambers, filters, and algorithms will be relevant. Key questions here should focus on how to reengage people who feel alienated and create opportunities for individuals to be exposed to and interact with people from different backgrounds, partisan affiliations, or racial groups. Ethnographic and sociological studies that focus on understanding why and how people become alienated, and the activities that they find most engaging, will be paramount in this area. The use of pilot programs that explore ways in which people can be encouraged to interact with others in different social, economic, political, or ethnic groups would also be valuable. Examples include community service programs that combine or swap volunteers across district lines and interfaith religious services. Finally, research on the role that diversity might play in overcoming the challenges associated with Truth Decay could prove relevant here.

Research priority 4.E (harnessing new technologies) seeks to capitalize on the benefits of technological advances to advance and promote fact-based information, civil discourse, and civic engagement. Research should explore ways that new technologies, such as social media, can be used to build trust, fight polarization, and drive civil discourse and civic participation. This might involve research to identify the most-significant advantages and disadvantages of online political participation and the development of applications or forums that exploit these advantages while minimizing disadvantages. The use of technology to pursue civics and media literacy curricula that rely on adaptive learning would also be relevant. Research in this stream could also focus on the possible benefits and opportunities of a democratized information system and identify ways to address challenges that this access raises. This work might build on existing research that seeks to identify and remove false information from social media platforms, or it might branch off in a different direction and consider alternative social media environments structured to reduce the problems in existing ones. Research that looks at how technology might improve the efficiency of democratic processes (such as online town halls with political representatives and even secure online voting) would also be valuable. Finally, research in this area could also explore ways that new technologies can be used to advance and promote a reliance on fact-based analysis and to champion and disseminate facts and evidence that are central to key debates. This might build on such efforts as Steve Ballmer's USAFacts website, which aims to provide a centralized source for facts on a range of different topics.[16] Rather than promoting fact-checking, research in this area might explore ways to promote the visibility and importance of objective facts and to shift attitudes toward such data from one of skepticism to one of trust and value.

Research priority 4.F (behavioral economics, psychology, and cognitive science) could be relevant in a number of ways. First, identifying ways to encourage people to approach issues with an open mind, con-

---

[16] USAFacts, "About Us," webpage, undated.

sider alternatives, seek disconfirming views, and be willing to change their minds could help address some of the more-negative effects of cognitive biases. This might include studies that consider how frames, cues, or other tools could be used to support a more effective use of facts and evidence in decisionmaking and interpersonal debate. One area of useful research would be the ways in which policy changes or a restructuring of the media industry might foster a different type of media environment and information system that places higher value on facts and data and that seeks out and rewards transparency and objectivity. This type of study might offer solutions to such issues as the blurring of the line between opinion and fact. Behavioral economics and cognitive science might also help identify ways to shift or update individual and social expectations for civic participation and engagement in activities such as local government and voting. Such an outcome could address at least one consequence of Truth Decay—alienation—and might encourage an increase in civil discourse at the local level.

Finally, research priority 4.G (organizational self-assessment) is an inward-looking research area that asks all institutions to consider ways in which practices and policies could be updated or revised to promote objectivity, transparency, facts, and data. This stream asks all institutions to increase intellectual and other types of diversity within their organizations, to identify areas that might be unintentionally exacerbating aspects of Truth Decay, and to develop solutions or responses to address such shortcomings. This self-assessment should consider institutional structure, policies, staff, products, and physical location to identify specific changes that might advance the fight against Truth Decay and determine how best to leverage its capabilities to contribute to the response.

## Summary and Way Ahead

The research agenda described in this report is ambitious. It will require an enduring commitment to addressing the challenges of Truth Decay for the purpose of improving the health of American democracy and continuing to realize its promise. The agenda will also require contributions from many organizations with specialized expertise, and it will likely benefit from the creation of partnerships that can capitalize on synergies and comparative advantages across organizations. Although the four research streams identified here need not be conducted entirely sequentially, there will be advantages to first establishing a foundation of evidence and data on Truth Decay, using these data to identify areas in which Truth Decay is new or most severe, then exploring causal mechanisms and processes, and finally looking for solutions. However, a single project could also focus on one aspect of Truth Decay across all research streams (e.g., exploring how polarization is related to distrust of institutions and increasing disagreement about facts, how it causes political stalemate and a loss of civil discourse, and ways to overcome it).

Figure 6.1 illustrates a possible implementation plan for the pursuit of this research agenda. We expect that research streams 1 and 2 can be conducted mostly in parallel, though perhaps by different teams. We also expect that research on data and trends might extend beyond that on historical and international analogues because the former is likely to be more time-consuming and to have many more moving

**Figure 6.1**
**Research Agenda Implementation Plan**

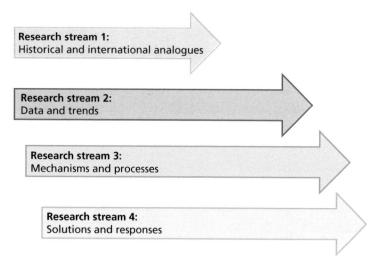

Research stream 1:
Historical and international analogues

Research stream 2:
Data and trends

Research stream 3:
Mechanisms and processes

Research stream 4:
Solutions and responses

RAND *RR2314-6.1*

pieces. Research stream 3 will rely and build on data collected as part of research stream 2, but commencement of research stream 3 need not wait until research stream 2 is complete (illustrated in Figure 6.1 by the short delay between the start of work on research streams 2 and 3). A team might begin collection of data on the volume of disinformation spread through social media sites and then move to an exploration of the technical and structural characteristics of individual sites that facilitate this. Similarly, we expect that the identification of solutions (research stream 4) will require that at least some work has been done on the prior research streams but can likely begin while other streams are ongoing, even within a single multiphase project. Continuing the previous example, the same team might conclude the project by identifying institutional or governance changes (or demand-side factors) that can reduce the spread of disinformation. Thus, a single project might combine tasks that touch on each research stream or it might dig more deeply into specific streams.

Research within this agenda is likely to proceed through research streams 2–4 based on topic area. Thus, work focused on social media or political polarization might start with a focus on data and trends, then consider mechanisms, then responses and solutions, in the scope of either one project or several. But, progress in any one topic area need not be constrained by that in other topic areas. A single research organization might be conducting work on social media concentrated in streams 3 and 4 (having already completed work in research stream 2) while just beginning work on political polarization.

Finally, we urge readers to remember that this research agenda should not be viewed as a static document but a living one—one that must be updated as the research progresses and as we learn more about Truth Decay.

As we have noted, the challenge of Truth Decay is both complex and urgent, and solutions will be multifaceted. The solutions must also be based on a clear and sound understanding of the problem, one grounded in careful research and analysis, solid data, and objective evidence. It is worth emphasizing that the focus of these solutions is unlikely to be an "undoing" or a "reversal" of the changes that have driven Truth Decay. American society will not be able to return to the way things were before the rise of social media, the advent of cable news, or the 2008 financial collapse. Instead, solutions must focus on ways to take advantage of the opportunities created by new developments and use these opportunities to champion facts and move beyond the challenges of Truth Decay.

RAND will pursue this research agenda with the objectivity and nonpartisanship that lie at the core of its organization. However, RAND's efforts and impact can be magnified if others join in, taking on pieces of the agenda and working with us to identify ways to fight Truth Decay. Because of the vital threat it presents to the health and future of American democracy, we urge interested individuals and organizations to join with RAND in working to promote the importance and necessity of facts, data, and analysis in civic and political discourse and in American public life more generally. The challenge posed by Truth Decay is great, but the stakes are too high to permit inaction.

# Additional Information About Our Methodology

This appendix provides additional technical details on the methodology used for the structured discussions and literature reviews conducted for this report.

## Structured Discussions

As the report notes, our discussions occurred most often in groups of eight to ten people, but we also conducted one-on-one discussions with people possessing particular areas of expertise who were unable to attend planned sessions. We conducted some separate sessions for people who work in RAND's Office of External Affairs (e.g., publications, communications, media and congressional relations) and with individuals in management roles. Other sessions mixed researchers from across disciplines and levels of seniority and experience. As noted in the body of the report, we also spoke with a number of RAND-affiliated and external audiences (including RAND donors and trustees and individuals who have been involved in RAND's many outreach events). We also presented earlier versions of this work to a variety of external audiences. Members of these external groups had varied economic and geographic backgrounds and political perspectives.[1]

All discussions covered the same basic topics and themes, but no two sessions were exactly alike; we allowed conversations to evolve nat-

---

[1] For a sampling of earlier remarks on Truth Decay by Michael Rich, see Rich, 2016a; Rich, 2016b.

urally within each group. The advantage of this strategy is that we were able to identify common emerging themes and to explore the issue from diverse perspectives. Before each meeting, we provided participants with some possible definitions of Truth Decay as a way to start the discussion and to give them some introduction to the topic. We also used a set of guiding questions, prompts, and activities to structure the discussions:

- Definitions
  - How would you define Truth Decay? What is the key element of a Truth Decay definition in your mind?
  - How is Truth Decay related to and different from "fake news"? From the concept of "post-truth"?
  - What aspects of Truth Decay are new? Which have always existed?
  - What types of evidence would provide support for an argument that Truth Decay is affecting contemporary life?
  - Does Truth Decay include only actions (e.g., dissemination of false information) that involve intent? Or is the proliferation of misinformation also an issue?
- Causes and consequences
  - What are the key causes and consequences of Truth Decay? Which seem most important?
  - Can we disentangle what is a cause and what is an effect? If not, why not?
  - How do agents like foreign actors or the media fit in?
- Risks, challenges, and opportunities
  - What challenges, risks, and opportunities does Truth Decay present?
  - What challenges, risks, and opportunities does Truth Decay present for RAND?
  - What are the implications if Truth Decay continues to worsen?
- Solutions and responses
  - Can Truth Decay be reversed? If so how? If not, why not?
  - What types of changes would be needed to reduce Truth Decay?

- What types of policy responses would be needed to address Truth Decay?
- What should RAND's role be in this issue space?
- Research agenda
  - What are some high-priority research questions that must be explored so that we can better understand and respond to Truth Decay? What are the methods you would use? What data would you collect or need? Who would be the audience? What contribution would this work make? What are the risks?
- Communication
  - What are the key aspects of a communication strategy about Truth Decay? How should it be described and presented?

The areas of "research agenda" and "communication strategy" were covered using activities during group discussions. For these activities, we asked individuals to break into groups of two. In early sessions, we asked groups to consider how they might explain and describe Truth Decay to various different audiences, such as a group of third-graders or a group of colleagues. This was intended to dig more deeply into the definition of Truth Decay and what it did and did not include. In later sessions, we asked participants to develop possible research questions for future exploration. This allowed us to think about possible sources of data and methods and also set the stage for the research agenda presented in Chapter Six.

## Coding Framework

As noted in the text, we used a list of key themes and concepts as a way to organize the key insights that emerged from our structured discussion and interviews. This coded material helped us to develop a working definition, to identify possible drivers and consequences, and then to propose a possible organizing framework. We later assessed this framework, testing its implicit hypotheses and refining it, through literature reviews and, where needed, expert discussions. The coding framework, therefore, helped us move from an "idea generation" phase to a "framework refinement" phase of the project. Our coding framework is outlined in the following list.

1. Definitions
    1.1 Truth Decay vs. "fake news"
    1.2 Distinction between fact, interpretation, and opinion
    1.3 Decline in trust in institutions
    1.4 Role of expertise, decline in trust in experts
    1.5 Fact versus experience or anecdote
    1.6 Are we talking about "truth"?
    1.7 Erosion of norms
    1.8 Evidence
        1.8.1   What types do we need?
        1.8.2   What types do we have?
    1.9 Role of intent
2. Drivers
    2.1 Social media and the internet
    2.2 Foreign actors
    2.3 Political actors
    2.4 The media and media market
    2.5 Cognitive bias and mental models (human nature)
    2.6 Polarization
    2.7 Role of critical thinking
    2.8 Economic inequality and recession
    2.9 Removal of gatekeepers
        2.9.1   Disinformation
        2.9.2   Educational system
        2.9.3   Cultural aspects
3. Consequences
    3.1 Disengagement
    3.2 Echo chambers
    3.3 Uncertainty
    3.4 Development and proliferation of stereotypes
    3.5 Weaponized information
4. Is it new?
    4.1 Factors that are new

4.1.1  Speed of information flow
4.1.2  Volume of information
4.1.3  Polarization
4.2  Factors that are old
4.2.1  Media spin
4.2.2  Political spin
4.2.3  Cognitive bias
4.3  Is it cyclical?
5.  International analogues
6.  Possible data sources
6.1  Survey data
6.2  Twitter data
6.3  Content coding
6.4  Other
7.  Responses
7.1  RAND
7.1.1  Internal
7.1.2  External
7.2  Other
8.  Research questions

## Literature Review

As described in the main report, we used literature reviews to explore ideas generated in brainstorming sessions and the working framework that we developed using these insights. We focused our literature reviews on the key elements of the framework and on related topics and insights that arose in our discussions. Table A.1 presents selected search terms used in the literature review. Because we conducted hundreds of searches, we focus here on the terms used to explore key aspects of the framework as well as closely related areas. The sample search terms provided were used with the topic area (or a derivative, if necessary) to conduct initial searches. We also used combinations of the search terms to provide more-targeted information where needed. From the returned hits, we focused on articles from peer-reviewed journals and used an initial screen of possible sources to narrow our list down to those that were most relevant to our hypotheses. We used information in these articles and books to refine the framework. Along the way, we conducted additional searches to fill in gaps or explore new topics.

**Table A.1**
**Selected Topic Areas and Search Terms Used in the Literature Review**

| Selected Topic Area | Sample Search Terms |
| --- | --- |
| Academia and research institutions | research, science, quality, retraction, bias, funding, transparency, objectivity, fraud, error, skepticism, diversity, standards, agenda |
| Alienation | civic engagement, institutions, trust, social capital, participation, discourse, online, social media, atomization, disengagement, trends, millennials, causes, effects |
| Atomization | civic engagement, institutions, trust, social capital, participation, discourse, online, social media, alienation, disengagement, trends, millennials, causes, effects |
| Cable and television news | bias, partisanship, profit, viewership, business model, accuracy, financing, regulation, trust, agenda, standards, "fake news," disinformation |
| Campaign finance | polarization, bias, partisanship, reform, influence, objectivity, transparency, engagement |
| Civics education | trends, standards, benefits, curriculum, democracy, social studies, media, outcomes, quality, engagement, voting, citizenship, media literacy, critical thinking, political knowledge, metrics, evaluation |
| Civil discourse | civics, partisanship, public, engagement, polarization, cross-group contact, communication, public engagement |
| Cognitive processing | cognitive bias, heuristics, overcoming, motivated reasoning, social networks, experience, mental models, mental schema, echo chambers, confirmation bias, cognitive dissonance, limitations, disinformation, susceptibility, trust |
| Critical thinking | teaching, training, testing, education, curriculum, common core, standards, media literacy, bias, science, citizenship, civic education |

## Table A.1—Continued

| Selected Topic Area | Sample Search Terms |
| --- | --- |
| Disinformation and propaganda | dissemination, consumption, weaponized, misinformation, Russia, China, effectiveness, consequences, causes, "fake news," profit, partisanship, bias, echo chamber, social media, types, detecting, removing, algorithm, filter, monitoring, evaluation |
| Echo chambers | social media, causes, effects, consequences, silos, filter bubble, polarization, disinformation, misinformation, filters, networks, consensus, bias |
| Economic inequality | recession, attitudes, polarization, changes, trends, causes, consequences, effects |
| Education standards | common core, science, math, reading, critical thinking, civics, political knowledge, quality, metrics, evaluation |
| Elections (laws and practices) | citizenship, voting, bias, information, partisanship, gerrymandering, financing, primary system, engagement, civic participation |
| "Fake news" | truth decay, post-truth, post-fact, volume, sources, types, detecting, removing, sources, effects, consequences, election, bias |
| Filters and algorithms | artificial intelligence, bias, echo chambers, information flow, information search, developing, "fake news" |
| Information gatekeepers | media, filters, information, access, democratization, quality, social media, newspapers, cable news, quantity, participation, engagement |
| Media literacy | Curriculum, teaching, skills, standards, metrics, trends, "fake news," benefits, social media, citizenship, engagement, metrics, evaluation |
| Newspapers | editorials, bias, partisanship, subscribers, readers, "fake news," investigative journalism, financing, accuracy, trust, disinformation, spin, "fake news" |
| Political paralysis | causes, consequences, cost, filibusters, laws enacted, judicial appointments, shutdown, diplomacy, risk, foreign policy, partisanship, polarizations, effects |
| Political polarization | causes, consequences, effects, elites, electorate, primaries, elections, attitudes, partisanship, increase, decrease, financing, media, sorting |
| Post-truth | "fake news," post-truth, measurement, metrics, data |

## Table A.1—Continued

| Selected Topic Area | Sample Search Terms |
| --- | --- |
| Quality of democracy | social capital, civic engagement, voting, representation, partisanship, polarization, alienation, atomization, social media, responsiveness, trust, well-being, information, citizenship |
| Science instruction | trends, standards, quality, assessment, metrics, critical thinking, inquiry, scientific method, next generation science standards |
| Social and demographic polarization | demographic clustering, echo chambers, causes, consequences, trends, landslide county, partisanship, values, mobility, sorting, attitudes, effects |
| Social capital | civic engagement, voting, participation, organizations, cross-cutting, reinforcing, cleavage, civic education, community, democracy, citizenship |
| Social media and the internet | information flow, volume, speed, changes, trends, Twitter, Facebook, bots, artificial intelligence, social networks, gatekeepers, "fake news," monitoring, access, disinformation, discourse |
| Trust in institutions | confidence, attitudes, trends, trusted institutions, distrusted institutions, partisanship |
| Trust in science | skepticism, climate change, vaccines, doubt, data, trends, metrics, partisanship, bias, mental models, education, critical thinking |
| Truth decay | "fake news," post-truth, measurement, metrics, data |
| Uncertainty (individual) | anxiety, causes, economic, political, security, consequences, effects, alienation, trends, metrics, engagement |
| Uncertainty (policy) | diplomatic, polarization, causes, foreign policy, economic, investment, costs, effects, trends, metrics |

# References

"1878–1899: Business and the Economy: Overview," *American Eras*, Vol. 8: *Development of the Industrial United States, 1878–1899*, Farmington Hills, Mich.: Gale Group, 1997, pp. 93–95. As of May 23, 2017: link.galegroup.com/apps/doc/CX2536601561/UHIC?u=oldt1017&xid=41df7b7e

Aaron, Paul, and David Musto, "Temperance and Prohibition in America: An Historical Overview," in Mark H. Moore and Dean R. Gerstein, eds., *Alcohol and Public Policy: Beyond the Shadow of Prohibition*, Washington, D.C.: National Academies Press, 1981.

Abrams, Samuel J., and Morris P. Fiorina, "'The Big Sort' That Wasn't: A Skeptical Reexamination," *PS: Political Science & Politics*, Vol. 45, No. 2, 2012, pp. 203–210.

Adamic, Lada A., Thomas M. Lento, Eytan Adar, and Pauline C. Ng, "Information Evolution in Social Networks," *Proceedings of the Ninth Association for Computing Machinery International Conference on Web Search and Data Mining*, 2016.

Alchin, Linda, "U.S. Immigration Trends 1880–1900," Emmigration.Info, 2017. As of June 4, 2017: http://www.emmigration.info/us-immigration-trends-1880-1900.htm

"Al-Jazeera Buys Al Gore's Current TV," Associated Press, January 3, 2013. As of July 10, 2017: https://www.usatoday.com/story/money/business/2013/01/02/al-jazeera-current-tv-al-gore/1805685/

Allcott, Hunt, and Matthew Gentzkow, "Social Media and Fake News in the 2016 Election," Cambridge, Mass.: National Bureau of Economic Research, NBER Working Paper No. 23089, January 2017, revised April 2017a.

———, "Social Media and Fake News in the 2016 Election," *Journal of Economic Perspectives*, Vol. 31, No. 2, Spring 2017b, pp. 211–236.

Altman, Micah, and Michael McDonald, "Redistricting and Polarization," in James Thuber and Antoine Yoskinaka, eds., *American Gridlock: The Sources, Character, and Impact of Political Polarization*, New York: Cambridge University Press, 2015.

American National Election Studies, homepage, undated. As of January 8, 2017: http://www.electionstudies.org

———, "Average Score on Index 1952–2012: External Political Efficacy," webpage, undated. As of June 4, 2017: http://www.electionstudies.org/nesguide/graphs/g5b_4_1.htm

Anderson, Monica, "More Americans Are Using Social Media to Connect with Politicians," Pew Research Center, May 19, 2015a. As of June 4, 2017: http://www.pewresearch.org/fact-tank/2015/05/19/more-americans-are-using-social-media-to-connect-with-politicians/

———, "5 Facts About Vaccines," Pew Research Center, July 17, 2015b. As of June 4, 2017: http://www.pewresearch.org/fact-tank/2015/07/17/5-facts-about-vaccines-in-the-u-s/

———, "For Earth Day, Here's How Americans View Environmental Issues," Pew Research Center, April 20, 2017. As of June 4, 2017: http://www.pewresearch.org/fact-tank/2017/04/20/for-earth-day-heres-how-americans-view-environmental-issues/

Annenberg Public Policy Center, "Science of Science Communication," webpage, undated. As of November 9, 2017: https://www.annenbergpublicpolicycenter.org/science-communication

Arceneaux, Kevin, Martin Johnson, and Chad Murphy, "Polarized Political Communication, Oppositional Media Hostility, and Selective Exposure," *Journal of Politics*, Vol. 74, No. 1, 2012, pp. 174–186.

Ashley, Christy, and Tracy Tuten, "Creative Strategies in Social Media Marketing: An Exploratory Study of Branded Social Content and Consumer Engagement," *Psychology & Marketing*, Vol. 32, No. 1, 2015, pp. 15–27.

Association of Centers for the Study of Congress, "Immigration and Nationalization Act," webpage, undated. As of April 6, 2016: http://acsc.lib.udel.edu/exhibits/show/legislation/immigration

Astin, Alexander W., and Linda J. Sax, "How Undergraduates Are Affected by Service Participation," *Journal of College Student Development*, Vol. 39, No. 3, 1998, pp. 251–263.

Auchard, Eric, and Bate Felix, "French Candidate Macron Claims Massive Hack as Emails Leaked," Reuters, May 6, 2017. As of July 10, 2017: http://www.reuters.com/article/us-france-election-macron-leaks-idUSKBN1812AZ

Authorea Team, "Do the Right Thing: 11 Courageous Retractions," webpage, undated. As of July 5, 2017:
https://www.authorea.com/users/8850/articles/126854-do-the-right-thing-11-courageous-retractions/_show_article

Baker, Scott, Nicholas Bloom, Brandice Canes-Wrone, Steven Davis, and Jonathan Rodden, "Why Has U.S. Policy Uncertainty Risen Since 1960?" Cambridge, Mass.: National Bureau of Economic Research, NBER Working Paper 19826, January 2014.

Baker, Scott R., Nicholas Bloom, and Steven J. Davis, "Measuring Economic Policy Uncertainty," Cambridge, Mass.: National Bureau of Economic Research, NBER Working Paper 21633, October 2015.

Bakshy, Eytan, Solomon Messing, and Lada A. Adamic, "Exposure to Ideologically Diverse News and Opinion on Facebook," *Science*, Vol. 348, No. 6239, 2015, pp. 1130–1132.

Bakshy, Eytan, Itamar Rosenn, Cameron Marlow, and Lada Adamic, "The Role of Social Networks in Information Diffusion," *Proceedings of the 21st International Conference on World Wide Web*, 2012.

Banilower, Eric R., P. Sean Smith, Iris R. Weiss, Kristen M. Malzahn, Kiira M. Campbell, and Aaron M. Weis, *Report of the 2012 National Survey of Science and Mathematics Education*, Chapel Hill, N.C.: Horizon Research, 2013. As of September 11, 2017:
http://www.horizon-research.com/2012nssme/wp-content/uploads/2013/02/2012-NSSME-Full-Report-updated-11-13-13.pdf

Barber, Michael, and Nolan McCarty, "Causes and Consequences of Polarization," in Jane Mansbridge and Cathie Jo Martin, eds., *Negotiating Agreement in Politics*, Washington, D.C.: American Political Science Association, 2013.

Barthel, Michael, "Newspapers Fact Sheet," Pew Research Center, June 1, 2017. As of June 4, 2017:
http://www.journalism.org/fact-sheet/newspapers/

Barthel, Michael, and Amy Mitchell, "Americans' Attitudes About the News Media Deeply Divided Along Partisan Lines," Pew Research Center, May 10, 2017. As of June 4, 2017:
http://www.journalism.org/2017/05/10/americans-attitudes-about-the-news-media-deeply-divided-along-partisan-lines/

Bennett, W. Lance, "Gatekeeping and Press-Government Relations: A Multigated Model," in L. L. Kaid, ed., *Handbook of Political Communication Research*, Mahwah, N.J.: Lawrence Erlbaum, 2004.

Berezow, Alex, "Are Liberals or Conservatives More Anti-Vaccine?" *RealClear Science*, October 20, 2014. As of July 10, 2017:
http://www.realclearscience.com/journal_club/2014/10/20/are_liberals_or_conservatives_more_anti-vaccine_108905.html

Berland, Gretchen K., Marc N. Elliott, Leo S. Morales, Jeffrey I. Algazy, Richard L. Kravitz, Michael S. Broder, David E. Kanouse, Jorge A. Munoz, Juan-Antonio Puyol, Marielena Lara, Katherine E. Watkins, Hannah Yang, and Elizabeth A. McGlynn, "Health Information on the Internet: Accessibility, Quality, and Readability in English and Spanish," *Journal of the American Medical Association*, Vol. 285, No. 20, 2001, pp. 2612–2621.

Berry, Jeffrey M., "Nonprofits and Civic Engagement," *Public Administration Review*, Vol. 65, No. 5, 2005, pp. 568–578.

———, *Lobbying for the People: The Political Behavior of Public Interest Groups*, Princeton, N.J.: Princeton University Press, 2015.

Berry, Jeffrey M., Kent E. Portney, and Ken Thomson, *The Rebirth of Urban Democracy*, Washington, D.C.: Brookings Institution, 1993.

Bertot, John, Paul Jaeger, and Justin Grimes, "Using ICTs to Create a Culture of Transparency: E-Government and Social Media as Openness and Anti-Corruption Tools for Societies," *Government Information Quarterly*, Vol. 27, No. 3, 2010, pp. 264–271.

Best, Paul, Roger Manktelow, and Brian Taylor, "Online Communication, Social Media and Adolescent Wellbeing: A Systematic Narrative Review," *Children and Youth Services Review*, Vol. 41, Issue C, 2014, pp. 27–36.

Beyerlein, Kraig, and John R. Hipp, "From Pews to Participation: The Effect of Congregation Activity and Context on Bridging Civic Engagement," *Social Problems*, Vol. 53, No. 1, 2006, pp. 97–117.

"Big Tobacco and Science: Uncovering the Truth," University of California, Davis, Health, webpage, undated. As of September 5, 2017: http://www.ucdmc.ucdavis.edu/welcome/features/20071114_cardio-tobacco/

Binder, Sarah A., and Forrest Maltzman, *Advice and Dissent: The Struggle to Shape the Federal Judiciary*, Washington, D.C.: Brookings Institution, 2009.

"Biographical Directory of the United States Congress, 1774–Present," Bioguide. Congress.Gov, undated. As of June 4, 2017: http://bioguide.congress.gov/biosearch/biosearch.asp

Bishop, Bill, *The Big Sort: Why the Clustering of Like-Minded America Is Tearing Us Apart*, Wilmington, Del.: Mariner Books, 2009.

Bittman, Bonnie, and William Russell III, "A Multiple Regression of Civics Education Scores," *Research in Social Sciences and Technology*, Vol. 1, No. 2, 2016, pp. 1–16.

Bleich, S., R. Blendon, and A. Adams, "Trust in Scientific Experts on Obesity: Implications for Awareness and Behavior Change," *Obesity*, Vol. 15, No. 8, 2007, pp. 2145–2156.

Blevins, Brooke, and Karon LeCompte, "Going Beyond the Games with iCivics. A Response to 'The Challenges of Gaming for Democratic Education: The Case of iCivics,'" *Democracy and Education*, Vol. 24, No. 2, 2016, Article 9.

Bodine-Baron, Elizabeth, Todd Helmus, Madeline Magnuson, and Zev Winkelman, *Examining ISIS Support and Opposition Networks on Twitter*, Santa Monica, Calif.: RAND Corporation, RR-1328-RC, 2016. As of September 12, 2017:
https://www.rand.org/pubs/research_reports/RR1328.html.

Boliek, Brooks, "FCC Finally Kills Off Fairness Doctrine," *Politico*, August 22, 2011.

Bolstad, Jorgen, Elias Dinas, and Pedro Riera, "Tactical Voting and Party Preference: A Test of Cognitive Dissonance Theory," *Political Behavior*, Vol. 35, No. 3, 2013, pp. 429–452.

Bonica, Adam, "The Punctuated Origins of Senate Polarization," *Legislative Quarterly*, Vol. 39, No. 1, February 2014, pp. 5–26.

Born, Kelly, "The Future of Truth: Can Philanthropy Help Mitigate Misinformation?" Hewlett Foundation, June 8, 2017. As of September 13, 2017:
https://www.hewlett.org/
future-truth-can-philanthropy-help-mitigate-misinformation/

Boxell, Levi, Matthew Gentzkow, and Jesse Shapiro, "Is the Internet Causing Political Polarization? Evidence from Demographics," Cambridge, Mass.: National Bureau of Economic Research, NBER Working Paper 23258, March 2017.

Bramlett, Brittany H., James G. Gimpel, and Frances E. Lee, "The Political Ecology of Opinion in Big-Donor Neighborhoods," *Political Behavior*, Vol. 33, No. 4, 2011, pp. 565–600.

Bresiger, Gregory, "The Great Inflation of the 1970s," Investopedia, undated. As of June 4, 2017:
http://www.investopedia.com/articles/economics/09/1970s-great-inflation.asp

Brookings Institution, "Report: Vital Statistics on Congress—Data on the U.S. Congress, Updated January 2017," webpage, January 9, 2017. As of June 29, 2017:
https://www.brookings.edu/multi-chapter-report/vital-statistics-on-congress/

Brossard, Dominique, Bruce Lewenstein, and Rick Bonney, "Scientific Knowledge and Attitude Change: The Impact of a Citizen Science Project," *International Journal of Science Education*, Vol. 27, No. 9, 2005, pp. 1099–1121.

Brossard, D., and M. C. Nisbet, "Deference to Scientific Authority Among a Low Information Public: Understanding U.S. Opinion on Agricultural Biotechnology," *International Journal of Public Opinion Research*, Vol. 19, No. 1, 2007, pp. 24–52.

Brosseau, Carli, "Executive Session: Civil Discourse in Progress," *Frankly Speaking*, Vol. 1, No. 2, October 27, 2011.

Brown, Abram, "Why All the Talk-Radio Stars Are Conservative," *Forbes*, July 13, 2015. As of June 4, 2017:
https://www.forbes.com/sites/abrambrown/2015/07/13/
why-all-the-talk-radio-stars-are-conservative/#76b2685b2788

Bryk, Anthony S., Louis Gomez, and Alicia Grunow, "Getting Ideas into Action: Building Networked Improvement Communities in Education," in M. Hallinan, ed., *Frontiers in Sociology of Education*, Dordrecht, The Netherlands: Springer Publishing, 2011.

Bureau of Justice Statistics, "Data Collection: National Crime Victimization Survey (NCVS)," webpage, undated. As of November 8, 2017:
https://www.bjs.gov/index.cfm?ty=dcdetail&iid=245

Burgess, Alexis G., and John P. Burgess, eds., *Truth*, Princeton, N.J.: Princeton University Press, 2011.

Burke, Marshall, "The Global Economic Costs from Climate Change May Be Worse Than Expected," Washington, D.C., Brookings Institution, December 9, 2015. As of June 4, 2017:
https://www.brookings.edu/blog/planetpolicy/2015/12/09/
the-global-economic-costs-from-climate-change-may-be-worse-than-expected/

Button, Mark, and Kevin Mattson, "Deliberative Democracy in Practice: Challenges and Prospects for Civic Deliberation," *Polity*, Vol. 31, No. 4, Summer 1999, pp. 609–637.

Calvert, Philip J., "Scholarly Misconduct and Misinformation on the World Wide Web," *The Electronic Library*, Vol. 19, No. 4, 2001, pp. 232–240.

Camarota, Steven, "Welfare Use by Immigrant and Native Households," Center for Immigration Studies, September 10, 2015. As of November 8, 2017:
https://cis.org/Report/Welfare-Use-Immigrant-and-Native-Households

Campbell, W. Joseph, *Yellow Journalism: Puncturing the Myths, Defining the Legacies*, Westport, Conn.: Praeger, 2001.

Carcasson, Martin, "Herbert Hoover and the Presidential Campaign of 1932: The Failure of Apologia," *Presidential Studies Quarterly*, Vol. 28, No. 2, Spring 1998, pp. 349–365.

Carr, Nicholas, *The Shallows: What the Internet Is Doing to Our Brains*, New York: W.W. Norton and Company, 2011.

Carson, Jamie L., Michael H. Crespin, Charles J. Finocchiaro, and David W. Rohde, "Redistricting and Party Polarization in the U.S. House of Representatives," *American Politics Research*, Vol. 35, No. 6, 2007, pp. 878–904.

Carson, Jamie L., Michael H. Crespin, and Ryan D. Williamson, "Reevaluating the Effects of Redistricting on Electoral Competition, 1972–2012," *State Politics & Policy Quarterly*, Vol. 14, No. 2, 2014, pp. 165–177.

Carter, Susan, Scott Sigmund Gartner, Michael Haines, Alan Olmsted, Richard Sutch, and Gavin Wright, eds., *Historical Statistics of the United States: Millennial Edition*, Cambridge, Mass.: Cambridge University Press, 2006.

Cassidy, John, "Why the Remain Campaign Lost the Brexit Vote," *The New Yorker*, June 24, 2016. As of June 4, 2017:
http://www.newyorker.com/news/john-cassidy/
why-the-remain-campaign-lost-the-brexit-vote

Centers for Disease Control and Prevention, "Vaccine Safety," webpage, August 14, 2017. As of November 8, 2017:
https://www.cdc.gov/vaccinesafety/index.html

Channell, Jason, Elizabeth Curmi, Phuc Nguyen, Elaine Prior, Alastair R. Syme, Heath R. Jansen, Ebrahim Rahbari, Edward L. Morse, Seth M Kleinman, and Tim Kruger, *Energy Darwinism II: Why a Low Carbon Future Doesn't Have to Cost the Earth*, Citi GPS: Global Perspectives & Solutions, August 2015.

Chase, Francis Seabury, *Sound and Fury: An Informal History of Broadcasting*, New York: Harper & Brothers, 1942.

Chetty, Raj, Nathaniel Hendren, Patrick Kline, and Emmanuel Saez, "Where Is the Land of Opportunity? The Geography of Intergenerational Mobility in the United States," *Quarterly Journal of Economics*, Vol. 129, No. 4, 2014, pp. 1553–1623.

*Citizens United v. Federal Election Commission*, 558 U.S. 08-205, 2009.

"CMO Today," *Wall Street Journal*, webpage, undated-a. As of July 5, 2017:
https://www.wsj.com/news/cmo-today

Cochrane, Sandra, and Joshua Cochrane, "Teacher Perceptions of the Common Core Performance Standards," *Georgia Education Researcher*, Vol. 12, No. 1, June 30, 2015, Article 1. As of June 12, 2017:
https://digitalcommons.georgiasouthern.edu/cgi/
viewcontent.cgi?article=1031&context=gerjournal

Cohen-Vogel, Lora, Ariel Tichnor-Wagner, Danielle Allen, Christopher Harrison, Kirsten Kainz, Allison Rose Socol, and Qi Wang, "Implementing Educational Innovations at Scale: Transforming Researchers into Continuous Improvement Scientists," *Educational Policy*, Vol. 29, No. 1, 2015, pp. 257–277.

Colleoni, Elanor, Alessandro Rozza, and Adam Arvidsson, "Echo Chamber or Public Sphere? Predicting Political Orientation and Measuring Political Homophily in Twitter Using Big Data," *Journal of Communication*, Vol. 64, No. 2, 2014, pp. 317–332.

Colletta, Paulo E., *William Jennings Bryan: Vol. I, Political Evangelist, 1860–1908*, Lincoln, Neb.: University of Nebraska Press, 1964.

Collins, Robert, *More: The Politics of Economic Growth in Postwar America*, New York: Oxford University Press, 2002.

Collins, Scott, *Crazy Like a Fox: The Inside Story of How Fox News Beat CNN*, New York: Portfolio Hardcover, 2004.

Common Core Standards Initiative, "Standards in Your State," webpage, undated-a. As of July 27, 2017:
http://www.corestandards.org/standards-in-your-state

———, "What Parents Should Know," webpage, undated-b. As of July 27, 2017:
http://www.corestandards.org/what-parents-should-know/

Conover, Pamela Johnston, and Donald D. Searing, "A Political Socialization Perspective," in Lorraine M. McDonnell, P. Michael Timpane, and Roger Benjamin, eds., *Rediscovering the Democratic Purposes of Education*, Lawrence, Kan.: University Press of Kansas, 2000, pp. 91–124.

Constine, Josh, "How Big Is Facebook's Data? 2.5 Billion Pieces and 500+ Terabytes Ingested Every Day," Techcrunch, August 22, 2012. As of November 8, 2017:
https://techcrunch.com/2012/08/22/how-big-is-facebooks-data-2-5-billion-pieces-of-content-and-500-terabytes-ingested-every-day/

Cook, M. B., and H. S. Smallman, "Human Factors of the Confirmation Bias in Intelligence Analysis: Decision Support from Graphical Evidence Landscapes," *Human Factors*, Vol. 50, No. 5, 2008, pp. 745–754.

Cook, Sarah, "Chinese Government Influence on the U.S. Media Landscape," testimony before the U.S.-China Economic and Security Review Commission, Hearing on China's Information Controls, Global Media Influence, and Cyber Warfare Strategy, May 4, 2017. As of September 5, 2017:
https://www.uscc.gov/sites/default/files/
Sarah%20Cook%20May%204th%202017%20USCC%20testimony.pdf

Cooper, Charlie, "EU Referendum: Immigration and Brexit—What Lies Have Been Spread?" *The Independent*, June 20, 2016. As of June 4, 2017:
http://www.independent.co.uk/news/uk/politics/
eu-referendum-immigration-and-brexit-what-lies-have-been-spread-a7092521.html

Costa, Daniel, David Cooper, and Heidi Shierholz, "Facts About Immigration and the U.S. Economy," Economic Policy Institute, August 12, 2014. As of November 8, 2017:
http://www.epi.org/publication/immigration-facts/

Cultural Cognition Project, homepage, undated. As of November 8, 2017:
http://www.culturalcognition.net

Dafoe, Allan, and Devin Caughey, "Honor and War: Southern US Presidents and the Effects of Concern for Reputation," *World Politics*, Vol. 68, No. 2, 2016, pp. 341–381.

D'Alessio, D., and M. Allen, "Media Bias in Presidential Elections: A Meta-Analysis," *Journal of Communication*, Vol. 50, No. 4, 2000, pp. 133–156.

Daniel, Marcus, *Scandal and Civility: Journalism and the Birth of American Democracy*, New York: Oxford University Press, 2009.

Darcy, Oliver, "Fox News' Now Retracted Seth Rich Story," CNN Money, August 10, 2017. As of September 5, 2017:
http://money.cnn.com/2017/08/10/media/seth-rich-fox-news-timeline/index.html

Davies, William, "The Age of Post-Truth Politics," *New York Times*, August 24, 2016. As of November 8, 2017:
https://www.nytimes.com/2016/08/24/opinion/campaign-stops/the-age-of-post-truth-politics.html

de Figueiredo, Rui J. P., Jr., "Electoral Competition, Political Uncertainty, and Policy Insulation," *American Political Science Review*, Vol. 96, No. 2, 2002, pp. 321–333.

DellaVigna, Stefano, and Ethan Kaplan, "The Fox News Effect: Media Bias and Voting," *Quarterly Journal of Economics*, Vol. 122, No. 3, 2007, pp. 1187–1234.

Delli Carpini, Michael X., "Gen. Com: Youth, Civic Engagement, and the New Information Environment," *Political Communication*, Vol. 17, No. 4, 2000, pp. 341–349.

Delli Carpini, Michael X., and Scott Keeter, *What Americans Know About Politics and Why It Matters*, New Haven, Conn.: Yale University Press, 1997.

Desilver, Drew, "U.S. Income Inequality, on Rise for Decades, Is Now Highest Since 1928," Pew Research Center, December 2013. As of June 4, 2017:
http://www.pewresearch.org/fact-tank/2013/12/05/u-s-income-inequality-on-rise-for-decades-is-now-highest-since-1928/

"Disinformation: A Primer in Russian Active Measures and Influence Campaigns," hearings before the Select Committee on Intelligence, United States Senate, 115th Congress, March 30, 2017. As of June 4, 2017:
https://www.intelligence.senate.gov/sites/default/files/documents/os-trid-033017.pdf

Dobbins, James, "Reining in Internet Abuse (Without Abusing the First Amendment)," *Tulsa World*, March 27, 2017. As of June 4, 2017:
http://www.tulsaworld.com/opinion/othervoices/james-dobbins-reining-in-internet-abuse-without-abusing-the-first/article_6380c695-4f7a-56aa-b539-f7c317c906e9.html

Downie, Leonard, and Michael Schudson, "The Reconstruction of American Journalism," *Columbia Journalism Review*, November/December 2009. As of July 1, 2017:
http://archives.cjr.org/reconstruction/the_reconstruction_of_american.php

Downs, Anthony, *An Economic Theory of Democracy*, New York: Harper & Row, 1957.

Downs, J. S., W. Bruine de Bruin, and B. Fischhoff, "Parents' Vaccination Comprehension and Decisions," *Vaccine*, Vol. 26, No. 12, 2008, pp. 1595–1607.

Drew, Sally Valentino, "Open Up the Ceiling on Common Core State Standards: Preparing Students for 21st Century Literacy—Now," *Journal of Adolescent & Adult Literacy*, Vol. 56, No. 4, December 2012/January 2013, pp. 321–330.

Drezner, Daniel, *The Ideas Industry*, Oxford and New York: Oxford University Press, 2017.

Drutman, Lee, "Political Divisions in 2016 and Beyond," Voter Study Group, June 2017. As of June 4, 2017:
https://www.voterstudygroup.org/reports/2016-elections/
political-divisions-in-2016-and-beyond

Dyck, Joshua J., and Shanna Pearson-Merkowitz, "To Know You Is Not Necessarily to Love You: The Partisan Mediators of Intergroup Contact," *Political Behavior*, Vol. 36, No. 3, 2014, pp. 553–580.

Eckes, Alfred E., Jr., *Opening America's Market: U.S. Foreign Trade Policy Since 1776*, Chapel Hill, N.C.: University of North Carolina Press, 1995.

Edwards, Jim, "Leaked Twitter API Data Shows the Number of Tweets Is in Serious Decline," *Business Insider*, February 2, 2016.

Eisenstein, Elizabeth, *The Printing Press as an Agent of Change*, New York: Cambridge University Press, 1980.

Engber, Daniel, "Is Science Broken?" *Slate*, August 21, 2017. As of September 5, 2017:
http://www.slate.com/articles/health_and_science/science/2017/08/
science_is_not_self_correcting_science_is_broken.html

Epstein, Diana, and John D. Graham, *Polarized Politics and Policy Consequences*, Santa Monica, Calif.: RAND Corporation, OP-197-PV/EMR, 2007. As of June 4, 2017:
https://www.rand.org/pubs/occasional_papers/OP197.html

Esparza, Jeffrey C., "The Personal Computer vs. the Voting Rights Act: How Modern Mapping Technology and Ethically Polarized Voting Work Together to Segregate Voters," *UMKC Law Review*, Vol. 84, No. 1, Fall 2015, pp. 235–260.

Fang, Ferric C., and Arturo Casadevall, "Retracted Science and the Retraction Index," *Infection and Immunology*, Vol. 79, No. 10, 2011, pp. 3855–3859.

Farand, Chloe, "French Social Media Awash with Fake News Stories from Sources 'Exposed to Russian Influence' Ahead of Presidential Election," *The Independent*, April 22, 2017. As of July 10, 2017:
http://www.independent.co.uk/news/world/europe/
french-voters-deluge-fake-news-stories-facebook-twitter-russian-influence-days-before-election-a7696506.html

Farkas Duffett Research Group, *Learning Less: Public School Teachers Describe a Narrowing Curriculum*, Washington, D.C.: Common Core, 2012.

Fazio, Lisa K., Nadia M. Brashier, B. Keith Payne, and Elizabeth J. Marsh, "Knowledge Does Not Protect Against Illusory Truth," *Journal of Experimental Psychology: General*, Vol. 144, No. 5, 2015, pp. 993–1002.

Federal Communications Commission, "Program Content Regulations," webpage, September 29, 2017. As of November 9, 2017: https://www.fcc.gov/media/program-content-regulations

Feldman, Lauren, Josh Pasek, Daniel Romer, and Kathleen Hall Jamieson, "Identifying Best Practices in Civic Education: Lessons from the Student Voices Program," *American Journal of Education*, Vol. 114, No. 1, 2007, pp. 75–100.

Felton, Emmanuel, "Are the Common Core Tests Turning Out to Be a Big Success or a Resounding Failure?" *The Hechinger Report*, April 2015. As of July 27, 2017: http://hechingerreport.org/are-the-common-core-tests-turning-out-to-be-a-big-success-or-a-resounding-failure/

Fiegerman, Seth, "Facebook's Global Fight Against Fake News," CNN, May 9, 2017. As of June 4, 2017: http://money.cnn.com/2017/05/09/technology/facebook-fake-news/

Fiorina, Morris, "Americans Have Not Become More Politically Polarized," *Washington Post*, June 23, 2014.

Flaherty, Lisa M., Kevin J. Pearce, and Rebecca B. Rubin, "Internet and Face-to-Face Communication: Not Functional Alternatives" *Communication Quarterly*, Vol. 46, No. 3, 1998, pp. 250–268.

Flaxman, Seth, Sharad Goel, and Justin Rao, "Filter Bubbles, Echo Chambers, and Online News Consumption," *Public Opinion Quarterly*, Vol. 80, Special Issue, 2016, pp. 298–320.

Flynn, D. J., Brendan Nyhan, and Jason Reifler, "The Nature and Origins of Misperceptions: Understanding False and Unsupported Beliefs About Politics," European Research Council, 2016.

Foner, Eric, *Give Me Liberty! An American History*, Vol. 2, 2nd ed., New York and London: W. W. Norton & Company, 2005.

Forest, Benjamin, "The Changing Demographic, Legal, and Technological Contexts of Political Representation," *Proceedings of the National Academy of Sciences*, Vol. 102, No. 43, 2005, pp. 15331–15336.

Franken, Al, *Giant of the Senate*, New York: Hachette Book Group, 2017.

Franklin, Christine, Gary Kader, Denise Mewborn, Jerry Moreno, Roxy Peck, Mike Perry, and Richard Schaeffer, *Guidelines for Assessment and Instruction in Statistics Education Report: A Pre-K–12 Framework*, Alexandria, Va.: American Statistical Association, 2007. As of September 6, 2017: http://www.amstat.org/asa/files/pdfs/GAISE/GAISEPreK-12_Full.pdf

Freedman, David, "The Truth About Genetically Modified Food," *Scientific American*, September 1, 2013. As of July 10, 2017: https://www.scientificamerican.com/article/ the-truth-about-genetically-modified-food/

Fridkin, Kim L., Patrick J. Kenney, Sarah Allen Gershon, and Gina Serignese Woodall, "Spinning Debates: The Impact of the News Media's Coverage of the Final 2004 Presidential Debate," *International Journal of Press/Politics*, Vol. 13, No. 1, 2008, pp. 29–51.

Friedman, John N., and Richard T. Holden, "The Rising Incumbent Reelection Rate: What's Gerrymandering Got to Do with It?" *Journal of Politics*, Vol. 71, No. 2, 2009, pp. 593–611.

Friesen, Justin P., Troy H. Campbell, and Aaron C. Kay, "The Psychological Advantage of Unfalsifiability: The Appeal of Untestable Religious and Political Ideologies," *Journal of Personality and Social Psychology*, Vol. 108, No. 3, 2015, pp. 515–529.

Frum, David, "Does Immigration Harm Working Americans?" *The Atlantic*, January 5, 2015a.

———, "The Coming Democratic Crack-Up," *The Atlantic*, September 21, 2015b.

Fukuyama, Francis, "America in Decay: The Sources of Political Dysfunction," *Foreign Affairs*, Vol. 93, No. 5, September/October 2014, pp. 5–26.

———, "The Emergence of a Post-Fact World," *Project Syndicate*, January 12, 2017. As of November 8, 2017: https://www.project-syndicate.org/onpoint/ the-emergence-of-a-post-fact-world-by-francis-fukuyama-2017-01

Funk, Cary, and Brian Kennedy, "Public Views on Climate Change and Climate Scientists," Pew Research Center, October 4, 2016a. As of June 4, 2017: http://www.pewinternet.org/2016/10/04/ public-views-on-climate-change-and-climate-scientists/

———, "Public Opinion About Genetically Modified Foods and Trust in Scientists Connected with Those Foods," Pew Research Center, December 1, 2016b. As of September 5, 2017: http://www.pewinternet.org/2016/12/01/public-opinion-about-genetically-modified-foods-and-trust-in-scientists-connected-with-these-foods/

Funk, Cary, and Lee Raine, "Public and Scientists' Views on Science and Society," Pew Research Center, January 29, 2015a. As of July 27, 2017:
http://www.pewinternet.org/2015/01/29/
public-and-scientists-views-on-science-and-society/

———, "Public Opinion About Food," Pew Research Center, July 1, 2015b. As of July 27, 2017:
http://www.pewinternet.org/2015/07/01/chapter-6-public-opinion-about-food/

Gainous, Jason, and Allison Martens, "Civics Education: Liberals Do It Better," *Journal of Political Ideologies*, Vol. 21, No. 3, 2016, pp. 261–279.

Gallup, "About Us," webpage, undated. As of October 4, 2017:
http://www.gallup.com/corporate/212381/who-we-are.aspx

———, "Confidence in Institutions," webpage, June 2016. As of June 4, 2017:
http://www.gallup.com/poll/1597/confidence-institutions.aspx

———, "Americans' Confidence in Institutions Edges Up," webpage, June 26, 2017. As of July 10, 2017:
http://www.gallup.com/poll/212840/americans-confidence-institutions-edges.aspx

Gauchat, Gordon, "Politicization of Science in the Public Sphere: A Study of Public Trust in the United States, 1974 to 2010," *American Sociological Review*, Vol. 77, No. 2, 2012, pp. 167–187.

General Social Survey, "About the GSS," webpage, undated. As of November 8, 2017:
http://gss.norc.org/About-The-GSS

Gentzkow, Matthew, "Polarization in 2016," Stanford, Calif.: Stanford University, Toulouse Network for Information Technology Whitepaper, 2016. As of July 10, 2017:
https://web.stanford.edu/~gentzkow/research/PolarizationIn2016.pdf

Gentzkow, Matthew, and Jesse M. Shapiro, "Media Bias and Reputation," *Journal of Political Economy*, Vol. 114, No. 2, 2006, pp. 280–316.

Gerber, Drew, "Spanish-Language Video Game Aims to Teach Students About Civil Rights," *Washington Post*, November 24, 2017. As of January 7, 2017:
https://www.washingtonpost.com/local/
spanish-language-video-game-aims-to-teach-students-about-civil-rights/2017/11/23/
72f20870-cfd2-11e7-9d3a-bcbe2af58c3a_story.html?utm_term=.9abadc184c80

Gerber, Theodore P., and Jane Zavisca, "Does Russian Propaganda Work?" *Washington Quarterly*, Vol. 39, No. 2, 2016, pp. 79–98.

Goldacre, Ben, "Trial Sans Error: How Pharma-Funded Research Cherry Picks Positive Results [Excerpt]," *Scientific American*, February 13, 2013. As of July 10, 2017:
https://www.scientificamerican.com/article/
trial-sans-error-how-pharma-funded-research-cherry-picks-positive-results/

Gore, D'Angelo, "Keeping Your Health Plan," FactCheck.Org, November 11, 2013. As of July 10, 2017:
http://www.factcheck.org/2013/11/keeping-your-health-plan/

Gottfried, Jeffrey, and Elisa Shearer, "News Use Across Social Media Platforms," Pew Research Center, May 16, 2016. As of September 5, 2017:
http://www.journalism.org/2016/05/26/
news-use-across-social-media-platforms-2016/

Gould, Lewis, *America in the Progressive Era, 1890–1914*, New York: Routledge, 2001.

GovTrack, "Statistics and Historical Comparison, Bills by Final Status," webpage, undated. As of June 4, 1978:
https://www.govtrack.us/congress/bills/statistics

Gramlich, John, "Voters' Perceptions of Crime Continue to Conflict with Reality," Pew Research Center, November 16, 2016. As of November 8, 2017:
http://www.pewresearch.org/fact-tank/2016/11/16/
voters-perceptions-of-crime-continue-to-conflict-with-reality/

Grant, S. G., "High-Stakes Testing: How Are Social Studies Teachers Responding?" *Social Education*, Vol. 71, No. 5, September 2007, pp. 250–254.

Gray, Maryann Jacobi, Elizabeth Heneghan Ondaatje, Ronald D. Fricker, Sandy A. Geschwind, Charles A. Goldman, Tessa Kaganoff, Abby Robyn, Melora Sundt, Lori Vogelgesang, and Stephen P. Klein, *Combining Service and Learning in Higher Education: Evaluation of the Learn and Serve America, Higher Education Program*, Santa Monica, Calif.: RAND Corporation, MR-998-EDU, 1999. As of June 4, 2017:
https://www.rand.org/pubs/monograph_reports/MR998.html

Greenstone, Michael, and Adam Looney, *Ten Economic Facts About Immigration*, The Hamilton Project, Washington, D.C.: Brookings Institution, September 2010. As of November 8, 2017:
https://www.brookings.edu/wp-content/uploads/2016/06/09_immigration.pdf

Groeling, Tim, "Who's the Fairest of Them All? An Empirical Test for Partisan Bias on ABC, CBS, NBC, and Fox News," *Presidential Studies Quarterly*, Vol. 38, No. 4, 2008, pp. 631–657.

Groseclose, Tim, and Jeffrey Milyo, "A Measure of Media Bias," *Quarterly Journal of Economics*, Vol. 120, No. 4, 2005, pp. 1191–1237.

Gross, Paul, Lawrence Lerner, Ursula Goodenough, John Lynch, Martha Schwartz, and Richard Schwartz, *The State of State Science Standards 2012*, Washington, D.C.: Thomas B. Fordham Institute, 2012.

Gurin, Patricia, Biren Ratnesh A. Nagda, and Gretchen E. Lopez, "The Benefits of Diversity in Education for Democratic Citizenship," *Journal of Social Issues*, Vol. 60, No. 1, 2004, pp. 17–34.

Guyette, Elise, Fern Tavalin, and Sarah Rooker, "A Brief Timeline of U.S. Policy on Immigration and Naturalization," Flow of History, 2013. As of June 4, 2017: http://www.flowofhistory.org/themes/movement_settlement/uspolicytimeline.php

Hair, William Ivy, *The Kingfish and His Realm: The Life and Times of Huey P. Long*, Baton Rouge, La.: Louisiana State University Press, 1996.

Hallin, Daniel C., *The Uncensored War: The Media and Vietnam*, Oxford and New York: Oxford University Press, 1986.

Hallman, William, Cara Cuite, and Xenia Morin, "Public Perceptions of Labeling Genetically Modified Foods," New Brunswick, N.J.: Rutgers School of Environmental and Biological Sciences, Working Paper 2013-01, November 1, 2013. As of September 5, 2017: http://humeco.rutgers.edu/documents_PDF/news/GMlabelingperceptions.pdf

Hamilton, Laura S., Brian M. Stecher, Julie A. Marsh, Jennifer Sloan McCombs, Abby Robyn, Jennifer Russell, Scott Naftel, and Heather Barney, *Standards Based Accountability Under No Child Left Behind: Experiences of Teachers and Administrators in Three States*, Santa Monica, Calif.: RAND Corporation, MG-589-NSF, 2007. As of December 18, 2017: https://www.rand.org/pubs/monographs/MG589.html

Hartz, Louis, *The Liberal Tradition in America*, New York: Harcourt Books, 1991.

Haselton, Martie G., Daniel Nettle, and Damian R. Murray, "The Evolution of Cognitive Bias," in David M. Buss, ed., *The Handbook of Evolutionary Psychology*, Hoboken, N.J.: John Wiley & Sons, Inc., 2005.

Hazlett, Thomas W., and David W. Sosa, "Was the Fairness Doctrine a 'Chilling Effect'? Evidence from the Postderegulation Radio Market," *Journal of Legal Studies*, Vol. 26, No. 1, 1997, pp. 279–301.

Heberlig, Eric, Marc Hetherington, and Bruce Larson, "The Price of Leadership: Campaign Money and the Polarization of Congressional Parties," *Journal of Politics*, Vol. 68, No. 4, 2006, pp. 992–1005.

Hebert, J. Gerald, and Marina K. Jenkins, "The Need for State Redistricting Reform to Rein in Partisan Gerrymandering," *Yale Law & Policy Review*, Vol. 29, No. 2, 2010, pp. 543–558.

"Help: Readers' Guide," New York Times, webpage, undated. As of November 8, 2017: https://www.nytimes.com/content/help/site/readerguide/guide.html

Hernandez, I., and J. L. Preston, "Disfluency Disrupts the Confirmation Bias," *Journal of Experimental Social Psychology*, Vol. 49, No. 1, 2013, pp. 178–182.

Herper, Matthew, "Would Trump's FDA Deregulation Create an Age of Miracles? Don't Bet on It," Forbes, March 1, 2107. As of July 5, 2017:
https://www.forbes.com/sites/matthewherper/2017/03/01/
would-trumps-fda-deregulation-create-an-age-of-miracles-dont-bet-on-it/
#541dd7023883

Hicks, John D., *The Populist Revolt: A History of the Crusade for Farm Relief*, Minneapolis, Minn.: University of Minnesota Press, 1931.

Hild, Matthew, *Greenbackers, Knights of Labor, and Populists: Farmer-Labor Insurgency in the Late-Nineteenth-Century South*, Athens, Ga., and London: The University of Georgia Press, 2007.

Hill, Kim Quaile, and Tetsuya Matsubayashi, "Civic Engagement and Mass-Elite Policy Agenda Agreement in American Communities," *American Political Science Review*, Vol. 99, No. 2, 2005, pp. 215–224.

Hiltzik, Michael, *The New Deal*, New York: Free Press, 2011.

Hirt, Edward R., and Keith D. Markman, "Multiple Explanation: A Consider-an-Alternative Strategy for Debiasing Judgments," *Journal of Personality and Social Psychology*, Vol. 69, No. 6, December 1995, pp. 1069–1086.

Ho, Shirley S., Dominique Brossard, and Dietram A. Scheufele, "Effects of Value Predispositions, Mass Media Use, and Knowledge on Public Attitudes Toward Embryonic Stem Cell Research," *International Journal of Public Opinion Research*, Vol. 20, No. 2, 2008, pp. 171–192.

Hoffman, Charles, *The Depression of the Nineties: An Economic History*, Westport, Conn.: Greenwood Publishing, 1970.

Hofstetter, C. Richard, David Barker, James T. Smith, Gina M. Zari, and Thomas A. Ingrassia, "Information, Misinformation, and Political Talk Radio," *Political Research Quarterly*, Vol. 52, No. 2, 1999, pp. 353–369.

Howard, Alex, "How Should History Measure the Obama's Administration's Record on Transparency?" The Sunlight Foundation, September 2, 2016. As of November 8, 2017:
https://sunlightfoundation.com/2016/09/02/
how-should-history-measure-the-obama-administrations-record-on-transparency/

Howard, Philip N., and Malcolm R. Parks, "Social Media and Political Change: Capacity, Constraint, and Consequence," *Journal of Communication*, Vol. 6, No. 2, 2012, pp. 359–362.

Hoyt, Carl, "The Blur Between Analysis and Opinion," *New York Times*, April 13, 2008.

Hutchinson, Amy, and David Reinking, "Teachers' Perceptions of Integrating Information and Communication Technologies into Literacy Instruction: A National Survey in the United States," *Reading Research Quarterly*, Vol. 46, No. 4, 2011, pp. 312–333.

iCivics, "Our Story," webpage, undated. As of June 4, 2017:
https://www.icivics.org/our-story

———, "iCivics Celebrates Gaming Milestone," webpage, October 21, 2010. As of
June 4, 2017:
https://www.icivics.org/news/icivics-celebrates-gaming-milestone

Insight Assessment, "California Critical Thinking Skills Test (CCTST)," webpage,
undated. As of November 9, 2017:
https://www.insightassessment.com/Products/Products-Summary/
Critical-Thinking-Skills-Tests/California-Critical-Thinking-Skills-Test-CCTST

Institute for Responsible Technology, "The Great GMO Cover-Up #2: Companies
Hide Dangers; Attack Scientists," *The Hill*, April 12, 2016. As of July 5, 2017:
http://thehill.com/sponsored/
content/276030-companies-hide-dangers-attack-scientists

Internet Live Stats, "Twitter Usage Statistics," webpage, undated. As of
September 5, 2017:
http://www.internetlivestats.com/twitter-statistics/

Ioannidis, John, "Why Most Published Research Findings Are False," *PLOS Med*,
Vol. 2, No. 8, August 30, 2005, pp. 696–701.

Ioannidis, John, T. D. Stanley, and Hristos Doucouliagos, "The Power of Bias
in Economics Research," *Economic Journal*, Vol. 127, No. 605, October 2017,
pp. F236–F265.

Irving, Doug, "Big Data, Big Questions," RAND Blog, October 16, 2017,
https://www.rand.org/blog/rand-review/2017/10/big-data-big-questions.html

Ishikawa, Mamoru, and Daniel Ryan, "Schooling, Basic Skills and Economic
Outcomes," *Economics of Education Review*, Vol. 21, No. 3, 2002, pp. 231–243.

Jensen, Jamie, Mark McDaniel, Steven Woodward, and Tyler Kummer, "Teaching
to the Test . . . or Testing to Teach: Exams Requiring Higher Order Thinking
Skills Encourage Greater Conceptual Understanding," *Education Psychology
Review*, June 2014.

Joinson, Adam N., "Self-Esteem, Interpersonal Risk, and Preference for E-Mail to
Face-to-Face Communication," *CyberPsychology & Behavior*, Vol. 7, No. 4, 2004,
pp. 472–478.

Jones, Bradley, "Americans' Views of Immigrants Marked by Widening Partisan,
Generational Divides," Pew Research Center, April 15, 2016a. As of June 4, 2017:
http://www.pewresearch.org/fact-tank/2016/04/15/americans-views-of-
immigrants-marked-by-widening-partisan-generational-divides/

Josephson, Matthew, *The Robber Barons*, New York: Houghton Mifflin, 1962.

Journell, Wayne, "The Influence of High-Stakes Testing on High School Teachers' Willingness to Incorporate Current Political Events into the Curriculum," *High School Journal*, Vol. 93, No. 3, Spring 2010, pp. 111–125.

Julio, Brandon, and Youngsuk Yook, "Political Uncertainty and Corporate Investment Cycles," *Journal of Finance*, Vol. 67, No. 1, 2012, pp. 45–83.

Jung, Donald J., *The Federal Communications Commission, the Broadcast Industry, and the Fairness Doctrine: 1981–1987*, New York: University Press of America, Inc., 1996.

Kahan, Dan M., "Ideology, Motivated Reasoning, and Cognitive Reflection: An Experimental Study," Yale Law School, Public Law Research Paper No. 272, 2012.

Kahan, Dan M., and Donald Braman, "Cultural Cognition and Public Policy," *Yale Law & Policy Review*, Vol. 24, No. 1, 2006, pp. 149–172.

Kahan, Dan M., Hank Jenkins Smith, and Donald Braman, "Cultural Cognition of Scientific Consensus," *Journal of Risk Research*, Vol. 14, No. 2, 2011, pp. 147–174.

Kahne, Joseph, and Benjamin Bowyer, "Educating for Democracy in a Partisan Age: Confronting the Challenges of Motivated Reasoning and Misinformation," *American Educational Research Journal*, Vol. 54, No. 1, February 2017, pp. 3–34.

Kahne, Joseph E., and Susan E. Sporte, "Developing Citizens: The Impact of Civic Learning Opportunities on Students' Commitment to Civic Participation," *American Educational Research Journal*, Vol. 45, No. 3, 2008, pp. 738–766.

Kann, Mark E., Jeff Berry, Connor Gant, and Phil Zager, "The Internet and Youth Political Participation," *First Monday*, Vol. 12, No. 8, 2007. As of December 18, 2017:
http://www.firstmonday.dk/ojs/index.php/fm/article/view/1977/1852

Kauffman, Bill, "When the Left Was Right," *The American Conservative*, May 19, 2008. As of June 4, 2017:
http://www.theamericanconservative.com/articles/when-the-left-was-right/

Kennedy, David M., *Freedom from Fear: The American People in Depression and War, 1929–1945*, Oxford and New York: Oxford University Press, 1999.

Kertzer, Joshua D., and Ryan Brutger, "Decomposing Audience Costs: Bringing the Audience Back into Audience Cost Theory," *American Journal of Political Science*, Vol. 60, No. 1, 2016, pp. 234–249.

Kimball, Roger, *The Long March: How the Cultural Revolution of the 1960s Changed America*, New York: Encounter Books, 2013.

Kirkham, Richard L., *Theories of Truth: A Critical Introduction*, Cambridge, Mass.: MIT Press, 1992.

Klar, Samara, "Partisanship in a Social Setting," *American Journal of Political Science*, Vol. 58, No. 3, July 2014, pp. 687–704.

Klein, Christopher, "10 Things You May Not Know About the Dust Bowl," The History Channel, August 24, 2012. As of October 3, 2017: http://www.history.com/news/10-things-you-may-not-know-about-the-dust-bowl

Kliff, Sarah, and Ezra Klein, "The Lessons of Obamacare," Vox, March 15, 2017. As of June 4, 2017: https://www.vox.com/policy-and-politics/2017/3/15/14908524/ obamacare-lessons-ahca-gop

Knack, Stephen, "Social Capital and the Quality of Government: Evidence from the States," *American Journal of Political Science*, Vol. 46, No. 4, October 2002, pp. 772–785.

Kolata, Gina, "Many Academics Are Eager to Publish in Worthless Journals," *New York Times*, October 30, 2017.

Kondik, Kyle, and Geoffrey Skelley, "Incumbent Reelection Rates Higher Than Average in 2016," Rassmussen Reports, December 15, 2016. As of June 4, 2017: http://www.rasmussenreports.com/public_content/ political_commentary/commentary_by_kyle_kondik/ incumbent_reelection_rates_higher_than_average_in_2016

Konnikova, Maria, "How a Gay Marriage Study Went Wrong," *The New Yorker*, May 22, 2015. As of July 10, 2017: http://www.newyorker.com/science/maria-konnikova/ how-a-gay-marriage-study-went-wrong

Kossinets, G., J. Kleinberg, and D. Watts, "The Structure of Information Pathways in a Social Communication Network," *Proceedings of the 14th Association for Computing Machinery Special Interest Group on Knowledge Discovery and Data Mining's International Conference on Knowledge Discovery and Data Mining*, 2008.

Krikorian, Raffi, "New Tweets per Second Record, and How!" Twitter Blog, August 16, 2013. As of November 8, 2017: https://blog.twitter.com/engineering/en_us/a/2013/ new-tweets-per-second-record-and-how.html

Krogstad, Jens Manuel, and Mark Hugo Lopez, "Black Voter Turnout Fell in 2016, Even as a Record Number of Americans Cast Ballots," Pew Research Center, May 12, 2017. As of June 4, 2017: http://www.pewresearch.org/fact-tank/2017/05/12/black-voter-turnout-fell-in-2016-even-as-a-record-number-of-americans-cast-ballots/

Kruglanski, Arie W., "Motivated Social Cognition: Principles of the Interface," in E. Tory Higgins and A. W. Kruglanski, eds., *Social Psychology: Handbook of Basic Principles*, New York: Guilford Press, 1996, pp. 493–520.

Kumar, K. P. Krishna, and Gopalan Geethakumari, "Detecting Misinformation in Online Social Networks Using Cognitive Psychology," *Human-Centric Computing and Information Sciences*, Vol. 4, No. 1, 2014. As of December 18, 2017: https://hcis-journal.springeropen.com/track/pdf/10.1186/s13673-014-0014-x?site=hcis-journal.springeropen.com

Kunda, Ziva, "The Case for Motivated Reasoning," *Psychological Bulletin*, Vol. 108, No. 3, 1990, pp. 480–498.

Künne, Wolfgang, *Conceptions of Truth*, Oxford: Clarendon Press, 2003.

Labonte, Marc, *The FY2014 Government Shutdown: Economic Effects*, Washington, D.C.: Congressional Research Service, September 11, 2015.

Lang, Corey, and Shanna Pearson-Merkowitz, "Partisan Sorting in the United States, 1972–2012: New Evidence from a Dynamic Analysis," *Political Geography*, Vol. 48, 2015, pp. 119–129.

La Raja, Raymond J., "Campaign Finance and Partisan Polarization in the United States Congress," *Duke Journal of Constitutional Law & Public Policy*, Vol. 9, No. 2, 2014, pp. 223–258.

La Raja, Raymond J., and Brian F. Schaffner, "The Effects of Campaign Finance Spending Bans on Electoral Outcomes: Evidence from the States About the Potential Impact of Citizens United v. FEC," *Electoral Studies*, Vol. 33, No. 1, 2014, pp. 102–114.

———, *Campaign Finance and Political Polarization: When Purists Prevail*, Ann Arbor, Mich.: University of Michigan Press, 2015.

Larochelle, Matthieu, Nicholas S. Downing, Joseph S. Ross, and Frank S. David, "Assessing the Potential Clinical Impact of Reciprocal Drug Approval Legislation on Access to Novel Therapeutics in the USA: A Cohort Study," *BMJ Open*, Vol. 7, No. 2, 2017, pp. 1–6.

Lazer, David, Matthew Baum, Nir Grinberg, Lisa Friedland, Kenneth Joseph, Will Hobbs, and Carolina Mattsson, "Combating Fake News: An Agenda for Research and Action," Cambridge, Mass.: Shorenstein Center on Media, Politics, and Public Policy, 2017. As of June 4, 2017: https://shorensteincenter.org/combating-fake-news-agenda-for-research/

Leonhardt, David, "Lesson from a Crisis: When Trust Vanishes, Worry," *New York Times*, September 30, 2008. As of July 27, 2017: http://www.nytimes.com/2008/10/01/business/economy/01leonhardt.html?mcubz=2

Lerner, Jennifer, Ye Li, Piercarlo Valdesolo, and Karim Kassam, "Emotion and Decision-Making," *Annual Review of Psychology*, Vol. 66, No. 1, 2015, pp. 799–823.

Lesher, Stephan, *George Wallace: American Populist*, Boston: Addison Wesley, 1994.

Leskes, Andrea, "A Plea for Civil Discourse: Needed, the Academy's Leadership," *Liberal Education*, Vol. 99, No. 4, 2013. As of December 18, 2017: http://www.marshall.edu/academic-affairs/files/A-Plea-for-Civil-Discourse.pdf

Levendusky, Matthew, *The Partisan Sort: How Liberals Became Democrats and Conservatives Became Republicans*, Chicago: University of Chicago Press, 2009.

———, "Affect Effects: Do Viewers Dislike and Distrust the Opposition After Partisan Media Exposure?" Philadelphia, Pa., University of Pennsylvania, working paper, 2012a.

———, "Do Partisan Media Polarize Voters?" Philadelphia, Pa., University of Pennsylvania, working paper, 2012b.

Levi, Margaret, and Laura Stoker, "Political Trust and Trustworthiness," *Annual Review of Political Science*, Vol. 2, 2000, pp. 475–507.

Levine, Peter, and Kei Kawashima-Ginsberg, *Civics Education and Deeper Learning*, Boston: Jobs for the Future, February 2015.

Lewandowsky, Stephan, Ullrich K. H. Ecker, Colleen M. Seifert, Norbert Schwarz, and John Cook, "Misinformation and Its Correction: Continued Influence and Successful Debiasing," *Psychological Science in the Public Interest*, Vol. 13, No. 3, 2012, pp. 106–131.

Lewis, Charles, *935 Lies: The Future of Truth and the Decline of America's Moral Integrity*, New York: Perseus Books, June 2014.

Library of Congress, "Rise of Industrial America, 1876–1900," webpage, undated. As of June 4, 2017: http://www.loc.gov/teachers/classroommaterials/presentationsandactivities/ presentations/timeline/riseind/city/

Lieu, Tracy, G. Thomas Ray, Nicola Klein, Cindy Chung, and Martin Kulldorff, "Geographic Clusters in Underimmunization and Vaccine Refusal," *Pediatrics*, Vol. 135, No. 2, February 2015, pp. 280–289.

Lipton, Eric, and Brooke Williams, "How Think Tanks Amplify Corporate America's Influence," *New York Times*, August 7, 2016. As of September 5, 2017: https://www.nytimes.com/2016/08/08/us/politics/think-tanks-research-and-corporate-lobbying.html?mcubz=0

Loevy, Robert, *The Civil Rights Act of 1964: The Passage of the Law That Ended Racial Segregation*, Albany, N.Y.: State University of New York Press, 1997.

Lowman, Rob, "Al Gore's Current TV Network Moves Toward Becoming a 24/7 Channel," *Daily Breeze*, January 29, 2012. As of July 10, 2017: http://www.dailybreeze.com/general-news/20120129/ al-gores-current-tv-network-moves-toward-becoming-a-247-channel

Luntz, Frank, *Words That Work: It's Not What You Say, It's What People Hear*, New York: Hachette Books, 2008.

MacLeod, Colin, Ernst H. W. Koster, and Elaine Fox, "Whither Cognitive Bias Modification Research? Commentary on the Special Section Articles," *Journal of Abnormal Psychology*, Vol. 118, No. 1, 2009, pp. 89–99.

Mahoney, James, and Kathleen Thelen, "A Theory of Gradual Institutional Change," in James Mahoney and Kathleen Thelen, eds., Explaining *Institutional Change: Ambiguity, Agency, and Power*, New York: Cambridge University Press, 2010.

Mascaro, Christopher M., and Sean P. Goggins, "Technologically Mediated Political Discourse During a Nationally Televised GOP Primary Debate," *Journal of Information Technology & Politics*, Vol. 12, No. 3, 2015, pp. 252–269.

Mason, Lilliana, "'I Disrespectfully Agree': The Differential Effects of Partisan Sorting on Social and Issue Polarization," *American Journal of Political Science*, Vol. 59, No. 1, 2015, pp. 128–145.

Massanari, Adrienne, "#Gamergate and the Fappening: How Reddit's Algorithm, Governance, and Culture Support Toxic Technocultures," *New Media & Society*, Vol. 19, No. 3, 2017, pp. 329–346.

Matsa, Katerina Eva, "Cable News Fact Sheet," Pew Research Center, June 1, 2017. As of June 4, 2017:
http://www.journalism.org/fact-sheet/cable-news/

Maues, Julia, "Banking Act of 1933," Federal Reserve Bank of St. Louis, November 22, 2013. As of July 27, 2017:
https://www.federalreservehistory.org/essays/glass_steagall_act

McAdam, Doug, "The U.S. Civil Rights Movement: Power from Below and Above, 1945–70," in Adam Roberts and Timothy Garton Ash, eds., *Civil Resistance and Power Politics: The Experience of Non-Violent Action from Gandhi to the Present*, Oxford and New York: Oxford University Press, 2009.

McCarty, Nolan, Keith T. Poole, and Howard Rosenthal, *Polarized America: The Dance of Ideology and Unequal Riches*, Cambridge, Mass.: MIT Press, 2008.

McCarty, Nolan, and Boris Shor, "Partisan Polarization in the United States: Diagnoses and Avenues for Reform," Cambridge, Mass.: Harvard University, working paper, 2015.

McCright, Aaron M., Sandra T. Marquart-Pyatt, Rachael L. Shwom, Steven R. Brechin, and Summer Allen, "Ideology, Capitalism, and Climate: Explaining Public Views About Climate Change in the United States," *Energy Research and Social Science*, Vol. 21, 2016, pp. 180–189.

McCright, Aaron, Chenyang Xiao, and Riley Dunlap, "Political Polarization on Support for Government Spending on Environmental Protection in the USA, 1974–2012," *Social Science Research*, Vol. 48, 2014, pp. 251–260.

McGhee, Eric, Seth Masket, Boris Shor, Steven Rogers, and Nolan McCarty, "A Primary Cause of Partisanship? Nomination Systems and Legislator Ideology," *American Journal of Political Science*, Vol. 58, No. 2, 2014, pp. 337–351.

Media Literacy Project, "About Us," webpage, undated-a. As of May 12, 2017: http://medialiteracyproject.org/about/

———, "What We Do," webpage, undated-b. As of May 12, 2017: http://medialiteracyproject.org/what-we-do/

Meirowitz, Adam, and Anne E. Sartori, "Strategic Uncertainty as a Cause of War," *Quarterly Journal of Political Science*, Vol. 3, No. 4, 2008, pp. 327–352.

Melchior, Alan, Joseph Frees, Lisa LaCava, Chris Kingsley, Jennifer Nahas, Jennifer Power, Gus Baker, John Blomquist, Anne St. George, Scott Hebert, JoAnn Jastrzab, Chuck Helfer, and L Lance Potter, *Summary Report: National Evaluation of Learn and Serve America*, Education Resources Information Center Clearinghouse, U.S. Department of Education, 1999.

Merriam-Webster, home page, undated. As of July 10, 2017: https://www.merriam-webster.com

Mitchell, Amy, Jeffrey Gottfried, Elisa Shearer, and Kristine Lu, "How Americans Encounter, Recall, and Act Upon Digital News," Pew Research Center, February 9, 2017. http://www.journalism.org/2017/02/09/how-americans-encounter-recall-and-act-upon-digital-news/

Moody, James, and Peter J. Mucha, "Portrait of Political Party Polarization," *Network Science*, Vol. 1, No. 1, 2013, pp. 119–121.

Moon, Soo Jung, and Patrick Hadley, "Routinizing a New Technology in the Newsroom: Twitter as a News Source in Mainstream Media," *Journal of Broadcasting & Electronic Media*, Vol. 58, No. 2, 2014, pp. 289–305.

Moriarty, Sandra Ernst, Nancy Mitchell, William Wells, Robert Crawford, and Linda Brennan, *Advertising: Principles and Practice*, Melbourne, Australia: Pearson Australia, 2014.

Morris, Jonathan S., "The Fox News Factor," *Harvard International Journal of Press/Politics*, Vol. 10, No. 3, 2005, pp. 56–79.

Morrow, James D., "Capabilities, Uncertainty, and Resolve: A Limited Information Model of Crisis Bargaining," *American Journal of Political Science*, Vol. 33, No. 4, November 1989, pp. 941–972.

———, "Alliances, Credibility, and Peacetime Costs," *Journal of Conflict Resolution*, Vol. 38, No. 2, 1994, pp. 270–297.

Mulligan, Casey, "How Many Jobs Does ObamaCare Kill?" *Wall Street Journal*, July 5, 2017.

Murphy, James E., "The New Journalism: A Critical Perspective," *Journalism Monographs*, No. 34, May 1974.

Musser, Rick, "History of American Journalism," University of Kansas, December 2007. As of June 4, 2017: http://history.journalism.ku.edu/1900/1900.shtml

Myers, Teresa A., Edward Maibach, Ellen Peters, and Anthony Leiserowitz, "Simple Messages Help Set the Record Straight About Scientific Agreement on Human-Caused Climate Change: The Results of Two Experiments," *PloS One*, Vol. 10, No. 3, 2015. As of December 18, 2017: http://journals.plos.org/plosone/article?id=10.1371/journal.pone.0120985

National Academies of Sciences, Committee on Science Communication, *Communicating Science Effectively: A Research Agenda*, Washington, D.C.: National Academies Press, 2017.

National Academies of Sciences, Engineering, and Medicine, *Genetically Engineered Crops: Experiences and Prospects*, Washington, D.C.: National Academies Press, 2016.

National Center for Education Statistics, "Are the Nation's Eighth-Graders Making Progress in Civics?" infographic, The Nation's Report Card, U.S. Department of Education, NCES-2015-112c, 2014.

National Research Council, *Scientific Research in Education*, Washington, D.C., National Academies Press, 2002.

National Science Teachers Association, "About the Next Generation Science Standards," webpage, undated. As of July 27, 2017: http://ngss.nsta.org/About.aspx

National Task Force on Civic Learning and Democratic Engagement, *A Crucible Moment: College Learning and Democracy's Future*, Washington, D.C., 2012.

Newell, Barbara, *A Quantitative Research Study on the Effects and Perceptions of the No Child Left Behind Legislation*, dissertation, University of Phoenix, 2014.

Newport, Frank, "In U.S., Percentage Saying Vaccines Are Vital Dips Slightly," Gallup, March 6, 2015. As of June 4, 2017: http://www.gallup.com/poll/181844/ percentage-saying-vaccines-vital-dips-slightly.aspx

News Literacy Project, "Program," webpage, undated. As of July 27, 2017: http://thenewsliteracyproject.org/about/program

"Newspapers," *Dictionary of American History*, Farmington Hills, Mich.: Gale Group, 2003.

Next Generation Science Standards, *Next Generation Science Standards: Executive Summary*, June 2013. As of July 27, 2017:
http://www.nextgenscience.org/sites/default/files/Final%20Release%20NGSS%20Front%20Matter%20-%206.17.13%20Update_0.pdf

Nguyen, Nam P., Guanhua Yan, and My T. Thai, "Analysis of Misinformation Containment in Online Social Networks," *Computer Networks*, Vol. 57, No. 10, 2013, pp. 2133–2146.

Nguyen, Nam P., Guanhua Yan, My T. Thai, and Stephan Eidenbenz, "Containment of Misinformation Spread in Online Social Networks," *Proceedings of the 4th Annual Association for Computing Machinery Web Science Conference*, New York: ACM, 2012. As of September 6, 2017:
http://dl.acm.org/citation.cfm?id=2380746

Nichols, Thomas, *The Death of Expertise: The Campaign Against Established Knowledge and Why It Matters*, New York: Oxford University Press, 2017.

Niemi, Richard G., and Jane Junn, *Civic Education: What Makes Students Learn*, New Haven, Conn.: Yale University Press, 2008.

Nikolov, Dimitar, Diego F. M. Oliveira, Alessandro Flammini, and Filippo Menczer, "Measuring Online Social Bubbles," *Peer Journal of Computer Science*, Vol. 1, 2015. As of December 18, 2017:
https://peerj.com/articles/cs-38.pdf

Noam, Eli, *Media Ownership and Concentration in America*, New York: Oxford University Press, 2009.

———, "Who Owns the World's Media?" Columbia Business School Research Paper, No. 13-22, September 2013.

Novak, Matt, "24 Hours of UberFacts: So Many Lies, So Little Time," Gizmodo, March 12, 2014. As of September 5, 2017:
https://paleofuture.gizmodo.com/uberfacts-is-full-of-lies-1541956164?utm_campaign=socialflow_gizmodo_twitter&utm_source=gizmodo_twitter&utm_medium=socialflow

Nyhan, Brendan, and Jason Reifler, "When Corrections Fail: The Persistence of Political Misperceptions," *Political Behavior*, Vol. 32, No. 2, 2010, pp. 303–330.

———, *The Roles of Information Deficits and Identity Threat in the Prevalence of Misperceptions*, manuscript, Dartmouth College, February 24, 2017. As of November 9, 2017:
https://www.dartmouth.edu/~nyhan/opening-political-mind.pdf

Office of the Director of National Intelligence, *Assessing Russian Activities and Intentions in Recent US Elections*, Washington, D.C., ICA 2017-01D, January 6, 2017. As of September 5, 2017:
https://www.dni.gov/files/documents/ICA_2017_01.pdf

Ohlheiser, Abby, "This Is How Facebook's Fake-News Writers Make Money," *Washington Post*, November 18, 2016. As of June 4, 2017:
https://www.washingtonpost.com/news/the-intersect/wp/2016/11/18/this-is-how-the-internets-fake-news-writers-make-money/

Okun, Arthur, "A Postmortem of the 1974 Recession," *Brookings Papers on Economic Activity*, No. 1, 1975.

Oreskes, Naomi, "The Scientific Consensus on Climate Change," *Science*, Vol. 306, No. 5702, 2004, p. 1686.

Osoba, Osonde A., and William Welser IV, *An Intelligence in Our Image: The Risks of Bias and Errors in Artificial Intelligence*, Santa Monica, Calif.: RAND Corporation, RR-1744-RC, 2017. As of July 10, 2017:
https://www.rand.org/pubs/research_reports/RR1744.html

Pace, Judith L., "The Complex and Unequal Impact of High Stakes Accountability on Untested Social Studies," *Theory & Research in Social Education*, Vol. 39, No. 1, 2011, pp. 32–60.

Pane, John F., Elizabeth D. Steiner, Matthew D. Baird, Laura S. Hamilton, and Joseph D. Pane, *Informing Progress: Insights on Personalized Learning Implementation and Effects*, Santa Monica, Calif.: RAND Corporation, RR-2042-BMGF, 2017. As of September 12, 2017:
https://www.rand.org/pubs/research_reports/RR2042.html

Patrick, Dennis, "Abolishing the Fairness Doctrine: A Policy Maker's Perspective," speech delivered to the George Mason University Information Economy Project, National Press Club, Washington, D.C., July 18, 2007.

Paul, Chris, and Miriam Matthews, *The Russian "Firehose of Falsehood" Propaganda Model: Why It Might Work and Options to Counter It*, Santa Monica, Calif.: RAND Corporation, PE-198-OSD, 2016. As of June 4, 2017:
https://www.rand.org/pubs/perspectives/PE198.html

Perkins, David, *Making Learning Whole*, San Francisco: Josey Bass, 2009.

Perkins, Lucy, "California Governor Signs School Vaccination Law," NPR, June 30, 2015. As of July 27, 2017:
http://www.npr.org/sections/thetwo-way/2015/06/30/418908804/california-governor-signs-school-vaccination-law

Pettigrew, Thomas F., "Generalized Intergroup Contact Effects on Prejudice," *Personality and Social Psychology Bulletin*, Vol. 23, No. 2, 1997, pp. 173–185.

———, "Intergroup Contact Theory," *Annual Review of Psychology*, Vol. 49, No. 1, 1998, pp. 65–85.

Pettigrew, Thomas F., and Linda R. Tropp, "A Meta-Analytic Test of Intergroup Contact Theory," *Journal of Personality and Social Psychology*, Vol. 90, No. 5, 2006, pp. 751–783.

————, *When Groups Meet: The Dynamics of Intergroup Contact*, New York: Psychology Press, 2011.

Pew Initiative on Food and Biotechnology, "Americans' Opinions About Genetically Modified Foods Remain Divided, but Majority Want a Strong Regulatory System," press release, December 8, 2004. As of January 7, 2018: http://www.pewtrusts.org/en/about/news-room/press-releases/2004/12/08/americans-opinions-about-genetically-modified-foods-remain-divided-but-majority-want-a-strong-regulatory-system2

Pew Research Center, "About Pew Research Center," webpage, undated. As of November 8, 2017: http://www.pewresearch.org/about/

————, "Public Knowledge of Current Affairs Little Changed by News and Information Revolutions," webpage, April 15, 2007. As of June 4, 2017: http://www.people-press.org/2007/04/15/public-knowledge-of-current-affairs-little-changed-by-news-and-information-revolutions/

————, "Press Widely Criticized, but Trusted More Than Other Information Sources," webpage, September 22, 2011. As of June 4, 2017: http://www.people-press.org/2011/09/22/press-widely-criticized-but-trusted-more-than-other-institutions/

————, "Civic Engagement," webpage, April 25, 2013. As of June 4, 2017: http://www.pewinternet.org/2013/04/25/civic-engagement/

————, "Political Polarization in the American Public," webpage, June 12, 2014. As of June 4, 2017: http://www.people-press.org/2014/06/12/political-polarization-in-the-american-public/

————, "Beyond Distrust: How Americans View Their Government—1. Trust in Government: 1958–2015," webpage, November 23, 2015a. As of June 4, 2017: http://www.people-press.org/2015/11/23/1-trust-in-government-1958-2015

————, "Beyond Distrust: How Americans View Their Government—9. Views of the Nation, How It's Changing and Confidence in the Future," webpage, November 23, 2015b. As of June 4, 2017: http://www.people-press.org/2015/11/23/9-views-of-the-nation-how-its-changing-and-confidence-in-the-future/

————, *State of the News Media*, Washington, D.C., June 15, 2016a. As of June 4, 2017: http://assets.pewresearch.org/wp-content/uploads/sites/13/2016/06/30143308/state-of-the-news-media-report-2016-final.pdf

———, "Politically Competitive Counties Have Become Even Less Common," webpage, June 29, 2016b. As of September 11, 2017:
http://www.pewresearch.org/fact-tank/2016/06/30/
electorally-competitive-counties-have-grown-scarcer-in-recent-decades/
ft_16-06-30_contestedcounties_chart/

———, "Even in an Era of Disillusionment, Many Around the World Say Regular Citizens Can Influence Government," webpage, October 24, 2016c. As of June 4, 2017:
http://www.pewglobal.org/2016/10/24/even-in-era-of-disillusionment-
many-around-the-world-say-ordinary-citizens-can-influence-government/
civic-participation-02/

———, "Public Trust in Government: 1958–2017," webpage, May 3, 2017b. As of September 5, 2017:
http://www.people-press.org/2017/05/03/public-trust-in-government-1958-2017/

Pillar, Paul, "Intelligence, Policy, and the War in Iraq," *Foreign Affairs*, Vol. 85, No. 2, March/April 2006, pp. 15–27.

Politifact, "Browse by Speaker," webpage, undated. As of September 5, 2017:
http://www.politifact.com/personalities/

Poniewozik, Jim, "Walter Cronkite: The Man with America's Trust," *Time*, July 17, 2009. As of July 27, 2017:
http://content.time.com/time/nation/article/0,8599,1911501,00.html

Poole, Keith, and Howard Rosenthal, "A Spatial Model for Legislative Roll Call Analysis," *American Journal of Political Science*, Vol. 29, No. 2, 1985, pp. 357–384.

"Popular Votes 1940–2012," Roper Center, webpage, undated. As of June 4, 2017:
https://ropercenter.cornell.edu/polls/us-elections/popular-vote/

Portman, Rob, "President Signs Portman-Murphy Counter-Propaganda Bill into Law," press release, December 23, 2016. As of June 4, 2017:
https://www.portman.senate.gov/public/index.cfm/2016/12/
president-signs-portman-murphy-counter-propaganda-bill-into-law

Primo, David M., and Jeffrey Milyo, "Campaign Finance Laws and Political Efficacy: Evidence from the States," *Election Law Journal: Rules, Politics, and Policy*, Vol. 5, No. 1, February 2006, pp. 23–39.

Prior, Markus, "Media and Political Polarization," *Annual Review of Political Science*, Vol. 16, No. 1, 2013, pp. 101–127.

Project for Excellence in Journalism, "The State of the News Media Report: 2004," Pew Research Center, undated. As of June 4, 2017:
http://assets.pewresearch.org/wp-content/uploads/sites/13/2017/05/24141554/
State-of-the-News-Media-Report-2004-FINAL.pdf

———, *Changing Definitions of News*, Washington, D.C., March 6, 1998. As of June 4, 2017:
http://www.journalism.org/files/legacy/ChangingDefinitionsofNews.pdf

Public Law 107–155, Bipartisan Campaign Reform Act of 2002, March 27, 2002.

Putnam, Robert D., *Bowling Alone*, New York: Simon & Schuster, 2000.

Puzzanghera, Jim, and E. Scott Reckard, "Citigroup to Pay Record Fine in $7-Billion Mortgage Settlement," *Los Angeles Times*, July 14, 2014. As of January 7, 2018:
http://www.latimes.com/business/
la-fi-citigroup-subprime-mortgage-settlement-20140714-story.html

Quinnipiac University Poll, "Trump Slumps as American Voters Disapprove 55%–38% Quinnipiac University National Poll Finds; Voters Trust Media, Courts More Than President," February 22, 2017a. As of June 4, 2017:
https://poll.qu.edu/images/polling/us/us02222017_Urj52hkb.pdf/

———, "GOP Health Plan Backers Could Feel Pain at the Polls, Quinnipiac University National Poll Finds; Only 20 Percent of U.S. Voters Support Plan," May 25, 2017b. As of June 4, 2017:
https://poll.qu.edu/national/release-detail?ReleaseID=2461.

Quintelier, Ellen, "Differences in Political Participation Between Young and Old People," *Contemporary Politics*, Vol. 13, No. 2, 2007, pp. 165–180.

Ramsey, Lydia, "5 Biggest Myths and Misconceptions About Zika Debunked," *Business Insider*, August 15, 2016. As of September 5, 2017:
http://www.businessinsider.com/
false-myths-about-zika-debunked-by-science-2016-8

RAND Corporation, "Diversity at RAND," webpage, undated-a. As of November 8, 2017:
https://www.rand.org/diversity.html

———, "Overview of RAND Staff," webpage, undated-b. As of November 8, 2017:
https://www.rand.org/about/staff.html

———, "Standards for High-Quality Research and Analysis," webpage, undated-c. As of September 5, 2017:
https://www.rand.org/standards/standards_high.html

———, "Welcome to the ALP Data Pages," webpage, undated-d. As of November 8, 2017:
https://alpdata.rand.org

———, "RAND Retracts Report About Medical Marijuana Dispensaries and Crime," news release, October 24, 2011. As of September 5, 2017:
https://www.rand.org/news/press/2011/10/24.html

———, "How We're Funded," webpage, March 22, 2017. As of September 5, 2017:
https://www.rand.org/about/clients_grantors.html

———, "RAND Corporation Board of Trustees," webpage, September 2017. As of January 8, 2017:
https://www.rand.org/about/organization/randtrustees.html

Ratkiewicz, Jacob, Michael D. Conover, Mark Meiss, Bruno Goncalves, Alessandro Flammini, and Filippo Menczer, "Detecting and Tracking Political Abuse in Social Media," *International AAAI Conference on Web and Social Media*, 2011.

Redlawsk, David, "Hot Cognition or Cool Consideration? Testing the Effects of Motivated Reasoning on Political Decision Making," *Journal of Politics*, Vol. 64, No. 4, November 2002, pp. 1021–1044.

Reisigl, Martin, and Ruth Wodak, *Discourse and Discrimination: Rhetorics of Racism and Antisemitism*, Abingdon, UK: Routledge, 2005.

Reston, Laura, "Immigrants Don't Drain Welfare. They Fund It," *New Republic*, September 30, 2015. As of November 8, 2017:
https://newrepublic.com/article/122714/
immigrants-dont-drain-welfare-they-fund-it

Rheingold, Howard, "Using Participatory Media and Public Voice to Encourage Civic Engagement," *Civic Life Online: Learning How Digital Media Can Engage Youth*, Cambridge, Mass.: MIT Press, John D. and Catherine T. MacArthur Foundation Series on Digital Media and Learning, 2008, pp. 97–118.

Rich, Michael D., *Erosion of Truth: Remarks from Politics Aside 2016*, Santa Monica, Calif.: RAND Corporation, CP-875, 2016a. As of September 13, 2017:
https://www.rand.org/pubs/corporate_pubs/CP875.html

———, "Policymaking in a Time of Truth Decay," UCLA Law School event (via YouTube), September 23, 2016b. As of November 8, 2017:
https://www.youtube.com/watch?v=wWxbO5hOI5o

Ries, Charles, Marco Hafner, Troy D. Smith, Frances G. Burwell, Daniel Egel, Eugeniu Han, Martin Stepanek, and Howard J. Shatz, *After Brexit: Alternate Forms of Brexit and Their Implications for the United Kingdom, the European Union and the United States*, Santa Monica, Calif.: RAND Corporation, RR-2200-RC, 2017. As of December 18, 2017:
https://www.rand.org/pubs/research_reports/RR2200.html

Romero, Daniel M., Brendan Meeder, and Jon Kleinberg, "Differences in the Mechanics of Information Diffusion Across Topics: Idioms, Political Hashtags, and Complex Contagion on Twitter," *Proceedings of the 20th International Conference on World Wide Web*, 2011.

Ruddick, Graham, "Experts Sound Alarms over News Websites' Fake News Twins," *The Guardian*, August 18, 2017. As of September 7, 2017: https://www.theguardian.com/technology/2017/aug/18/experts-sound-alarm-over-news-websites-fake-news-twins

Saez, Emmanuel, "Striking It Richer: The Evolution of Top Incomes in the United States (Update with 2007 Estimates)," Berkeley, Calif.: University of California, Department of Economics, 2009.

Saez, Emmanuel, and Gabriel Zucman, "Wealth Inequality in the United States Since 1913: Evidence from Capitalized Income Tax Data," *Quarterly Journal of Economics*, Vol. 131, No. 2, 2016, pp. 519–578.

Salzberg, Steven, "Nobelists to Greenpeace: Drop Your Anti-Science Anti-GMO Campaign," *Forbes*, July 4, 2016. As of July 10, 2017: https://www.forbes.com/sites/stevensalzberg/2016/07/04/nobelists-to-greenpeace-drop-your-anti-science-anti-gmo-campaign/#6ae3c3ab203a

"A Scary New Health Care Bill," *New York Times*, July 17, 2017. As of July 27, 2017: https://www.nytimes.com/2017/07/13/opinion/senate-health-care-bill-trumpcare.html?mcubz=2

Scheufele, D. A., "Agenda-Setting, Priming, and Framing Revisited: Another Look at Cognitive Effects of Political Communication," *Mass Communication and Society*, Vol. 3, Nos. 2–3, 2009, pp. 297–316.

Schudson, Michael, *The Power of News*, Cambridge, Mass.: Harvard University Press, 1996.

Schwarz, Norbert, Lawrence J. Sanna, Ian Skurnik, and Carolyn Yoon, "Metacognitive Experiences and the Intricacies of Setting People Straight: Implications for Debiasing and Public Information Campaigns," *Advances in Experimental and Social Psychology*, Vol. 39, 2007, pp. 127–161.

The Sentencing Project, *Immigration and Public Safety*, Washington, D.C., 2017.

Shao, Chengcheng, Giovanni Luca Ciampaglia, Alesssandro Flammini, and Filippo Menczer, "Hoaxy: A Platform for Tacking Online Misinformation," *Proceedings of the 25th International Conference Companion on World Wide Web*, April 11–15, 2016. As of September 6, 2017: https://dl.acm.org/citation.cfm?id=2890098

Shapiro, Herbert, ed., "The Muckrakers and American Society," *Problems in American Civilization*, Vol. 52, Lexington, Mass.: D. C. Heath, 1968.

Shearer, Elisa, and Jeffrey Gottfried, "News Use Across Social Media Platforms 2017," Pew Research Center, September 2017. As of November 8, 2017: http://www.journalism.org/2017/09/07/news-use-across-social-media-platforms-2017/

Sherman, D. K., and G. L. Cohen, "Accepting Threatening Information: Self-Affirmation and the Reduction of Defensive Biases," *Current Directions in Psychological Science*, Vol. 11, No. 4, 2002, pp. 119–123.

Sherman, Ryland, and David Waterman, "Technology and Competition in U.S. Television: Online vs. Offline," working chapter, September 21, 2013.

Short, Marc, and Briane Blase, "The Fundamental Error in the CBO's Health-Care Projections," *Washington Post*, July 14, 2017. As of July 27, 2017:
https://www.washingtonpost.com/opinions/
the-fundamental-error-in-the-cbos-health-care-projections/2017/07/14/
25f0d8a4-67ee-11e7-a1d7-9a32c91c6f40_story.html?utm_term=.203115c0c21c

Singer, Jane B., "User-Generated Visibility: Secondary Gatekeeping in a Shared Media Space," *New Media and Society*, Vol. 16, No. 1, 2014, pp. 55–73.

Siracusa, Joseph M., and David G. Coleman, *Depression to Cold War: A History of America from Herbert Hoover to Ronald Reagan*, Santa Barbara, Calif.: Praeger, 2002.

Skrentny, John, *The Minority Rights Revolution*, Cambridge, Mass.: Belknap Press of Harvard University Press, 2002.

Smith, Aaron, "Part 2: Political Engagement on Social Networking Sites," Pew Research Center, April 25, 2013. As of June 4, 2017:
http://www.pewinternet.org/2013/04/25/
part-2-political-engagement-on-social-networking-sites

Smith, Dorothy E., "A Peculiar Eclipsing: Women's Exclusion from Man's Culture," *Women's Studies International Quarterly*, Vol. 1, No. 4, 1978, pp. 281–295.

Smith, Kit, "Marketing: 47 Facebook Statistics for 2016," Brandwatch, May 12, 2016. As of November 8, 2017:
https://www.brandwatch.com/blog/47-facebook-statistics-2016/

Snyder, Jack, and Erica D. Borghard, "The Cost of Empty Threats: A Penny, Not a Pound," *American Political Science Review*, Vol. 105, No. 3, 2011, pp. 437–456.

Soule, George H., *The Prosperity Decade: From War to Depression: 1917–1929*, New York: Holt, Rinehart, and Winston, 1947.

Spector, Ronald H., "The Vietnam War and the Media," *Encyclopedia Britannica*, April 27, 2016. As of June 4, 2017:
https://www.britannica.com/topic/The-Vietnam-War-and-the-media-2051426

Stamos, Alex, "An Update on Information Operations on Facebook," Facebook Newsroom, September 6, 2017. As of November 8, 2017:
https://newsroom.fb.com/news/2017/09/information-operations-update/

Stevens, Dana, "Invasion of the Pod People," *Slate*, August 3, 2005. As of July 10, 2017:
http://www.slate.com/articles/news_and_politics/surfergirl/2005/08/
invasion_of_the_pod_people.html

Stocker, Thomas F., and Dahe Qin, eds., *Climate Change 2013: The Physical Science Basis*, Working Group I Contribution to the Fifth Assessment Report of the Intergovernmental Panel on Climate Change, New York: Cambridge University Press, 2013.

Stocking, Galen, "Digital News Fact Sheet," Pew Research Center, August 7, 2017. http://www.journalism.org/fact-sheet/digital-news/

Stony Brook University Happenings, "'Making Sense of the News: News Literacy Lessons for Digital Citizens' Online Course from the Center for News Literacy," webpage, December 2016. As of July 27, 2017:
http://www.stonybrook.edu/happenings/alumni/making-sense-of-the-news-news-literacy-lessons-for-digital-citizens-online-course-from-the-center-for-news-literacy/

Stratmann, Thomas "Campaign Finance: A Review and Assessment of the State of the Literature," *Oxford Handbook of Public Choice*, April 20, 2017. As of December 18, 2017:
https://papers.ssrn.com/sol3/papers.cfm?abstract_id=2941870

Sussell, Jesse, "New Support for the Big Sort Hypothesis: An Assessment of Partisan Geographic Sorting in California, 1992–2010," *PS: Political Science & Politics*, Vol. 46, No. 4, 2013, pp. 768–773.

Sussell, Jesse, and James A. Thomson, *Are Changing Constituencies Driving Rising Polarization in the U.S. House of Representatives?* Santa Monica, Calif.: RAND Corporation, RR-896-RC, 2015. As of June 4, 2017:
https://www.rand.org/pubs/research_reports/RR896.html

Swanberg, W. A., Pulitzer, New York: Charles Scribner's Sons, 1967.

T Brand Studio, "Cities Energized: The Urban Transition," *New York Times*, undated.

Tankard, J., L. Hendrickson, J. Silberman, K. Bliss, and S. Ghanem, "Media Frames: Approaches to Conceptualization and Measurement," paper presented at the annual convention of the Association for Education in Journalism and Mass Communication, Boston, August 1991.

Tau, Byron, Georgia Wells, and Deepa Seetharam, "Lawmakers Warn Tech Executives More Regulation May Be Coming for Social Media," *Wall Street Journal*, November 1, 2017.

Terhune, Chad, and Julie Appleby, "Uncertainty over Obamacare Leaves Next Year's Rates in Limbo," National Public Radio, July 19, 2017. As of September 11, 2017:
http://www.npr.org/sections/health-shots/2017/07/19/538099050/uncertainty-over-obamacare-leaves-next-years-rates-in-limbo

"Texas Judge Kicks Exxon Climate Lawsuit to New York Court," Reuters Business News, March 29, 2017. As of November 9, 2017:
http://www.reuters.com/article/us-exxon-mobil-climatechange/texas-judge-kicks-exxon-climate-lawsuit-to-new-york-court-idUSKBN1710AC

Theiss-Morse, Elizabeth, and John R. Hibbing, "Citizenship and Civic Engagement," *Annual Review of Political Science*, Vol. 8, No. 1, 2005, pp. 227–249.

Theriault, Sean M., "Party Polarization in the U.S. Congress: Member Replacement and Member Adaptation," *Party Politics*, Vol. 12, No. 4, 2006, pp. 483–503.

Thomsen, Jacqueline, "Three Resign from CNN After Russia Story Retraction," *The Hill*, June 26, 2017. As of July 10, 2017:
http://thehill.com/media/339564-three-resign-from-cnn-over-russia-story-retraction

Timberlake, Richard H., Jr., "Panic of 1893," in David Glasner and Thomas F. Cooley, eds., *Business Cycles and Depressions: An Encyclopedia*, New York: Garland Publishing, 1997, pp. 516–518.

Toor, Amar, "France Has a Fake News Problem, But It Is Not as Bad as the U.S.," *The Verge*, April 21, 2017. As of June 4, 2017:
https://www.theverge.com/2017/4/21/15381422/france-fake-news-election-russia-oxford-study

Troia, Gary, and Steve Graham, "Common Core Writing and Language Standards and Aligned State Assessments: A National Survey of Teacher Beliefs and Attitudes" *Reading and Writing*, Vol. 29, No. 9, November 2016, pp. 1719–1743.

Tseng, V., "Studying the Use of Research Evidence in Policy and Practice," *Social Policy Report*, Vol. 26, No. 2, 2012, pp. 3–16.

Tull, Charles J., *Father Coughlin and the New Deal*, Syracuse, N.Y.: Syracuse University Press, 1965.

Tversky, Amos, and Daniel Kahneman, "Judgment Under Uncertainty: Heuristics and Biases," *Science*, Vol. 185, No. 4157, 1974, pp. 1124–1131.

Twitter Engineering, "200 Million Tweets per Day," Twitter Blog, June 30, 2011. As of September 6, 2017:
https://blog.twitter.com/official/en_us/a/2011/200-million-tweets-per-day.html

Tyack, David, and Larry Cuban, *Tinkering Toward Utopia: A Century of Public School Reform*, Cambridge, Mass.: Harvard University Press, 1997.

Unger, Irwin, *The Best of Intentions: The Triumphs and Failures of the Great Society Under Kennedy, Johnson, and Nixon*, New York: Doubleday, 1996.

*United States v Philip Morris*, Civil Action No. 99-2496, 2004.

USAFacts, "About Us," webpage, undated. As of September 12, 2017:
https://www.usafacts.org/about

U.S. Census Bureau, *Census of Population and Housing 2010*, 2012. As of June 4, 2017:
https://www.census.gov/population/censusdata/table-4.pdf

U.S. Department of Commerce, Bureau of Economic Analysis, "GDP: One of the Great Inventions of the 20th Century," from the January 2000 Survey of Current Business, January 2000. As of September 5, 2017:
https://www.bea.gov/scb/account_articles/general/0100od/maintext.htm

U.S. Department of Labor, *Bulletin of the Department of Labor*, No. 29, U.S. Government Printing Office, July 1900.

U.S. Senate Historical Office, "Cloture Motions," webpage, undated-a. As of December 18, 2017:
https://www.senate.gov/pagelayout/reference/cloture_motions/clotureCounts.htm

———, "Party Division," webpage, undated-b. As of December 18, 2017:
https://www.senate.gov/history/partydiv.htm

———, "Select Committee on Presidential Campaign Activities," webpage, undated-c. As of July 10, 2017:
https://www.senate.gov/artandhistory/history/common/investigations/Watergate.htm

Valli, Linda, and Robert Croninger, "High Quality Teaching of Foundational Skills in Mathematics and Reading," Chicago: Data Research and Development Center, undated. As of June 16, 2017:
https://drdc.uchicago.edu/community/project.php?projectID=79

Vaughn, Stephen, ed., *Encyclopedia of American Journalism*, New York: Routledge, 2008.

Verba, Sidney, and Norman H. Nie, *Participation in America*, New York: Harper & Row, 1972.

Vice Chairman's Staff of the Joint Economic Committee, *What We Do Together: The State of Associational Life in America*, SCP Report No. 1-17, May 2017. As of June 4, 2017:
https://www.lee.senate.gov/public/_cache/files/b5f224ce-98f7-40f6-a814-8602696714d8/what-we-do-together.pdf

Voorhies, John, Nolan McCarty, and Boris Shor, "Unequal Incomes, Ideology, and Gridlock: How Rising Inequality Increases Political Polarization," working paper, August 2015.

"Voter Turnout," United States Election Project, webpage, undated. As of November 9, 2017:
http://www.electproject.org/home/voter-turnout/voter-turnout-data

Vultee, Fred, "Audience Perceptions of Editing Quality: Assessing Traditional News Routines in the Digital Age," *Digital Journalism*, 2014.

Wagner, Tony, *The Global Achievement Gap: Why Even Our Best Schools Don't Teach the New Survival Skills Our Children Need—and What We Can Do About It*, New York: Basic Books, 2008.

Walker, Jack L., *Mobilizing Interest Groups in America: Patrons, Professions, and Social Movements*, Ann Arbor, Mich.: University of Michigan Press, 1991.

Wang, William Yang, "'Liar, Liar Pants on Fire': A New Benchmark Dataset for Fake News Detection," *Proceedings of the 55th Annual Meeting of the Association for Computational Linguistics*, Vancouver, July 30–August 4, 2017, pp. 422–426.

Wardle, Claire, "Fake News: It's Complicated," *First Draft*, February 16, 2017. As of September 6, 2017:
https://firstdraftnews.com/fake-news-complicated/

Wasserman, David, "2016 National Popular Vote Tracker," Cook Political Report, January 2, 2017a. As of June 4, 2017:
http://cookpolitical.com/story/10174

———, "Purple America Has All But Disappeared," FiveThirtyEight Blog, March 8, 2017b. As of June 4, 2017:
https://fivethirtyeight.com/features/purple-america-has-all-but-disappeared/

Weil, Kevin, "Measuring Tweets," Twitter Blog, February 22, 2010. As of September 6, 2017:
https://blog.twitter.com/official/en_us/a/2010/measuring-tweets.html

West, Darrell, *How to Combat Fake News and Disinformation*, Washington, D.C.: Brookings Institution, December 18, 2017. As of December 18, 2017:
https://www.brookings.edu/research/
how-to-combat-fake-news-and-disinformation/

Westheimer, Joel, "No Child Left Thinking," *Colleagues*, Vol. 12, No. 1, 2015, pp. 37–46.

White, Stephen, "The Effectiveness of Political Propaganda in the USSR," *Soviet Studies*, Vol. 32, No. 3, 1980, pp. 323–348.

Wilson, Suzanne, Heidi Schweingruber, and Natalie Nielsen, eds., *Science Teachers' Learning: Enhancing Opportunities, Creating Supportive Contexts*, Washington, D.C.: National Academies of Sciences, Engineering, and Medicine, 2015.

Wineburg, Sam, Sarah McGrew, Joel Breakstone, and Teresa Ortega, "Evaluating Information: The Cornerstone of Civic Online Reasoning," Stanford Digital Repository, 2016. As of October 23, 2017:
http://purl.stanford.edu/fv751yt5934

Wood, Thomas, and Ethan Porter, "The Elusive Backfire Effect: Mass Attitudes' Steadfast Factual Adherence," *Political Behavior*, forthcoming.